FOUR
KILLINGS

FOUR KILLINGS

LAND HUNGER, MURDER AND FAMILY IN THE IRISH REVOLUTION

MYLES DUNGAN

An Apollo Book

This is an Apollo book, first published in the UK in 2021 by
Head of Zeus Ltd

9 7 5 3 2 4 6 8

A catalogue record for this book is available from
the British Library.

ISBN (TPB): 9781800244849
ISBN (E): 9781800244870

Typeset by Adrian McLaughlin
Maps by Jeff Edwards

Printed and bound in Great Britain by
CPI Group (UK) Ltd, Croydon CR0 4YY

Head of Zeus Ltd
First Floor East
5–8 Hardwick Street
London EC1R 4RG

WWW.HEADOFZEUS.COM

For…

T.P. McKenna (1858–1929) and
Sarah Clinton (1867–1904)

Mary Teresa McKenna (1894–1983) and
Terence P. O'Reilly (1889–1945)

Máire O'Reilly (1920–2012) and
William Niall Dungan (1906–1964)

Without whom…

And for my beloved brother Niall Dungan (1943–2019) –
'without whom' in so many different ways…

Contents

Acknowledgements

Research and writing are normally very solitary occupations. You become accustomed to the company of dusty files in archives where, although you are surrounded by other readers, their preoccupations are not yours. They are inching down pathways that will lead to a fresh evaluation of the fraught interactions of de Valera and Churchill, or the catastrophic consequences of the nineteenth-century subdivision of Irish agricultural land.

Researching and writing *Four Killings*, however, has been utterly unlike anything I have ever attempted before. There were a few dusty files, and the usual dollop of solitude when it came to producing eighty thousand words, give or take. But this volume feels as if it has been written by a committee, many of whom did not even attend the same meetings, and some of whom live eight thousand kilometres apart.

Four Killings could not have been written without the generous contributions of time and expertise from a huge number of people. Since this is not an Oscar speech, I have the space to apportion full credit to each.

First, to my various McKenna and Clinton relatives.

On the Irish Clinton side, I owe a huge debt of gratitude to the two Mark Clintons, namesakes of the murdered IRA Volunteer, both of whom hail from Sutton. One is in the Sutton adjacent to Howth in north County Dublin, the other – who also looked after my big brother in his first year at boarding school – has been domiciled in Sutton Coldfield in the English midlands since the 1970s. A huge *buíochas* is due.

Both Marks were rather like the TV detective Lieutenant Columbo. Just as they walked out the door, they would turn back with a 'Just one more thing!' What followed would always be pure gold. I found out about Jack Clinton in a hurried *post scriptum* in a letter from Mark of Sutton Coldfield. Talk about burying the lede!

The feisty Rose Clinton's youngest offspring, the genial Patrick Travers, was responsible for a couple of late revisions to the text when he brought some interesting material to my attention, as was Brian Flaherty, a relative of Jack Clinton's wife Delia Varley, who has spent a considerable amount of time among the Clintons of Arizona (and makes very tasty desserts for a living).

Half a world to the west, and in the middle of the Old West itself, are those Clintons of Arizona: Roseanne Feeback and Mary Frances Clinton. Mark de Sutton (Ireland) just happened to mention them in one of those Columbo moments, and their input has been invaluable. Both have an acute sense of their fascinating family history, of which I have been able to include only the most dramatic incident and its ramifications.

The McKennas of Mullagh (and the wider world) are integral to this story. My beloved maternal grandmother was equal parts Clinton and McKenna, but she spent the early part of her life in Mullagh, County Cavan, surrounded by the descendants of the wild MacCionnaith clan, rather than the slightly more patrician

Clintons, whose homestead overlooked the beautiful lake outside the town.

Two members of the pugnacious MacCionnaith sept have guided me on this journey. Stephen McKenna, based in London but a man who never strays far from his roots, has made his own insightful contribution to the historiography of the extended family with his poignant biography of our mutual grand-uncle, the ill-fated T.P. McKenna. I have relied heavily on *A Gallant Soldier of Ireland: The Life and Times of T.P. McKenna Jr.*, and on the counsel and expertise of Stephen himself. The son of one of Ireland's most accomplished actors (the third T.P. McKenna), Stephen adds an innate flair for the theatrical to his peerless abilities as a researcher.

In trying to get a sense of the personality of John McKenna, I had a template to work from – his son Joe. In one of the quirks of genealogy, Joe, although five years my junior, is actually a first cousin of my late mother. Were we one degree more closely related, he would be my uncle. Joe spent hours talking to me about his father – one of the central characters in this narrative – and escorting me around the highways and byways of County Meath, identifying some of the sites that figure prominently in the McKenna story. I am eternally grateful.

Joe enlisted the aid of his brother T.P. – a storied name in this narrative – who also offered some valuable guidance, as did Joe's sister Margaret and her husband Michael Farrelly of the warrior clan from Clonagrowna, Carnaross, whose uncles feature heavily in this narrative and who now lives in the original family homestead. At a much earlier juncture, before beginning to get into the traumatic details of the McKennas' War of Independence, my interest had been aroused by some written material gifted to me by Erna McKenna, daughter of Justin. This included the poignant poetry of her uncle, T.P. McKenna Jr.

When it came to the intricate details of the Anglo-Irish War in County Meath, I was fortunate in being able to enlist the aid of the men I have come to think of as the Three Amigos: Frank Cogan, Ultan Courtney and Danny Cusack. As with many of the others mentioned above, all three have obliged me by reading most of the text (including some chapters subsequently excised for reasons of space). The email conversations resulting from a query on my part have been fascinating and have made me aware that these three gentlemen have forgotten more about the War of Independence in the north midlands than I will ever know. On the rare occasions when I managed to come up with a piece of research with which they were not already familiar, I felt like an eager Leaving Certificate student who had just been marked as an A+.

Also offering invaluable information about his father, General Seán Boylan, was the legendary Seán Boylan Jr., who like his dad is a leader on and off the field.

Padraig Óg Ó Ruairc has no valid excuse of consanguinity or geography for his involvement in this project, just an overweening curiosity and a cooperative spirit. Only he and I know the extent to which I relied on his expertise and his collaborative instincts. As they say in California (where at least half this book was written), 'Thank you for sharing, Padraig.'

To all at Head of Zeus publishers I am most profoundly grateful. To my editor, Neil Belton, for his faith in this project, for his vision in seeing the potentially wider ramifications of a family memoir, and for his creative patience in guiding, pruning and expanding the narrative. To Clare Gordon and Matilda Singer for nudging me gently through some of the essential byways of publication. To Declan Heeney, publicist extraordinaire, whose only previous experience of my work has been as an annoying radio host.

To Captain Daniel Ayiotis, Cécile Gordon, Rob McEvoy and all at the Military Archives in Rathmines for their help with this volume and its precursor, the RTÉ Radio 1 *History Show* programme 'Three Killings', and to the great-great-grandson of T.P. McKenna Sr., Philip Boucher Hayes, for being a good sport in the latter enterprise. Also a heartfelt thanks to Lorcan Clancy and Liz Gillis of said *History Show* for forcing me into acquiring a more detailed knowledge of the revolutionary period than might otherwise have been the case.

When it came to active encouragement/cheerleading, I turned to Wales and to the Williamses. I am currently married to both. To Nerys (cariad), in a literal sense. She has been an acute sounding board, warm-hearted supporter and incisive counsellor. While I may not have actually walked down the aisle with Jonathan Williams, he has been more than an agent on this and other projects. Although not technically a spouse, he is certainly a diligent and insightful midwife.

Buíochas ó chroí daoibh go léir.

This volume has in part been written for my own immediate family, in the hope of connecting them to a generation with which they have had no direct contact, so that Amber, Rory, Lara, Ross and Gwyneth – and in future years Oliver, Sadie and little Sophie (and, with luck, one or two more) – can read about the role their ancestors played in the dramatic events of the Irish revolutionary decade.

Dramatis Personae

(Not all family members are included, only those
who feature prominently in the narrative)

The Clintons

(Cloggagh, County Meath)

Joseph Clinton (inherited the Cloggagh, Cormeen, County Meath farm in 1892)

Kate (Osborne) Clinton – his wife

Patrick Clinton, b.1893 – 1st Eastern Division Intelligence Officer

Peter Clinton, b.1894 – IRA Volunteer, present at Garryard Wood, 2/3 July 1921

Rose Clinton, b.1895 – Cumann na mBan member, gun smuggler and keeper of a safe house

Mark Clinton, b.1897 – IRA Volunteer, murdered 10 May 1920

Bridget Clinton, b.1900 – Cumann na mBan member

(Palominas, Arizona)

John (Jack) Clinton – murdered 18 June 1915

Delia (Varley) Clinton – his wife, died 1929

Annie Clinton – sister of Jack, farmed close to the Palominas Clintons

Rose Clinton – witnessed her father's killing and gave evidence at the trials of his alleged killers

Francis Mark Clinton – also witnessed his father's killing

The McKennas

T.P. McKenna (1858–1929) – businessman, local politician, chairman of Cavan GAA

Sarah (Clinton) McKenna (1867–1904) – died after the birth of her tenth child, Una

Anna (Schiebel) McKenna – widow of Dr P.J. McKenna of Salt Lake City, second wife of T.P. McKenna, died in 1944

John McKenna, b.1892 – Mullagh IRA quartermaster, present at Garryard Wood, 2/3 July 1921

Justin McKenna, b.1897 – Kells solicitor, member of Second Dáil, voted for the Anglo-Irish Treaty in January 1922

Raphael McKenna, b.1895 – Meath 3rd Brigade intelligence officer

Mary Teresa McKenna, b.1893 – non-combatant, grandmother of the author

T.P. McKenna b.1903 – Meath 3rd Brigade Adjutant, present at Garryard Wood, 2/3 July 1921

The Meath IRA

Seán Boylan – O/C 1st Eastern Division

Seán Farrelly – Carnaross IRA, 3rd Brigade deputy O/C

Séamus Finn – Deputy O/C 1st Eastern Division

Non-family victims

William Gordon – ex-RAF, member of Cormeen Gang, killer of Mark Clinton, executed by the IRA in Salestown, Dunboyne, August 1920

Patrick Keelan – Crown forces 'identifier', executed by the IRA on the night of 2/3 July 1921 in Garryard Wood

Maps

Arizona and Cochise County

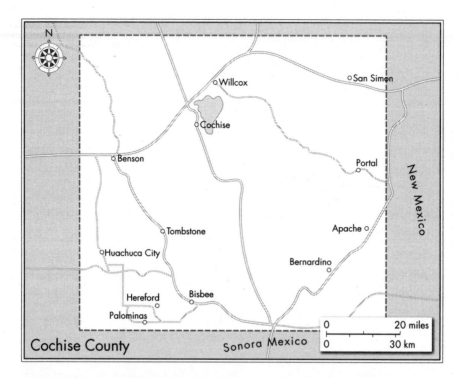

Cochise County

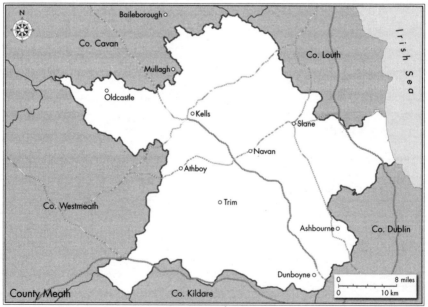

County Meath

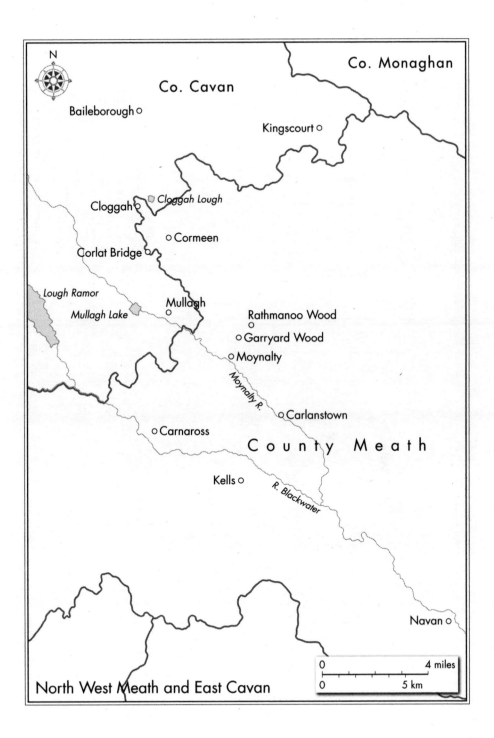

N

Co. Monaghan

Co. Cavan

Baileborough ○

Kingscourt ○

Cloggah ○ Cloggah Lough

○ Cormeen

Corlat Bridge ○

Lough Ramor

Mullagh Lake

Mullagh ○

Rathmanoo Wood ○

○ Garryard Wood

○ Moynalty

Moynalty R.

○ Carlanstown

○ Carnaross

County Meath

Kells ○

R. Blackwater

Navan ○

0   4 miles

0   5 km

North West Meath and East Cavan

Prologue

'Every man is a quotation from all his ancestors.'

Ralph Waldo Emerson

It comes as a surprise to realise that she had such intense youthful beauty. In the posed black-and-white photograph, more than a century old, she stares sceptically at the camera, flanked by her nine brothers and sisters, her glowering father and her new American stepmother, who is gazing enigmatically into the middle distance.

It is 1906. Edward VII is on the English throne. San Francisco has just experienced a devastating earthquake. Alfred Dreyfus is about to be exonerated and reinstated by the French army. Arthur Griffith is attempting, with scant success, to spread the separatist gospel of a new political party called Sinn Féin.

She is just twelve years old. The last traces of puppy fat are still evident on her cheeks. She wears a long white pinafore and an expression of jaded wisdom, disturbing in one so young. You can read a lot into that jaundiced gaze. The eldest of four daughters, she is still mourning her mother – Sarah Clinton McKenna is barely two years dead. Now, with the arrival from the United

States of Anna Schiebel as her stepmother, she has relinquished her unlooked-for status as woman of the house.

But the real shock is her youth. The fact that Mary Teresa 'May' McKenna (born 27 December 1893) had ever been twelve years old comes as a revelation. To me she was Mama, a frail, stately, punctilious elderly lady who would descend upon our household once a year and stay for four weeks. Not three weeks and the odd day. Not a calendar month. Four weeks precisely.

She would arrive from our cousins in Newry, a raucous household of six granddaughters and a lone grandson, all with gentle lilting northern accents. After spending twenty-eight days with us, among the broad, flat, uvular tones of the north midlands, she would move on to our cousins in Cork, a smaller establishment enlivened by a girl and two younger boys with gentle lilting southern accents.

When bedding down with us in Kingscourt, County Cavan or Kells, County Meath, she would visibly ensconce. The word could have been invented to describe Mama's annual domestic ritual. The summer campaign over, this aging general in the body of an old dear would winter with her youngest daughter and son-in-law in Drumshanbo, County Leitrim. Every year, for two decades or more, she traipsed majestically across each of the Irish provinces in turn.

She disappointed me only once in the thirty-odd years I knew her. That was when she sided with my aunt, Nóirín, who was looking after me for a few days, in crushing my obsessive intention (as a six-year-old) to travel to the Himalayas, to the foothills of Mount Everest, in search of the Abominable Snowman. I could barely pronounce – and certainly could not spell – the word 'abominable', but in preparation for the pilgrimage I had already appropriated a linen sheet to serve as a tent and stolen some pots and pans.

Over my raucous entreaties, which quickly mutated into shrieks, the sheet was folded and the pots returned to their cupboard.

She would awaken each day shortly after dawn, make tea, toast two slices of bread to semi-carbonised aridity and return to bed to spend the rest of the morning reading the previous day's paper. When you were in your seventies, she probably reasoned, it was vital to be sufficiently well informed to venture opinions upon the business of the day, but it was no longer imperative to be bang up to date. News of the perennially dominant Fianna Fáil's latest perfidy (she was an unreconstructed Blueshirt, a diehard supporter of Fine Gael, the other party that had emerged from the chaos of the Civil War) or another of Gay Byrne's sabre-rattling sorties on *The Late Late Show* could wait for twenty-four hours.

I saw Mama for the last time in a nursing home in Newry. She had suffered a stroke and was comatose. My brother Niall had driven us north and was in bad humour. One of the British squaddies who stopped us en route and searched the car with the southern registration had enquired, 'Is that your son in the passenger seat?' I never did let him forget that.

It wasn't until I got back to Dublin a few hours later that it dawned on me that I would never see my sweet and engaging grandmother alive again. It occurred to me for the first time that I should not have taken her for granted, that I was going to miss her, and that I had been too obtuse, self-absorbed and blasé to sit down and record some of the memories she had shared with me when I was younger.

I did not make the same mistake with my mother, but her reminiscences, while gratifying and idiosyncratic, were banal by comparison. Sadly, Mama's often disquieting memories are now mostly irrecoverable, though fragments can be recreated and verified through the recollections of others.

Before I had reached adolescence, Mama told me hair-raising stories of the War of Independence. These involved nocturnal visits by the terrifying Black and Tans, the ill-trained special police recruited to suppress the IRA. She related how her young family, which by then included my infant mother, would be rousted out of bed and made to watch as their house was rigorously searched by loutish men with English accents. The family's belongings would be tossed about carelessly, but with a definite purpose – to intimidate. She told me that she had feared their home would be burned to the ground, something she knew had happened to the houses of others during those dangerous times.

I listened intently and nurtured an unhealthy loathing for the men who had frightened my benign and charming grandmother. The aversion has modified with age but has never entirely dissipated. More than half a century later, the only occasion on which I have ever been able to cheer on a team dressed in white with a three lions logo on their shirts has been the Men's Coxless Four final at the 2000 Sydney Olympics. Steven Redgrave was going for a unique fifth consecutive gold medal. This validated my disloyalty. Finally getting over myself in this way probably helped my television commentary, which ended in a primal scream as Redgrave, Pinsent, Cracknell and Foster held off the fast-finishing Italian four by less than half a length.

Since then, even in a neutral setting, I have reverted to the discreditable stance of hoping for a German win on penalties or a late Welsh try to snatch an undeserved victory. I blame my grandmother entirely for this reprehensible chauvinism.

But then, as a teenager, I acquired a little more knowledge of our country's troubled history and doubts began to creep in. Was she embroidering? Was she plagiarising? Why would the Black and Tans be interested in terrorising my inoffensive grandmother, her husband – Dr Terence P. O'Reilly, later County Cavan medical officer – or her four young children (the number would quickly expand to eight)?

They certainly weren't looking for her brother Justin. Although he was elected as a Sinn Féin TD in 1921 – in time to cast his vote in favour of the Anglo-Irish Treaty – he always hid in plain sight. Justin was never compelled to go on the run, and he spent the period before his elevation to the Second Dáil exactly where the Crown forces could keep a beady eye on him. For more than six months in 1921, he was a guest of His Majesty in the Rath internment camp in the Curragh.

Justin was the only one of Mama's brothers I remember ever being discussed in any detail in the context of the War of Independence. She somehow neglected to mention that three other brothers, John, Raphael and T.P. Junior, were all serving members of the IRA. It wasn't until a conversation many years later with Justin's daughter Erna that I made this discovery.

This knowledge, and the online release in 2017 of the first War of Independence files from the Military Service Pensions Collection, led to an epiphany, and to the beginning of a journey that has proved infinitely more rewarding than my aborted quest for the Yeti in the early 1960s.

May McKenna's brother T.P. Junior, who died of tuberculosis in Argentina in 1929 at the age of twenty-six, had applied for a military pension shortly after the relevant legislation was passed in 1924. His file was one of the first of around 100,000, encompassing all the pension and medal applications, to go online. Sitting on my living room couch, I could browse through the terse responses in Military Service Pensions Collection (MSPC) file number

24SP12899 to the many administrative questions demanded of this long-dead veteran of the Anglo-Irish War.

I learned how young he was – fourteen – when he became active in the Irish Volunteers, and that he was still in his teens when he joined the IRA as a medical student. He was a classmate of Kevin Barry in University College, Dublin. Barry, at the age of eighteen, was hanged for the killing of three equally callow British soldiers in a disastrous ambush, and in death became a Republican martyr.

I read, in neat cramped handwriting, his own condensed account of the four years of a short life spent in the (metaphorical) uniform of the IRA and the (actual) uniform of the National Army. There followed a number of what were called MSP7 forms, filled out 'by a person testifying to the service, if any, of an applicant for a certificate of military service'. One of these had been completed by a Captain D. Smith on behalf of T.P. Junior. It was largely a repetition of the information contained in earlier forms.

My attention was already beginning to wander, and I was scrolling upwards with increasing speed. I suppose I had been hoping for something dramatic. That was when a line in Smith's submission leapt out at me. On page five, under the heading 'Continuous service from 1st April, 1921 to 11th July, 1921', there were five questions printed in columns down the left-hand side. The first was: 'What military services did applicant render?'

Just in case there was any doubt about what constituted military services, the bureaucrats who had devised the form offered some prompts. 'Insert particulars of attacks on enemy forces or positions; destruction of enemy property; manufacture, purchase or disposal of munitions; collection of information to enable these acts to be done; or organising or training to the same ends.' The Free State government was not going to hand over £110 per annum of taxpayer money – this was the sum to which T.P.'s rank in the Civil War National Army entitled him – without chapter and verse.

In the space opposite this first query, however, the taxpayer got lethal value for the expenditure of the £500 or more that Colonel T.P. McKenna would receive from a grateful state before his premature death. Smith had written 'Executed spy at Carlanstown'. The shock that travelled through my entire body almost sent the laptop flying.

I had found something dramatic after all.

My grandmother never told me much about her cousins either. The Clintons of Cloggagh House were from the tiny village of Cormeen, County Meath, close to the Cavan border. Three of them, Pat, Peter and Mark, were in the north Meath IRA, and two more, Rose and Bridget, were quintessential fellow travellers, members of Cumann na mBan, the women's auxiliary of the IRA. For the duration of the War of Independence, Rose carried weapons and despatches and ran the safest of safe houses in County Meath for IRA men on the run. Bridget clung to her extreme Republican beliefs, often to the dismay of her family, to her dying day.

Nor, as far as I can recall, did Mama ever talk about Sarah Clinton, her mother. Sarah was born in a sprawling farmhouse overlooking a beautiful lake on the outskirts of the village of Mullagh, County Cavan. Perhaps, as an elderly woman, May McKenna no longer had any clear memories of the most important figure in her young life. Her mother died a few weeks after giving birth in 1904 to her tenth child, Una. May was ten years old at the time, the same age at which I lost my own father. I can claim some insight into memories occluded by grief.

My grandmother certainly never mentioned her stepmother, a German-American named Anna Schiebel. Anna was the widow of my great-grandfather's cousin Dr P.J. McKenna, an Irish-American surgeon. He had suffered a truly dreadful death – falling from a moving train – in Salt Lake City, Utah, three years before Sarah Clinton's death. Anna Schiebel McKenna – she did not even require a change of surname – had been cajoled or wooed into taking on the mind-numbing responsibility of rearing ten stepchildren in a sleepy Irish village. Some of her new charges were already old enough to take exception to her arrival.

Neither did my grandmother mention the bad blood between the Clintons of Mullagh House and the McKennas, prosperous merchants of the nearby village. One version of the origins of this feud has it that a drunk T.P. McKenna Sr. peremptorily ordered his ailing wife from her sickbed to recommence her domestic chores too soon after the birth of her last child. Sarah Clinton caught a chill and died shortly thereafter. Mark Clinton of Mullagh House, so the story goes, never forgave his brother-in-law.

The alternative version suggests that the Clintons, whether or not with just cause, felt that allowing less than two years to pass after the death of Sarah Clinton before remarrying had been a mark of disrespect on the part of T.P. McKenna. Hamlet expresses it unforgettably: 'The funeral baked meats did coldly furnish forth the marriage tables.'

I never did find out if my grandmother sympathised with the resentment of the Prince of Denmark. The blood cannot have been that toxic, however, because Mark and Catherine Clinton are listed in the *Meath Chronicle* as gift-givers at the nuptials of May McKenna and my grandfather Dr T.P. O'Reilly on 11 April 1915.

Why this silence, I have often wondered? Why did a garrulous septuagenarian with an attentive audience keep such a remarkable narrative to herself? Her suggestible young witness would have accepted hearsay or embellishment as gospel.

Perhaps we were distracted by discussing George Best's alcoholism and womanising, Cavan or Meath's All-Ireland prospects, or why an Irishman hadn't managed to win the British Open since Fred Daly. She was the perfect grandmother for a little boy, because when she read the previous day's newspaper, she read it from cover to cover, right down to the death notices – especially the death notices! – and the small ads. She could discourse as effortlessly on soccer, GAA and golf as she could on the Anglo-Irish War.

She never actually watched much sport on television; she just read about it. She thought soccer looked like a very gentlemanly game. I never disillusioned her. Her husband had played golf, and her son-in-law (my father) had dropped dead on a golf course less than a kilometre away from where most of our conversations took place. I dare say that at the time I was more interested in discussing sport with this opinionated old lady than 'old, unhappy, far-off things, and battles long ago'.

Or perhaps it was a natural reticence that prevented her from discussing the details of the roles played in the Anglo-Irish War by many of her closest relatives. She might have shied away from telling one so young about the May 1920 murder of her cousin Mark Clinton, an IRA Volunteer, and the subsequent execution of the man who killed him, William Gordon. She would certainly have been aware of his death, one of the most egregious and well-publicised killings of a period often defined by its callousness.

If she knew anything about the matter, she would definitely have had far too much delicacy to draw my attention to the role played by two of her brothers and one of her cousins in the killing of an alleged informer by the Meath IRA a year later. She may not have been privy to all the details or have been aware of what is reported to have happened to the body of the unfortunate Patrick Keelan after his execution. Had she known, would she have countenanced the burial of my unnamed infant brother and sister in the same cemetery plot two decades later?

Aware as she was of my nascent obsession with the history of the American Far West – though we just called it playing Cowboys and Indians back then – I am surprised she never related the tragic narrative of her cousin Jack Clinton, cut down in his own backyard in Arizona in 1915 by two mounted assassins, despatched in all likelihood by the representatives of an insatiable corporation. Jack Clinton was a victim of primogeniture, of desire for some land of his own – collateral damage of one of the many simmering wars of the American frontier. He was Van Heflin in *Shane*, but without the satisfying ending.

Mama, wisely perhaps, restricted her war chronicles to the range of her own direct experience. Most of this concerned the depredations of the Black and Tans. However, it didn't make for a very rounded picture of the period. Between 1915 and 1921, six members of her extended family were involved in four killings, in two instances as victims.

I was wrong to doubt her memories of those vindictive rampages by a paramilitary police militia, heavily armed, alcohol-fuelled agents of a powerful colonising state. They were mercenaries, mostly devoid of ideology, tasked with the preservation of a union that had been shipping water for generations. But had she widened her scope, without even straying beyond the bounds of family memory, she might have managed to impress on an impressionable boy that

Irish history was more than a chain of binary clashes – separatist versus loyalist; landlord against tenant; peaceful constitutionalist in opposition to violent militarist.

I remember, as a child, being exposed to my little sister's chickenpox as a substitute for inoculation. Had Mama trusted me, or herself, with a fuller narrative, she might have inoculated me against simple-minded and unipolar interpretations of Ireland's jagged history (and an unreasonable, atavistic antipathy to those white shirts sporting three lions). Ultimately it was the likes of Professors Kevin B. Nowlan, F.X. Martin and Robin Dudley Edwards who administered that particular vaccine in the History Department of University College, Dublin in the 1970s.

She might also have personalised the otherwise impersonal, and highlighted the private tragedies and sacrifices strapped to the romance of revolution and nationhood. But that would have broken the silence demanded by the necessity to forget, as an aid to healing. Instead, she adhered to the rigidity of that very Irish axiom: 'Whatever you say, say nothing.'

Mama would have reckoned that she had a perfect right to share her own memories with her ten-year-old grandson, but not the far more harrowing experiences of other family members. Because even in a region of the country that never succumbed to complete mayhem, as parts of Cork and Clare did, the violence of the War of Independence cast dark shadows over the lives of many of her relatives still living in the Irish north midlands.

A word here to the wise and the wary. While there actually is an 'I' in history, in the case of *Four Killings* it will not be found wandering beyond this prologue. The author will not be tempted to insert himself any further into events a century old in which he played no part. He is fully prepared to acknowledge that had he actually been around a hundred years ago, it is highly improbable that he would have been a willing protagonist in any of the episodes described here. Some are born to observe, and to describe the histories of those who are destined to take action. There is, however, an obvious biological, if not a compelling philosophical, connection.

Had T.P. McKenna not married Sarah Clinton, then Mary Teresa (May) McKenna would not have been born. Had May (McKenna) O'Reilly not given birth to her daughter Máire (who always stridently insisted on the Gaelic *fada*) while one of her brothers was imprisoned, one was on the run, one was pretending he had never heard of the IRA, and a fourth was trying to convince the Royal Irish Constabulary (RIC) that he thought policemen were exceptional fellows, I would not now be imposing on the reader's time.

The McKennas and the Clintons will be treated much like any other family of the Irish revolutionary period. The Bureau of Military History Witness Statements, the applications for campaign medals, the Military Service Pension files, credible folklore and oral family history, copious newspaper cuttings and scholarly secondary sources will be allowed to do their work with as little hindrance as possible.

There are myriad ways of charting the course of the original Troubles, now broadly rechristened 'the revolutionary decade' and book-ended by those profoundly incompatible bedfellows, the 1913 Dublin Lockout, in which striking trade unionists were disowned by the Volunteers and beaten by the Dublin Metropolitan Police, and the triumphant 'conservative revolution' of the Irish Free State. Some studies of the crucial 1919–22 segment of that remarkable decade have adopted the broadest of approaches (the surveys of Charles Townshend or Lorcan Collins, for example). Others have concentrated on particulars, examining topics like the contribution of noteworthy individuals to the independence struggle (T. Ryle Dwyer, Richard English); the experience of the IRA Volunteer (Joost Augusteijn); localised city or county narratives (John Borgonovo, Liz Gillis, David Fitzpatrick); the role of women in general, and of Cumann na mBan in particular (Mary McAuliffe); the physical violence meted out to women by both sides (Linda Connolly); allegations of ethnic cleansing (Andy Bielenberg, Peter Hart); the pall cast by the ubiquity of death, violence and trauma (Anne Dolan, Eunan O'Halpin); oral testimony and memory (Tomás MacConmara); the influence of newspapers (Ian Kenneally); the minor miracle of the Dáil courts (Mary Kotsonouris, Heather Laird); the onset and reinforcement of partition (Michael Laffan); the byzantine Treaty negotiations (Frank Pakenham); the final activism of the days and weeks before the 1921 Truce (Padraig Óg Ó Ruairc); and, on the most micro-cosmic of levels, the legacy of a painful family history (Fergal Keane). Many other casements have already been opened in this particular house, and more remain to be investigated.

Chronicling the experience of two families, both resident in the Irish north midlands – a part of the country usually seen as becalmed during the Anglo-Irish War – may not at first sight appear to add much to the sum of our understanding of the conflict, especially when an unrelated 1915 killing in the American south-west is introduced into the mix. But the Anglo-Irish War of the Clintons of County Meath and their cousins, the McKennas of County Cavan, was both enthrallingly exceptional and typical. While they may have been physically situated in the doldrums of the war, at no point did they float aimlessly, hoping for a breath of liberating wind.

On the contrary, the four McKenna brothers and the five Clintons from Cloggagh were highly active. While some of their number might have maintained a semblance of normality by continuing in the practice of their jobs or professions, those diurnal banalities masked substantial sacrifice, tribulation and trauma. Even in the apparent activist wastelands of Cavan and Meath, there was no shortage of Black and Tans and Auxiliaries to mete out threats, verbal abuse, beatings, arson and death. It is certainly valid to view the conflict, though not in its totality, through the prism of these two families.

In addition to reflecting the brutality of those times, the experience of the Clinton family of Cloggagh in particular resonates with a rather neglected aspect of the Anglo-Irish War, the violent struggle for land redistribution with which it often overlapped. This parallel conflict was a function of the enduring bitterness brought about by memories of old injuries and injustices stretching back to the Land War of the 1880s. One of my objects in writing this book is to highlight this unsung aspect of the Troubles. In a country as economically dependent on agriculture as Ireland during this period, it would be unwise to ignore the consequences of a 'land hunger' that had not abated for two generations. In the case of Mark Clinton, those consequences would prove fatal.

Where the casual savagery of the Crown forces was absent, their role was often supplied by a home-produced variant. For many months the predatory Cormeen Gang operated with relative impunity in north Meath, under the less than watchful gaze of a distracted RIC. Until the murder of Volunteer Mark Clinton provoked the IRA into an overwhelming response, their activities – a throwback to the agrarian turmoil of the late nineteenth century – added a complex and feral layer to the primary conflict. North Meath was not unique when it came to this subset of the prevailing anarchy, so the experience of the Clintons is instructive.

Casualty figures might have been far lower in the north midlands than in the feted cockpits of the conflict (Dublin, Cork, Tipperary, Kerry, Limerick, Clare), but Cavan and Meath still managed to run the gamut of distressing Anglo-Irish War experiences. Even the murder of Jack Clinton in Arizona, recounted in the first two chapters of this narrative, is of circumstantial relevance. It was the grim certainties of Irish land tenure that drove him and much of his family away from the Barony of Kells Lower to the barrenness of southern Arizona.

Those same tenurial realities, allied to the ugly Irish history of forced dispossession, also informed the activities of the Black Hand Gang of Cormeen. Their agrarian acquisitiveness equates, albeit on a diminished scale and with an entirely inverted class perspective, to the baronial capitalism of Jack Clinton's corporate nemesis, the Boquillas Land and Cattle Company of southern Arizona. As we shall see, in issuing threats in May 1920 against the Clintons and their relatives the Smiths, the Cormeen Gang actually genuflected towards the murder of Jack Clinton, threatening to replicate Arizonan vigilantism in rural County Meath.

There is much we can learn by exploring the doldrums.

Ireland's most courageous, ruthless and efficacious generation continue to tell their own stories through the witness statements and pension applications stored in the Military Archives in Cathal Brugha Barracks in Rathmines. The former are more colourful, but the latter, with independent verification of claims mandatory, are more reliable. My task has been to unlock and record, and, in the absence of certainty, to offer some reasonable speculation about two ordinary families pummelled by extraordinary events. For any missteps, let me apologise in advance.

I now believe Mary Teresa McKenna. I know she wasn't exaggerating. I know the Tans were looking for her brothers, or terrorising her because she was Justin, John, Raphael and T.P. McKenna's sister. Having a Clinton for a mother probably didn't help either.

But there was much she didn't tell me. She probably felt that she couldn't, because others, more directly involved, had remained silent for decades. Their experiences still hovered over them, out of sight but never entirely out of mind.

Perhaps she wanted to tell me everything. I was a good listener. I loved hearing those stories from the past. They fired my imagination and made me want to find out more. Was that her greatest gift to her grandson?

Now, while these stories are important to my extended family, and while the events described have had repercussions far beyond the 1920s, it is only right to paraphrase Humphrey Bogart as the evasively eloquent Rick in *Casablanca* and point out that 'It doesn't take much to see that the problems of [these] little people don't amount to a hill of beans in this crazy world.' So the tone and style of this narrative will not attempt to suggest otherwise. My hope is that it reads in a way that might have tempted my grandmother to abandon the *Irish Independent* for a few hours.

Part One

THE CLINTONS
OF CLOGGAGH

1

Arizona, 1915

I.

It was approaching dusk as the two riders jogged their horses across the needle grass and sagebrush. Stars were already beginning to appear through the thickening daylight. They would soon have the North Star at their backs. When darkness fell, the crescent moon would offer little help in guiding them to their destination. They would have to rely on whatever feeble glow was provided by the distant ranch house.

The lead rider, an unremarkable-looking man somewhere in his mid-thirties, was displaying more urgency than his companion. The latter hung back, as if uncertain what he was doing on horseback in open country close to the Mexican border, with twilight descending. Calvin Cox had agreed to play his part, but he wasn't sure exactly what he had agreed to. Had he been cajoled or coerced? Either way, he had not resisted Ed Scarborough's summons. The former lawman, Cox mused, was not someone who took no for an answer.

Cox knew they were heading for Jack Clinton's farmhouse near Palominas, but that was all he knew. Scarborough hadn't shared his intentions, or much else for that matter. He hadn't even spoken since they left behind the San Pedro River. Scarborough's moody silence, and the descending dusk, were making Cox uneasy. He liked to know where he was going and why, and he liked doing it in daylight.

At least he didn't have to worry about Apaches any more. Geronimo had been thrown from his horse and killed six years earlier in Oklahoma, still a prisoner of the federal government after more than two decades.

Make no mistake, Cox had no time for Jack Clinton, particularly after the Irishman had the gall, earlier that very day, to turn away a few head of Boquillas cattle at the Wilcox auction. He had challenged the authenticity of their brands. That was the last straw. Was this upstart Irish nester trying to make out that the Boquillas cowboys had altered the brand of one of his squatter friends? That would make them no better than rustlers.

But just because Cox had already threatened to kill the man didn't mean he actually intended to. He wasn't so sure about Scarborough though. The former Arizona Ranger had once pulled a gun on Clinton and warned him to keep his steers off Boquillas land. Cox was fairly certain that Clinton and some of his Irish neighbours had been building up their own herds by rustling the unbranded wandering calves of the Boquillas Land and Cattle Company. Scarborough was convinced of it.

Cox knew that Scarborough had killed men in the past, but that was when he had had the protection of a badge. This was different.

Clinton and the other homesteaders were a perennial irritant to the big cattle company for which Cox and Scarborough now worked. Aside altogether from trespass and theft, they fenced off their land and drew water from the San Pedro river. They were bugs who needed swatting, but you couldn't just squash them under your foot. They were not rustlers, who needed to be lynched or shot out of hand. Cox hoped Scarborough felt the same way.

But if he did, why wait until after dark to confront this small-time rancher and scare the hell out of him? Amateur rustlers could be intimidated just as easily during business hours.

2.

To get an idea of the size of Cochise County, the southernmost section of the then newly created state of Arizona, you need to aggregate Rhode Island and Connecticut. Or most of Ireland west of the Shannon. The county had come into existence in 1881, named after the great Chiricahua Apache military leader.

Cochise ('strength of an oak') had defied the federal government for more than a decade. Between 1861 and 1872, he outwitted and outrode the US cavalry, using the sort of hit-and-run tactics that would be emulated by the IRA flying columns of the Irish War of Independence. The fact that he had an entire county named after him might explain why Cochise was one of the first prominent Native American guerrilla fighters to get a fair crack of the whip from Hollywood. He would be portrayed sympathetically by Jeff Chandler in *Broken Arrow* (1950).

From 1881 until 1931, the administrative seat of Cochise County was Tombstone, site of that great misnomer 'the gunfight at the OK Corral'. Although three men died there, it wasn't really much of a gunfight – more a brawl between the Clantons and McLaurys, a group of unruly cowboys, and the three Earp brothers and John Henry 'Doc' Holliday, who were rather dubious federal marshals. It lasted about thirty seconds and a number of the contending parties were probably dead before getting off a second shot.

Thirty years later, Cochise County, though no longer the stuff of western legend, was still what American historian Richard Slotkin calls a 'fatal environment'.[1] In 1915, this environment had already proven fatal for seven men. This had prompted an irate editorial, 'Red Record of Cochise', in the local *Bisbee Daily Review* on 26 June that year.

> Within little more than a week, three unusually revolting murders have been done in Cochise County. Within the ensuing week the July term of the Superior Court will convene at Tombstone. The cases on the calendar number about forty, and they are all criminal

cases. Included in this number are four [more] murder cases...
Cochise County feels a sense of shame which is the more acute
because of an accompanying sense of helplessness to combat the
situation. Inside its boundaries live approximately 50,000 people, or
a fourth of the entire population of Arizona. It is therefore a matter
of more than county concern, this record of violence. The entire
State of Arizona is justified in resenting what cannot be other
than a blot on her fair name. It is a stain made by human blood.

The *Daily Review* called on the state governor, one George
Washington P. Hunt – 'conservator of those aids to law enforce-
ment which work to the end of inculcating respect for law' – to
enforce the death penalty for murder in Arizona. The squeamish
Hunt had thus far ignored the popular vote on a recent proposition
to that effect. The *Daily Review* demanded that he stop dragging
his feet and commence dragging some of those convicted of
murder to the gallows. Their crimes, it harrumphed, 'seem to indicate that the perpetrators harbored no wholesome fear of the law;
respect for the law was not in them'.[2]

Was the *Daily Review* correct? While Bisbee and its environs
was no Quaker settlement, was the murder rate in Cochise County
really so excessive? The criterion on which such statistical questions
are usually assessed is murders per 100,000 of the population. On
that basis, with a total population of around 50,000, the 1915 murder
rate in Cochise county was 14/100K. Compare that with nearby
Gila County (150/100K), the infamous cow-towns of Wichita,
Dodge City and Abilene (a combined 155/100K) and the Black
Hills morgue that was Deadwood, South Dakota (442/100K), and
the *Daily Review* seems guilty of over-reaction.[3]

Not that Cochise County was exactly sedate, as the Clinton
family of Palominas was about to find out.

3.

John Clinton, Jack to friends and family, must often have wondered why he ever traded the low, rain-soaked hills of north Meath for the arid badlands of southern Arizona. He would have missed the trundling clouds of north Leinster, not merely for their surreal shapes, but for what they brought in their wake – that most precious of all commodities, rainfall. In County Meath, it was sometimes a boon, though often a curse that you just took for granted. In southern Arizona, it was an infrequent guest welcomed on bended knees. The region's casual relationship with precipitation meant that even with a small corner of Cochise County to call his own, Jack Clinton was glad he did not have to rely entirely on farming for a living.

Born on 25 July 1862, Clinton had finally abandoned rural Meath during the violent upheavals of the Land War, the mass movement of Irish peasants against the Anglo-Irish proprietors who owned most of the country's agricultural land. He arrived in the USA in 1882, just as the Land League and the Liberal government of William E. Gladstone were coming to terms after three years of agrarian anarchy. He could have placed his trust in the capacity of Michael Davitt, the tireless originator of the Land League, and Charles Stewart Parnell, the charismatic leader of the Irish Home Rule movement, to deliver on the League's slogan, 'the land for the people', but he put more faith in the emigrant ship.

The nature of Irish land tenure had, mercifully, changed in the aftermath of the devastating Great Famine. Tenants still did not own their own farms, which mostly belonged to the aristocratic landlord class, but the endless subdivision of holdings between the sons of tenant farmers had ended. The practice, already in decline before the Famine, had played a central part in the pauperisation of rural Ireland. With each generation, holdings had become smaller and more uneconomic. Only the availability of the life-supporting potato, which seemed to grow anywhere and in great quantities, staved off tragedy. This eventually struck in 1845 when *Phytophthora infestans* (potato blight) caused the crop that year, and for most of the next four, to rot in the ground.

After the Great Famine – and the loss through starvation, disease and emigration of some two million people – there would be no more subdivision of Irish holdings. Only one of the ten children of Patrick Clinton and Rose Smith of Cloggagh, near Cormeen, County Meath, would take over the family farm. That, as it turned out, would be John's younger brother Joe, when the paterfamilias died in 1892 – but not before Joe had accompanied his brothers John, Mark and Francis to the United States. They would later be joined by their sisters Anna (Annie), Brigid (Bee Agnes) and Mary. John, a highly intelligent young man, had contemplated a career in medicine, but was forced to abandon any thoughts of tertiary education when it became clear that his father could not afford to pay his fees.

Like an increasing number of Irish immigrants as the nineteenth century wore on, the Clintons decided against settling down in one of the many Irish ghettoes of the great cities of the eastern seaboard. Instead, along with 100,000 of their countrymen, they headed for the Far West, in their case to the very Irish city of San Francisco. From there the Clinton men first travelled to Montana where, like thousands of other Irishmen, they worked in the mining industry, an activity dominated by among others Marcus Daly from Ballyjamesduff in County Cavan, one of the legendary Copper Kings of Butte. It was in Silverbow County, Montana that Jack Clinton became a US citizen in 1896.

The three Clinton women settled in Colorado Springs, where all became nurses. In 1897/98 they were joined in Colorado by their mother, Rose. She had opted not to continue sharing the farmhouse in Cloggagh with her new daughter-in-law, Kate Osborne, when Kate and Joe Clinton married after his return from America. With most of her children now living in the western states of the US, Rose chose instead to join her daughters there.*

When the Spanish-American war broke out in 1898, Jack Clinton joined up and was sent to the Philippines to play his part in the first overseas war fought by the United States. He was despatched to the Pacific from the Presidio in San Francisco, where he was fortunate not to contract a debilitating disease from the cramped conditions in that crowded military base. In the Philippines, however, his luck ran out. There he contracted the dysentery that would continue to incapacitate him from time to time for the rest of his life. He was invalided out of the army and returned to San Francisco. By 1902 he was living with his sisters in Colorado Springs, working as a lineman for a local power company.

By 1903 he had returned to California and found work in Pasadena as an electrician. It was in the Pasadena Hibernia Club that he met a young woman from Cong, County Mayo named Delia Varley. She was twenty-four years old and worked as a domestic servant for a wealthy southern Californian family. Delia's

* *The Giles Directory* of Colorado Springs records Rose, Anna, Mary and Brigid as resident in Colorado Springs in 1903. Bee Agnes departed the household in 1906 to get married (she died in 1917), but the others were still living there in 1910, according to that year's US census. Around 1912, Annie moved to Arizona. Rose Clinton, by then nearly ninety years of age, died in Colorado Springs in October 1925, 'at the home of her daughter', Mary (*Colorado Springs Gazette and Telegraph*, 18 and 19 October 1925). Mary left Colorado in 1925 and settled with Annie in Arizona shortly before the death of Jack Clinton's widow, Delia.

passage to the US had been paid for by an aunt in Indianapolis, Kate Crane, and most of her wages went to pay for passage to America for her brothers and sisters in Ireland. The ending of subdivision was double-edged. Only her brother Patrick remained in Mayo, working the family farm.

Jack Clinton was forty-one years old when he married Delia Varley on 23 February 1903 at St Andrew Catholic Church in Pasadena. Within a year their daughter, named Rose after her paternal grandmother, was born. A year after that, the family moved to Arizona and Jack filed a homestead claim.

One of the many successors to the Homestead Act of 1862, the Desert Land Act of 1877 enabled a married couple to acquire between 160 and 640 acres (one square mile) of Arizona. This was not as generous as it might appear. The land of southern Arizona was mostly sub-desert, and the larger the grant, the worse the soil. On some homesteads it could take fifteen to twenty acres to sustain a single cow.

Before securing tenure, homesteaders were given five years to irrigate and develop their property, though the definition of irrigation was flexible. In one instance it involved depositing buckets of water around a ranch in the hope that it would pass the federal inspection. Even with such levels of ingenuity, up to half the homesteaders of the American west failed to make it to the 'patent stage' when they could safely call their farm their own.[4]

The Clintons did enough with their 160 acres of relatively promising soil to retain their holding and build a modest wooden farmhouse in the Hereford-Palominas area. Domestic dwellings were no longer quite as rough and ready as in the frontier days of the late nineteenth century. Back then, homesteaders lived in shacks with sod or thatched roofs that often didn't survive desert winds or cloudbursts. Along with the human inhabitants, these glorified *bothàns* could house tarantulas, scorpions, rats and snakes. If you were fortunate, the snakes would devour the rats.

The small Palominas ranch was near the township of Huachuca, a thirty-minute stroll from the Mexican border, not that the searingly hot environment was conducive to walking. The Clintons began to raise a small number of cattle. As required by both law and common sense, these had to be branded. The couple, unwilling to waste time and money having a brand designed for them, chose one 'off the shelf' in Tombstone Courthouse from among retired Arizona brands no longer in use. They were struck by one in particular, JDC, which could well stand for John and Delia Clinton. The family discovered only in the late 1970s that the brand had been that of the Clanton family of Billy Clanton, shot dead at the OK Corral.[5]

Jack Clinton was under no illusions about the economic potential of his newly acquired land. To supplement his income, he found work in the local mining industry, principally in the nearby town of Bisbee. He also travelled for work across the Mexican border to Cananea in the province of Sonora, a sixty-mile round trip.

There, shortly after his arrival in Arizona, trouble was brewing. The local mine, whose origins went back to the Jesuit missions of the eighteenth century, had been acquired by the American-owned Cananea Consolidated Copper Company. On 1 June 1906, local miners went on strike in protest at being paid half the wages of American employees for doing the same work.

In the US itself, in similar circumstances, the mine's owners would probably have lobbied successfully for the National Guard to be pitched against the strikers. If the state governor proved reluctant to unleash the militia, muscular agents of the more expensive Pinkerton Detective Agency could be used as a battering ram instead.

In the case of the Cananea strike, the American mine owners, against the wishes of the governor, managed to recruit a large posse (almost 300 men) of the Arizona National Guard and sundry Spanish-American war veterans to cross into Mexico and protect the owners' interests. This border incursion, not unexpectedly, led to a violent response. Thirty-four deaths later (four American and thirty Mexican), the Arizonans crossed back into the US before Mexican forces could block their withdrawal.

By 1910, according to that year's census, Jack Clinton was no longer in the mining business. His census entry describes him as an electrician working in a lighting plant. The upkeep of the ranch and the care of the small herd of cattle was left largely to Delia. This was not uncommon in the inhospitable landscape of southern Arizona, especially among members of the Hispanic farming community.[6]

By 1915, however, Jack was being described as a 'farmer and a rancher'. It probably made more sense to the *Bisbee Daily Review* to treat him as such, rather than labelling him an electrician. On 16 February 1915, the *Review* noted that 'John Clinton, a farmer and rancher of the San Pedro valley, was a business visitor in Bisbee yesterday. Clinton declares that the conditions at the crossings of the San Pedro are frightful and that they demand some improvement in them in the neighbourhood.'

If Clinton was a 'rancher', the scale of his operations was small and unthreatening. Most of his neighbours in the Palominas de San Pedro section of Cochise County could also be so described. However, the aggregate herd made up of these small undertakings challenged the dominance of big cattle companies like the Cananea Cattle Company – once owned by the late William Cornell Greene, the man who enticed the Arizona National Guard into Mexico – and the Boquillas Land and Cattle Company.

Boquillas owned and laid claim to thousands of acres of well-watered land in the San Pedro Valley, and was very particular about access to the river. A water dispute involving 'riparian rights', in which the Boquillas Company was plaintiff, had gone all the way to the US Supreme Court in 1909.[7] The company was actually owned by a huge ranching and mining conglomerate based in California, the Kern County Land and Cattle Company, which had vast land holdings all over Arizona, New Mexico and Mexico itself. It had been part-controlled, up to the time of his death in 1891, by the ruthless San Franciscan mining tycoon and US Senator George Hearst (father of William Randolph Hearst, the model for Orson Welles's *Citizen Kane*).[8]

Since few of the valley homesteaders – though the big cowmen generally preferred to think of their new neighbours as squatters – had sizeable herds, their animals often roamed freely. Unconstrained, they would frequently trespass on the property of the Boquillas Company, whose local cowmen were not the kind to live and let live. They were highly litigious, had little tolerance for 'squatters' and, where legal processes ground too slowly, had employees who were more than willing to take the law into their own hands.

By the time Europe went to war in 1914, Arizona, one of the last untamed regions of the Old West, had been a state for only two and a half years. The rugged territory achieved statehood on 14 February 1912, the forty-eighth and last contiguous state to shed its territorial status – only Alaska and Hawaii came later. By then Jack and Delia Clinton had added two more boys to their growing family, Francis Mark (1909) and Joseph (1912). Clinton first names tended to commemorate ancestors.

In December 1914, Delia gave birth to a little girl they named Mary, after Jack's sister who lived with her mother in Colorado

Springs. It soon became apparent that all was not well with young Mary and, after an illness lasting five days, she succumbed to pneumonia on 30 January 1915.[9] Delia quickly became pregnant again and, later in the year, gave birth to a son called John, named for a husband who tragically would never see his fifth child.

Delia Clinton spent the first half of 1915 in mourning for her little daughter. The second half of the year would be spent grieving for her dead husband.

4.

By the late nineteenth century, the hierarchical practice of feudalism had in theory been dead for nigh-on two hundred years. It certainly had no official standing in the American republic.

But from the point of view of the US wage slave or the impoverished homesteader of the so-called Gilded Age – the gilt being spread rather unevenly – American capitalism must have looked a lot like medieval feudalism. While the members of the rapidly expanding underclass might not have had to provide actual military service to their local overlords, their predicament certainly felt like vassalage. As if to rub it in, their masters were even popularly dubbed with mock-medieval titles. If you were an industrialist with a virtual monopoly of some vital sector of the economy – a Carnegie or a Rockefeller – you were a robber baron. If you commanded millions of acres of western land and raised hundreds of thousands of steers, like the steely magnate Charles Goodnight, monarch of the Texas Panhandle, you were a cattle baron.

'Commanded' is the *mot juste*, because although your vast cattle herds roamed freely over an immense acreage, you might have legal title to only a few hundred of those acres. Most of the land being grazed by your cattle was probably owned by the federal government. Cattle barons, while they could subsume swathes of private land by purchase, were legally permitted to file claim only for the acreage of government-owned land to which they were entitled under the 1862 Homestead Act.*

That was the theory. In practice, enterprising ranchers often exercised 'possessory rights', 'cow custom', 'range privilege' or half a dozen other euphemisms for grand theft over thousands of acres to which they had no title. They would graze their herds over land in the public domain, defend their 'property' against interlopers as if they actually owned it, frequently fence it off and, in the spirit of gritty entrepreneurial independence, defy the authorities to do anything about it.

Irritating impediments to this coercive seizure of public land were the one and a half million homesteaders who, over almost a century, filed legitimately for their quota of federal land, territory mostly acquired by purchase from France or conquest from Mexico in the first half of the nineteenth century. Homesteaders lacked the ambition, the capital, the scale and the avarice of the cattle barons. They were farmers who wanted to plant corn, raise pigs or sheep, perhaps even graze some cattle of their own, and support their families in peace and in as much comfort as was feasible. The magnitude of their undertaking was modest, but their numbers often made them a threat to the activities of the robber barons of the mesa and the plains.

---

* Big ranchers could increase the extent of their legally held land by persuading others (their employees or even war widows on the east coast) to file for their 160 acres under the Homestead Act and then convey the land to their favourite cowman. William H. Forbis, *The Old West: The Cowboys – Time Life* Books Series (New York, 1973), p. 61.

There is a choral exchange in the Rodgers and Hammerstein musical *Oklahoma!*, set in the so-called Indian Territory in 1906 as it metamorphosed into a new state, that sums up the mutual antipathy between farmer and cowman, who, as ironically suggested in the eponymous song, 'should be friends'. In one verse the farmer speaks up on behalf of his kind by pointing out that the humble homesteader has brought many positive changes to the American frontier. The nettled cowman responds, 'He come out west and built a lot of fences / And built 'em right across our cattle ranges.'

This was an ironic claim, given the countless miles of illegal barbed wire erected by the big cattle ranchers themselves all across the Great Plains. The right of the small farmer to delineate his newly acquired boundaries with his own fencing did not sit well with the cowmen. The bad odour in which the small farmer was often held is encapsulated in the announcement of an election result in the joyously named Deaf Smith County in Texas, returning 'two Democrats, two Republicans, and a sheepman'.[10]

The ubiquitous western cowboy, though in theory a free-spirited, buccaneering type with no real stake in this particular quarrel, in practice sided with the employer, who generally underpaid and overworked him. In the nineteenth- and early twentieth-century 'range versus grange' wars, the cowboy could be relied upon to do the bidding of his baronial chieftain when it came to homesteaders whose activities inhibited the free passage of the rancher's steers. Interventions designed to discourage the 'grangers' went all the way up to the level of cautionary lynchings. And if the cowboy was unwilling to act as an assassin, the local Stock Growers' Association could easily recruit more orthodox mercenaries, as occurred in the murderous Johnson County War in Wyoming from 1889 to 1893.

At the height of his fame, Charles Goodnight, one of the richest and most influential cattle barons of the late nineteenth century, 'commanded' more than a million acres around Palo Duro Canyon in the Texas Panhandle, the vast north-western area of the state. He had only actually purchased 24,000 acres from the federal government, at 75c an acre.[11] While building up his fortune, Goodnight never saw a rustler he didn't care to lynch or a homesteader he didn't wish to intimidate into heading back east (or to lynch alongside the rustler, if it came to that). He was once asked by a reporter how he felt about the settlement and enclosure of rangelands by 'nesters'. Goodnight's response, which appeared to undermine his own calling, was politic but utterly disingenuous:

> I am strongly against the free-grass idea. It simply means the use of the grass to the strongest arm. The six-shooter and free grass go hand in hand… To monopolise free grass a man must have a tough set of hands, whom he has to keep around him all the time, and they will eat up the profits and make every blade of grass cost him more than if he had it leased and fenced.[12]

It was sound bite as threat, a reminder of the firepower that cattle barons like Goodnight had at their disposal, and a hint of his own previous record in this regard. Once, when Goodnight's wife drew his attention with genuine horror to the fact that some neighbouring homesteaders had been strung up from a telegraph pole, he made sympathetic noises that indicated more of a concern for the welfare of the pole. He neglected to mention to his wife that he himself had been the instigator of the lynchings.[13]

While cattle barons depended on the population east of the Mississippi for their livelihood and were unwelcoming to human freight travelling in the opposite direction, other interests were intent on persuading as many easterners and mid-westerners as possible to respond to the dictum of the *New York Tribune* editor, Horace Greeley, to 'Go west, young man, and grow up with the country.' The new mercantile aristocrats of the western states – railroad men, retailers, bankers, administrators – wanted settlers, as taxpayers, consumers and borrowers, to arrive in droves. They were prepared to gild the lily with fool's gold to entice them.

The boosters advertising the benefits and charms of this vast open prairie land bank failed to mention drought, disease, infestation, lawlessness or the overwhelming need for significant start-up capital, when selling the west to potential settlers. They also glossed over the reality that the farmer would be selling wholesale whatever he produced, while buying retail whatever he required.

Then there were the unstated start-up expenses. A rough estimate of the cost of building a home, purchasing animals, digging a well, fencing a newly acquired property and acquiring seed grain for that vital first crop was somewhere in the region of $1,000. This was a lifetime's wages to many – lifetimes were short in those days, and wages were low. If you could find a bank prepared to lend you that amount of cash, it would take decades of bumper crops to pay off the debt.

The land to the west of the Great Plains, often called the Great American Desert, gets about 30cm of rainfall a year, a tenth of the precipitation in the Amazon Rainforest, or a quarter of the rain produced by the mizzly showers that soak the Irish north midlands forsaken by Jack Clinton. Conveniently, the American west experienced higher than average rainfall in the 1870s and 1880s. This gave rise to the booster myth that the very act of cultivation promoted precipitation, that rainfall 'follows the plough'. Later generations were to discover that rainfall did no such thing.

If you happened to find yourself in financial difficulties, the banks would have the patience and forbearance of buzzards introduced to a fresh carcass. If you had no available cash to transport all your produce, the railroads would be happy to remove your freight, dump it carelessly in a siding, invite you to come and collect it, and charge you for the privilege.

It was said of the Great American West that 'farmers... raised three crops, corn, freight and interest'.[14] Or, as Richard Slotkin has more prosaically put it, 'The greatest beneficiaries of the Homestead legislation were railroad, banking and landholding corporations.' By the turn of the century, 'Land ownership in the Great Plains states was being steadily consolidated in fewer and fewer hands.'[15]

And there was no point in looking to government for assistance when times were tough. Once enticed to a semi-arid western state with promises of 'nesting' profitably, you were on your own. According to the prevailing Manichean mindset of the Far West, you were either hard-working and self-reliant or a mendicant of doubtful moral character. In the first instance, you needed no assistance from the public coffers; in the second, you received none.

Jack Clinton, had he a mind to do so, would have looked in vain for an Arizonan workhouse for his family to fall back on *in extremis*. In Ireland, they were much-loathed and stigmatised establishments whose prison-like facilities were availed of only as a last resort. In the south-western US there was no such thing as a last resort, outside of prison or a hole in the ground on Boot Hill.

This was the landscape in which the Clintons chose to make their home.

2

The First Killing

'George Scarborough's son Ed was no good…
They should have hung him when he was a pup.'

Judge James C. Hancock, Arizona, 23 August 1936

I.

No one knows precisely what Ed Scarborough and Calvin Cox wanted with Jack Clinton on the night of 18 June 1915. Their intentions were certainly not amicable. It is probable that they wanted to discuss Clinton's rejection of a number of Boquillas cattle in his role as a brand inspector at that day's auction in Wilcox, a small town halfway between Tucson and the New Mexico border. As an official brand inspector for the state of Arizona, Clinton had the right to intervene in the sale of cattle when he was unhappy with the branding or the condition of the animals.[1] To the cow-men, a squatter with such discretionary authority was like a slave with a gun. The Boquillas cowboys had acquired another reason to dislike Jack Clinton.

Little enough is known about Cal Cox, who played only a supporting role in the events of that night. But much is known about George Edgar Scarborough, a truculent man with a violent pedigree and a personal history of criminality.

If one applies the Frigyes Karinthy 'six degrees of separation' template, George Edgar 'Ed' Scarborough was halfway along the scale to the most notorious killer in the Old West. As the son of the man who killed the man who shot dead John Wesley Hardin, Scarborough was separated by three degrees from the famous gunslinger. Hardin was the verified murderer of more than twenty victims and self-confessed slayer of twenty more, and merits an impressive thirteen columns in the *Encyclopedia of Western Outlaws* – James Butler 'Wild Bill' Hickok is deemed to be worth only nine.

Hardin terrorised the state of Texas for most of the 1870s.[2]

Jailed for twenty-five years for a single manslaughter in 1877, he 'reformed', wrote his autobiography – in which he claimed that the twenty-one kills with which he was credited was a gross underestimate – studied law and bided his time. He was released after sixteen years at the age of forty-one. He survived until just beyond his forty-second birthday, before being shot in the back of the head in the Acme Saloon in the border town of El Paso, Texas by one John Selman Sr., father of a local lawman.

Selman's lawyer, Albert Fall, managed to force a retrial by convincing enough members of the jury that Selman had killed Hardin in self-defence. Despite Hardin having been shot dead while his back was turned, it would not have taken much to convince a jury that the murderous John Wesley, who had issued threats to both Selman and his son, had lethal intentions.

Unfortunately, while awaiting his second trial, Selman fell out with the celebrated Texas lawman George Scarborough, Ed's father. He accused Scarborough of stealing money from the corpse of a cattle rustler who had been lured back from Mexico and shot dead. The two men (Scarborough and Selman) met in an alleyway in El Paso, and Selman did not emerge alive. Scarborough shot the older man four times.

As Selman died, he was heard to declare, 'I never drew my gun.' A jury, however, found Scarborough not guilty of murder.[3] Juries could be surprisingly lenient when it came to the western equivalent of eighteenth-century duelling.

On the same Karinthy scale, Ed Scarborough was separated from another famous western outlaw by only two degrees – he was the son of the man shot and killed by Harvey Logan. Better known as Kid Curry, Logan was an intimate of Robert LeRoy Parker and Harry Longabaugh, much better known as Butch Cassidy and the Sundance Kid.

On 5 April 1900, George Scarborough, now working for the Grant County Cattleman's Association in south-western New Mexico, tracked Logan and other members of the so-called Wild Bunch to a canyon near the town of San Simon, Arizona. Chasing the outlaw into the canyon, he was shot in the leg by the fleeing Logan. Scarborough was carried to safety and the leg was amputated, but he died the following day in Deming, New Mexico.[4] An alternative narrative suggests that the killing was not mere happenstance and that Scarborough had been successfully lured into a trap by Butch Cassidy himself.[5]

Ed Scarborough, born on 12 January 1879, looked destined to follow in his father's footsteps. As a teenager, he had been recruited by his father to work alongside him chasing down rustlers and outlaws in the interests of the Grant County cattlemen. After the murder of his father, Ed joined in the search for the killers. Later he was frequently deputised as an *ex officio* member of posses hunting rustlers or other outlaws.

Within months of his father's death, Ed Scarborough had killed his first alleged criminal. In August 1900, as part of a posse escorting a suspected murderer named Ralph Jenks to Silver City on the Arizona-New Mexico border, the prisoner seized Scarborough's shotgun. When Jenks tried to use the weapon, it jammed. Scarborough killed Jenks with three shots from his revolver.

The posse escorting Jenks, which had been scouring the countryside for rustlers, included a number of men – Scarborough was one – who had been deputised at the instigation of the South-western New Mexico Cattle Protective Association. The *Silver City Independent* defended the local sheriff, James K. Blair, against accusations that this was in effect a public-private vigilante force operating at the behest of wealthy cattle interests. The *Independent* claimed on 9 October 1900 that: 'The commissions were applied for by the executive committee of the cattle association in order that its men might have proper authority to carry out the work which they were employed to do.'

To which the response of critics might have been that this was precisely the point: the power of the cattlemen was such that they could influence the commissioning of deputies by the local county sheriff. The men thus deputised were paid not from local tax revenues, but from the funds of the concerned cowmen.

To many New Mexicans, the Jenks 'escort' had amounted to little more than a murder squad, and the reports of the circumstances of his death were widely disbelieved. The assumption was that Scarborough had simply gunned down Jenks on behalf of his *de facto* employers. Later that year Blair lost the election for county sheriff, and his successor revoked the appointment of Ed Scarborough as a deputy.

Scarborough then went about his father's business and began working for the cattlemen, though he was deemed to be over-enthusiastic in his pursuit of alleged rustlers. In January 1901 he became the main object of discord at a meeting in Silver City, New Mexico that almost culminated in an outbreak of fisticuffs, or worse. According to the *Lordsburg Western Liberal*, 'The chief point of discussion seemed to have been ... [Edgar] Scarborough [who has] arrested many men for stealing cattle but was unable to present enough evidence to warrant indictments, and the men arrested had to be turned loose. It looked to the citizens as though the rangers were trying to bulldoze men more than they were trying to secure convictions of cow thieves.'[6]

The reference to rangers – a state-wide police force actually defunct for almost twenty years – was something of a self-fulfilling prophecy, because in 1901 the Arizona Rangers, a force last seen on horseback in 1882, was re-established by Governor Nathan Oakes Murphy. Created in the main to deal with the scourge of rustling, impinging largely on the business interests of the prosperous cowmen of Arizona, the Rangers had a complement of one captain, one sergeant and a dozen privates. Edgar Scarborough, twenty-two, already married and a father, was recruited as a private. The first captain of the Arizona Rangers was Burton C. Mossman of Bisbee. Mossman's previous employment had been as superintendent of the two-million-acre Aztec Land and Cattle Company spread, where he had a reputation for unrivalled ferocity when it came to dealing with alleged cattle thieves.

Scarborough, one of the youngest recruits, was described by the *Tucson Citizen* as 'a determined fellow and much like his father'.[7] Given his father's cynical killing of John Selman, that was an even more accurate description than the *Citizen* could have suspected. Ed Scarborough's career as an Arizona Ranger lasted a mere nine months. He was thrown out for brawling with a civilian and pulling a gun on Mossman.

Continuing to channel the career path of his father, Ed Scarborough immediately signed up as a hand with a cattle outfit, the so-called Wagon Rods of the Boquillas Land and Cattle Company, which operated across a vast tract of Cochise County. Over the next thirteen years he left a nomadic, rackety trail of petty crimes in his wake. In December 1902 he was charged in Deming, New Mexico with 'unlawfully carrying a deadly weapon'; two years later he was identified as the hold-up man in the robbery of a restaurant. His lawyer requested a change of venue from Deming to Silver City, and hedged adroitly to the point where charges were dropped.[8]

In 1909, this erstwhile nemesis of the rustler was alleged to have been engaged in stealing horses. He fled New Mexico for California and spent the next few years in Los Angeles. By February 1915, however, Scarborough was back in the south-west and working once again for the Boquillas Land and Cattle Company.

By then the superintendent of the Wagon Rods was Henry K. Street, an uncompromising cattleman of the old school.[9] Street's education would inevitably have included the axiom that 'nesters' were to be tolerated only until a pretext could be found to treat them like the rustlers they almost inevitably were. Street did not need to pass on the benefit of his schooling to Scarborough. The former ranger knew what his employers required of him.

And Jack Clinton had transgressed the unwritten code of the cowmen. His very presence in the San Pedro Valley was a first misdemeanour. Having filed for his legitimate allotment of federal land in Cochise County, Clinton was an unavoidable irritant. Like his Palominas neighbours the Foudys (Jack Clinton and Michael Foudy had met in San Francisco), he was legally entitled to fence off his property and curtail the grazing of corporate steers previously encouraged to roam at will. The corollary was his legal obligation to confine his own JDC-branded cattle to the land secured from Washington, DC.

It was a combative and litigious environment. In April 1915, Clinton was listed as plaintiff in an Arizona Superior Court appeal involving the Cananea Cattle Company, owners of 700,000 acres of US and Mexican land. For the small farmers and homesteaders of the San Pedro Valley, life involved a struggle against elemental forces other than that of nature itself.

Clinton ran a small herd which Ed Scarborough was convinced was grazing on Boquillas land. There was at least one recorded confrontation between the two, during which Scarborough took out his gun and threatened to use it if Clinton didn't restrict the movements of his nomadic JDC cattle. On that occasion, Clinton had 'laughed the cowboy out of the notion of shooting'.[10]

There would be no laughter on the evening of 18 June 1915.

That night, Scarborough arrived at the camp of fellow Boquillas hand Calvin Cox and asked him to saddle up and join him in a visit to Clinton's farm. Cox was another cowboy with an axe to grind with the Irishman, and had also threatened to kill him. Their altercation had taken place in front of witnesses, who would come forward at his subsequent trial.

Throughout the aftermath, Cox would claim that Scarborough had been solely responsible for what happened. He, Cox, was an innocent abroad with no inkling of Scarborough's intentions, and had remained detached throughout the proceedings. Unlikely as this might seem, it was supported in court by the testimony of the only uninvolved witness, eleven-year-old Rose Clinton.

2.

It was Rose Clinton who answered the knock on the door.

Darkness had almost fallen, the family had finished its evening meal, and Jack Clinton, just back from the Wilcox auction, had removed his boots before retiring for the night.* Rose told her father that there were two men in the yard. One was sitting on his horse, the other was standing on the porch. The second man wanted to talk to him.

Jack Clinton slipped on a pair of moccasins and went outside,

---

* Rose Clinton recited the details of what occurred in evidence at John Clinton's inquest and at Ed Scarborough's trial. Her evidence appeared in the *Bisbee Daily Review* of 20 June 1915 and 4 December 1915.

unarmed. His wife, Delia, was busy preparing her two boys for bed. Temporarily distracted, she failed to notice that Rose was watching her father and the stranger.

What the eleven-year-old saw was Jack Clinton engaged in animated conversation with Ed Scarborough. They were walking towards the gate of the ranch house yard, arguing heatedly as they went. Looking on was Calvin Cox, who remained on his horse throughout the exchange. By the time they had reached the first of the ranch's two garden gates, both men were swearing loudly at each other. Then Scarborough produced a gun and fired four shots into Clinton's body. One hit him in the right side of his chest, two more entered his stomach, the fourth lodged in his right leg.

Clinton slumped to the ground. Scarborough and Cox fled.

By the time Delia Clinton reached her husband, he was barely clinging to life. Rose Clinton, who lived into her mid-nineties, dying only in 2002, always maintained that her father had managed to mutter a few words before he died: 'Mama, bring the rifle and kill him. He has shot me.'

Thankfully, Delia Clinton did not try to exact immediate retribution. Had she attempted to do so, there might have been no innocent witnesses to the original crime left alive.

The pursuit of Scarborough and Cox began almost immediately. Both men rode towards the Mexican border two miles away, but separated before reaching it. Cox crossed into Mexico, while Scarborough doubled back and rode towards the town of Benson, where his intention seems to have been to board a Southern Pacific train and get as far away as possible. He was foiled by two deputies of the Cochise County sheriff, Harry C. Wheeler, who arrested him at Benson railway station, sixty miles from Clinton's farm.

Judge George R. Smith of Lowell, Arizona, was meanwhile conducting an inquest into the death of John Clinton at the JDC ranch. After listening to the testimony of Rose Clinton, the *Bisbee Daily Review* of 20 June 1915 concluded that 'Scarborough will have a difficult time in clearing himself before the courts.'

Calvin Cox did not remain at large much longer than Scarborough. He crossed back into Arizona and by 21 June was under lock and key in Tombstone, charged as an accessory to murder. Cox protested his innocence and claimed to have had no foreknowledge of Scarborough's intentions. On 27 June, he was transferred by car from Tombstone to Bisbee by two sheriff's deputies.

He was not the only passenger. Also being ferried to Bisbee, as a courtesy, was one of Jack Clinton's sisters, Annie, who lived on her own spread a few miles from the Palominas ranch. Well aware of the identity of the front-seat passenger, she sat stoically in the back.

The stoicism did not endure for long. The *Bisbee Daily Review* reported with some morbid satisfaction that at some point along the road from Tombstone, Annie Clinton leaned forward in her seat, 'reached over and started to choke the man. It was with some trouble that the officers in charge released Cox from the grasp of the enraged woman.'[11]

Cox wasn't finished with the Clinton women either. On 4 September in Tombstone, at a bail hearing, Delia Clinton spotted an opening, sprang from her seat in the courtroom and lunged at Cox in the dock. According to the *Bisbee Daily Review* of 5 September, 'She sought his throat and it was some minutes before court attendants could force her to release her hold from the accused man.'

The presiding judge ordered Delia to be removed from the court, but a short time later she slipped back in and was thrown out all over again. Cox's claim to have been an uninformed and innocent onlooker at the murder of Jack Clinton did not impress the doughty female members of the Clinton family.

There was a clear division of opinion in southern Arizona about what had actually occurred on the evening of 18 June in Palominas. If you had a vested interest in large-scale cattle ranching, your presumption would be that the unarmed Jack Clinton had pro-voked or intimidated Ed Scarborough into shooting him dead. If, on the other hand, you were a small farmer or rancher, you would trust in the more credible theory. As far as his fellow 'nesters' were concerned, Clinton was the victim of an assassination commissioned by the beneficial owners of the Boquillas Land and Cattle Company and carried out by two of the corporation's employees, Scarborough and Cox, because he had finally pushed the cowmen too far.*

Clinton, a well-educated man, had long been a thorn in the side of the southern Arizona cattle barons through a series of political and legal disputes undertaken on behalf of fellow homesteaders. Logically, therefore, a San Pedro Valley minus Jack Clinton was a highly desirable outcome for the powerful cattlemen.

To quell the persistent rumours swirling around Cochise County, the Boquillas Land and Cattle Company adopted a 'nothing to see here' approach. Henry K. Street, company super-intendent, issued a statement denying any involvement and insisting that:

---

* A Clinton family anecdote has it that when Scarborough was arrested in Benson, he was carrying $1,500 in his pocket. If this is true, it was a large sum of money for a wrangler engaged solely in bovine conveyance and husbandry. There is, however, no documentary evidence in any contemporary accounts to back up the assertion.

29

None of the employees of this company has ever had a dispute with Mr. Clinton over the rights of his property, or over any other question until this affair came up between him and Scarborough last Friday. And I know absolutely nothing about that, only hearsay. I have heard so many stories about it that I have come to the conclusion that the only thing we can do is to await the preliminary examination and see what that brings out. I am sure that if the newspapers and Mr. Clinton's friends will take the trouble to investigate or wait until the preliminary examination, before rendering a decision, they will find out that these erroneous reports are doing the Boquillas Land & Cattle Company a great injustice. Personally, I never knew Mr. Clinton, and could not possibly have had any ill-feeling towards him.'[12]

The following month, Scarborough's attorney, Eugene R. Ives, was forced to deny rumours that he had been retained by the Boquillas Land and Cattle Company to defend the accused man. He told the *Tombstone Epitaph* that 'he was retained to defend Scarborough by the defendant himself'.[13]

3.

The trial of Ed Scarborough began in Tombstone on 3 December 1915. Proceedings were expected to last a week. After more than an hour of preliminaries, in which a number of potential jurors were successfully challenged by both sides, twelve men were chosen from the twenty-nine originally sworn. Coincidentally, two of those serving on Scarborough's trial jury bore the surname Gordon. As we shall see in subsequent chapters, it is richly ironic that anyone of that name should preside over the fate of a man who had murdered a member of the Clinton family.

The main prosecution witness was young Rose Clinton. Her testimony was an ordeal for a girl not yet in her teens who had seen her father brutally murdered. The *Tombstone Epitaph* was tremendously impressed with the manner in which she stood up to direct questioning and cross-examination. 'Rose Clinton, daughter of the deceased, was on the stand for several hours. This little girl is considered one of the star witnesses, having witnessed the alleged affair and for several hours this afternoon answered without a falter the queries of the attorneys for both sides.'[14]

Scarborough, though not obliged to do so, testified on his own behalf. He denied premeditated murder and pleaded self-defence. He claimed that he had not visited the JDC ranch with any intention of killing Jack Clinton, but simply to remonstrate with him. He had seen Clinton steal a cow and had gone to the Clinton ranch to, as he told the jury euphemistically, 'talk the matter over with him'.[15]

According to the court report in the *Bisbee Daily Review* of 10 December 1915:

He stated he got Cal Cox to accompany him but that he did not tell Cox what he was going over there for, and that Cox did not know what he went for. He stated that after he went over to the Clinton place he left Cox on the outside and called Clinton out and started to talk to him and that Clinton said: 'Mamma bring the gun and we will get rid of one of the witnesses.'

It was a clever ploy if Scarborough was going to mitigate the crime of shooting an unarmed man. He also denied statements already made by a number of witnesses who had testified that he had threatened Clinton's life. Proceedings then became somewhat more theatrical as Scarborough re-enacted the drama, from his point of view, for the benefit of the jury.

> At the same time Clinton grabbed him by the left arm, he pulled his gun from the small scabbard that he had in the pocket of his chaps and fired three shots at Clinton. At that time Scarborough says he heard a door close. He had the gun in his hand and accidentally pulled the trigger, hitting Clinton the fourth time. He demonstrated with one of the jurors as to the manner in which Clinton grabbed him at the time.

The potential witness most notable for his absence was the only living person, other than Rose Clinton and Ed Scarborough, who had seen the confrontation: Calvin Cox. Eugene Ives feigned shock and surprise at the state's failure to produce the man who, by all accounts, should have been their star witness. He was challenged by the attorney for the State of Arizona, experienced trial lawyer W. B. Cleary, as to why the defence had not subpoenaed Cox if they were implying that his statement would exonerate the defendant. Ives got the better of that exchange by declaring, 'We did not have to, as we have already proved Scarborough innocent!'[16] Cleary, despite his acknowledged ringcraft, had walked into a haymaker.

Ives also presented an expert witness to challenge the veracity of Rose Clinton's statement about her father's last words. Dr H.H. Hughart told the court that in his expert medical opinion, this was a physical impossibility. 'Clinton,' Hughart averred, 'would have died almost immediately or would have had such haemorrhages that would have prevented him from making any such statement.'

After a couple of prosecution rebuttal witnesses and final

statements from prosecution and defence counsel, Judge Alfred C. Lockwood sent the case to the jury room. It took the twelve yeomen of Cochise County an entire night of animated discussion to deliver a verdict. Initially, ten of the twelve voted to send Scarborough to the gallows (executions having resumed in Arizona a few weeks before). Then one of the hold-outs caved in, leaving only a single juror crediting Scarborough's version of events. But that was enough to prolong the deliberations.

At 10 a.m. on the morning of 11 December, the jury returned with a series of questions and a request for instructions. They retired once again and returned with a verdict of second-degree murder. Ives immediately gave notice of appeal and filed for a retrial. Bail was denied, and Scarborough was returned to prison.

Scarborough, who faced sentencing (of a minimum ten years in jail) that afternoon, seemed peculiarly unperturbed by the outcome of the trial. His wife and mother, both in court, broke down in tears, but the killer himself appeared insouciant. The *Bisbee Daily Review*, which had covered the case from start to finish, noted that 'Scarborough was not in the least affected by the verdict of the jury and seemed to be the least concerned of any of those who were interested in the case'.[17]

As it turned out, he was right to be blasé.

The trial of Calvin Cox, indicted as Scarborough's accomplice, began on 15 December.

Cox's defence was straightforward. He was a waif and stray, hard of hearing and with no agency worthy of consideration. Ed Scarborough, a known killer and thief (albeit with no convictions), bore complete responsibility for the entire tragedy. That had been Cox's line since the preliminary hearing back in July, when:

In his own behalf, Cox made a voluntary statement. He declared that on the night of the killing Scarborough came to his camp and suggested that he ride with him to Clinton's place. Cox agreed. He declared that when the gate was reached Scarborough dismounted and entered the yard. Cox said he heard voices indistinctly as he was partly deaf. A moment later he heard and saw the flash of a gun. Scarborough then ordered him to ride to the international boundary.[18]

Cox was not forced to explain why he had failed to come to the assistance of Jack Clinton before or after his death, or why, if he was an innocent man, he had agreed to Scarborough's injunction that they both ride for the Mexican frontier. Cox's case, however, was strengthened by the evidence of Rose Clinton that he had not dismounted throughout the quarrel between the two men.

The presiding justice in the case, Judge O'Connor of Nogales in the south-west corner of Arizona, was precise in his direction to the jury. He instructed them that they had only two options: acquittal, or the conviction of Cox of first-degree murder.

He was guilty of deliberate, premeditated murder, with malice aforethought, or not of anything, as he did not fire the shot that killed Clinton and unless he had prearranged the matter with Scarborough he was not guilty of the lesser offenses, as the testimony showed that he did not get off his horse or take any physical part in the affair that led to the killing of Clinton.[19]

The jury, unsurprisingly, opted to acquit. Calvin Cox left the Tombstone courthouse a free man.

Ed Scarborough could have gone to jail for up to forty years. The shortest sentence available to Judge Lockwood was ten years in prison, and that was the tariff he opted to impose. Assuming that Scarborough's appeal was dismissed, he would probably spend just over half that time in jail. He was likely to serve only six years, seven at most, for the murder of Jack Clinton, a man in his moccasins, carrying no weapon, gunned down in front of his eldest child.

But it might have been worse. The *Arizona Republican* viewed the verdict and the sentence as a sign that the more disorderly regions of the state were at last putting law and order ahead of anarchic individualism:

> Considering the verdicts of Cochise County jurors in the recent past in murder cases, where cold-blooded slayers have been acquitted because they stated that they thought that their unarmed victims had 'motioned toward their hip pockets', we think this verdict of second-degree murder is something of an advance.[20]

4.

Fortune, or something suspiciously closer to home, favoured Ed Scarborough in the end. The *Bisbee Daily Review*, in the same issue in which it reported on the carnage of the Easter Rising in Dublin – 'Bitter aftermath to Irish revolt' – drew attention to the fact that Scarborough had lost his appeal and would be serving his sentence.

Except that he did no such thing.

His wife Ruby divorced him and took up with an El Paso and Southwestern Railroad brakeman, O.A. Ash. From his prison cell, Scarborough swore that he would wreak vengeance on the heads of both. It was not the language of penitence, or a pathway to parole.[21]

The latter option, however, proved unnecessary. On 25 May 1917, just over a year after he had begun serving his time in Arizona State Prison in Florence, Scarborough somehow contrived to break out of jail. He was one of three escapers, but the only one to remain at large after four weeks.

He was expected to arrive at the Ash residence to express his displeasure at his ex-wife's new domestic arrangements, but he never showed up. Instead, he simply disappeared. A reward of one hundred dollars for his apprehension went unclaimed. Rumour had it that, unlike his abortive flight in the immediate aftermath of the killing of Jack Clinton, Scarborough had fled to Mexico and remained there. He was said to cross the frontier from time to time, incognito, to visit his mother and sisters.

In the course of reporting on the killing of Jack Clinton, the 20 June 1915 *Bisbee Daily Review*, published in a town a few miles north-east of Palominas, informed its readers that 'Clinton was comparatively well-to-do. He had a considerable number of cattle and a well-appointed ranch. It is understood he leaves his family fairly well off.'

That is certainly not the narrative of the extended Clinton clan, which suggests that Jack Clinton's family was anything but prosperous, and was largely left to shift for itself after his death. From the age of seven, when he was orphaned, Frank Clinton 'hunted all kinds of wild game with his .22 rifle to put food on the table... It was a hard life, but the family survived.'[22] Life would have been harder still but for the fact that Jack's sister Annie, the would-be strangler of Calvin Cox, helped Delia raise her four children.

Delia Clinton, who had lost her second daughter to pneumonia in January 1915, was pregnant once again when her husband was murdered in their own back yard. She gave birth to her fourth surviving child, John, in December of that year.

Three of the Clinton children spent the rest of their lives in Arizona. Rose married, became a teacher and died at the age of ninety-five, still on the Palominas property where she had witnessed her father's murder. Joe married a widow, Mabel Stevenson, and died in Hereford, Arizona at the age of eighty-five in 1997. John Clinton never married; he died in 1990, aged seventy-four. Frank Clinton became a successful engineer, lived and worked in Idaho and California, and died in 1986 at the age of seventy-seven.

Delia Clinton, worn out by grief and the exhaustion of looking after her young family alone, remarried in August 1918. Aged thirty-eight, she married Ralph Hart of Hereford, six years her junior. Father Mardin, the Roman Catholic priest who had buried her first husband, officiated at their wedding.

Sadly, Delia had precious little time to enjoy her new life. She died at the age of only forty-six in 1926. Working on a haystack on the family farm, she lost her balance and broke her neck in the fall.[23] She left four distraught children, the oldest in her twenties, the youngest not yet in his teens. They had now lost both parents to sudden and violent death. Annie, by now married herself, formally adopted the two young boys, Joe and John.

Jack Clinton, transplanted from the moist green fields of north Leinster, escaped the agrarian turmoil of his native Ireland in the

1880s only to perish of gunshot wounds in the arid, inhospitable wilderness of southern Arizona. Born on the border between the ancient provinces of Leinster and Ulster, he died violently within a few miles of the Mexican-American frontier. On 18 June 1915, he became a victim of two of the unresolved issues of the fast-vanishing American frontier: infatuation with gun violence, and perennial quarrels over the nature of land ownership. He was one of a dozen Cochise County murder victims that year.

On 29 January 1916, the *Bisbee Daily Review*, newspaper of record for the administrative seat of Cochise County, was once again exercised about the local murder rate. A January editorial lamented the fact that sixteen men had been murdered in the previous thirteen months. It echoed the sentiments of the 'Red record of Cochise' editorial from the previous June, shortly after the murder of John Clinton.

Jack Clinton's killer – or killers, assuming you take a less than charitable view of Cox's credibility and the complicity of the Boquillas Land and Cattle Company – went almost entirely unpunished.

The killer of Jack Clinton's cousin Mark five years later would not be so fortunate.

3

The Second Killing

'In the spring of 1920… all bonds were broken and
the fever swept with the fury of a prairie fire over
Connacht and portions of the other provinces, sparing
neither great ranch nor medium farm and inflicting, in its
headlong course, sad havoc on man, beast, and property.'

Kevin O'Shiel, 'The last land war', *Irish Times*,
22 November 1966

'The people in my district, except in agrarian disputes,
are well disposed towards the law and each other.'

Kilkee resident magistrate, 1914[1]

I.

Then there was that other war.

This was the one that hid its light under a bushel of flying column raids and RIC indifference. It was almost as ubiquitous as the one for which the campaign medals (with a fetching black and tan ribbon) were issued. It spread over half the counties of Ireland in the early months of 1920.[2]

For reasons that will become plain, this parallel conflict tended not to prosper in regions where the IRA was at its most active. This is because it was a war of dearth and desperation, an artless brawl for land, rather than a poetic struggle for political freedom. It was largely conducted in inverse proportion to the parallel contest of nationalism and imperialism. In the real hot-spots of the 'Tan War', where the IRA maintained a ruthless hegemony, there was little room for the distraction of reheated agrarian battles from the 1880s, or the gratification of a craving for land.

The onset of the Anglo-Irish War did not miraculously bring about an armistice in the stamina-sapping and multi-faceted agrarian *pas d'armes* that had plagued rural Ireland for four decades. Thousands of disillusioned smallholders, angry at the economic power of the new grazier class – breeders of livestock and occupiers of vast tracts of land – did not suddenly put aside their economic grievances and rally to a higher cause. Some did, but others saw opportunity in upheaval.

To many smallholders in the west and the midlands, with all due respect to the struggle for an independent Irish republic, there was no higher cause than that of land redistribution. This had been the case during the Great War, when prosperous graziers, not dastardly Germans, had been the enemy. The ostensible change of combatants was of little consequence to this militia of the dispossessed, determined to shrug off their serfdom.

The Sinn Féin of 1920 liked to think that it had moved beyond the struggles of the Land War (1879–82) and its sequel, the Ranch War (1906–09). The former conflict is usually represented as a classic peasant revolt, combining elements of quasi-legal popular agitation with violent subversion. Passionate speeches by day, punitive raids after dark. But late Victorian Irish rural society fell far short of the idyllic. Reality ran counter to the prevailing mythos of a noble and beleaguered Irish peasantry, more sinned against than sinning, whose occasional descent into intimidation was entirely justified by the unjust tenurial system against which it struggled.

Far from being an agrarian uprising prosecuted by the Irish Land League on behalf of an indigent but heroic rural populace, the land struggle of the 1880s was a complex palimpsest of interacting class antagonisms. It was as much about debt resolution as it was about land tenure. The competing interests were driven by complex overlapping animosities between landowner, tenant, shopkeeper and labourer.

The conflict was characterised by stirring slogans like 'the land for the people' (Land League founder Michael Davitt) and 'keep a firm grip of your homesteads' (Irish Nationalist Party leader Charles Stewart Parnell), and by that most ingenious device, the boycott. This was a process of social ostracism visited on landlords, 'land grabbers' who moved onto farms from which the original tenants had been evicted, and all others adjudged by agrarian activists to be transgressors. They were despatched, in Parnell's words, to 'a sort of moral Coventry'.

But the Land War was also a confrontation between the gentry and the rising Irish merchant class. The prize was a golden share in the dwindling assets of the peasant. The early 1880s was a period of severe economic depression. Irish farmers had been faring better since the Great Famine than received wisdom suggests,[3] but even after two decades of rising expectations, they were not in a position to pay their debts to both landlord *and* shopkeeper.

The Irish Land League, often led by the rural petit-bourgeoisie, while undoubtedly championing the small farmer, was also a combatant in a putsch, a play to annex the resources of the Irish peasantry. Breach of contract campaigns, like the No Rent Manifesto of 1881 in which farmers were advised by the Land League to withhold rent, were messages from merchant to tenant: 'If you can't pay the landlord and reimburse the shopkeeper, then default on your rent, not your commercial debts.'

Decades of late nineteenth-century remedial land legislation from Westminster had managed to pull some of the teeth of agrarian agitation, which then grew a few new ones. Land purchase legislation framed by successive British governments seeking to spend less parliamentary time pacifying the Irish countryside had, by the first decade of the twentieth century, brought about a revolution in Irish land tenure. The ten thousand-strong landlord class had gradually given way to peasant proprietors remitting manageable sums in loan repayment annuities to a British government that had effectively abandoned the Irish Ascendancy, the old Anglo-Irish elite.

But it was all very far from the idealistic 'land for the people' sloganeering of the League. If the 'people' included landless labourers, then the mantra was a platitude. The truth was that in the new dispensation of tenant ownership, the self-styled cream had risen to the top. Many of the more prosperous farmers had been enabled to purchase the land that they and their families had worked for generations. Having done so, some had gone on to acquire additional holdings to which many others felt they had no entitlement.

Those landlords who had opted to buck the trend and retain their holdings had also discovered imaginative ways of circumventing decades of agrarian legislation making it more difficult to evict inconvenient tenants. This had led to the ubiquity of the 'eleven-month' system of landholding. Under this practice, auctioneers would sell short-term leases for agricultural land to the highest bidder. Many of these leases were acquired not by farming families eager to expand their holdings, but by dilettantes with no agricultural background whatever. The merchants and shopkeepers who had often led the battle against landlord dominance in the 1880s now donned the robes of the aristocracy and added 'eleven-month' land, adorned by herds of pedigree cattle, to their expanding portfolio of assets.

The fissures of the late nineteenth century were thus still in evidence three decades later. In some respects they had widened as the fundamentals of Irish agricultural practice changed. There was a rapid movement from tillage to livestock farming. A prerequisite for this development was an increase in the size of farms and the acquisition of supplementary land by a growing grazier class often derided as 'ranchers' – the term had more pejorative connotations in the Irish midlands than it had in Arizona – and one of the consequences of the growth of the large beef or dairy farm was the reduced need for farm labourers. Both phenomena fuelled an increased land hunger among the members of the lower socioeconomic agricultural class to whom few benefits had accrued from the onset of peasant proprietorship.

In the first decade of the twentieth century, ad hoc groups like the Back to the Land movement attempted to mitigate the drift towards pastoral agriculture. This organisation sought to purchase estates, divide the land into modest but viable parcels, and distribute farms to landless labourers or other aspiring agriculturalists.

But there was a darker side to this activism in the emerging practice of cattle-driving, the nocturnal scattering of an offending grazier's herd across a few parishes. The ability of 'ranchers' to acquire additional land by purchase or rental, often at premium prices, shut out both the landless and the purchasing agents of the Back to the Land movement.[4] The growth of the eleven-month system encouraged some landlords to retain their holdings, and prevented Back to the Land, and the British administration, from expediting the disintegration of large estates.

Leading and exemplifying the cattle-driving crusade was the maverick nationalist MP Laurence Ginnell from Westmeath. Elected as an Irish Parliamentary Party (IPP) MP in 1906, Ginnell never quite settled into political subservience. His advocacy of cattle-driving as an antidote to the social implications of increasing pastoralism set him at odds with party leadership, and their ways parted in 1909 when he was denied access to the party accounts. He sat as an independent nationalist until 1918, when he made the logical leap to Sinn Féin and became a TD after the Republican landslide in the December election of that year.

The battle cry adopted by the cattle-drivers and often articulated by Ginnell, 'The land for the people, and the bullock for the road', was a subversive variation of the famous slogan of the Land League. The Ranch War prospered in Ginnell's bailiwick of County Westmeath. Since one of his allies was the MP for South Meath, David Sheehy, the same applied to the neighbouring county.

Sinn Féin, eager to please all constituencies, had exploited the issue to harvest votes in the 1918 election by campaigning vociferously for an end to the dominance of the ranch. It helped that the graziers were mostly supporters of the old IPP. The cattle-drivers needed little encouragement, and the practice of 'driving' resumed with élan. This prompted the unsympathetic *Sligo Champion* of 2 March 1918 to observe, a few months after Lenin had managed to install an unlikely communist regime in Russia, that 'a reign of terror similar to that of the Bolsheviks [has] been unleashed on the Irish countryside'. More Narodnik than Bolshevik in its essentials, perhaps, but the *Sligo Champion* was reflecting an anxiety that identified any radical undertaking post-1917 as communist to the core.

Ironically, Sinn Féin itself might have become the victim of the renewed wave of rural agitation that swept across Connacht and the north midlands in 1920. The agrarian passions that the party unleashed in 1918, which boosted it in the intra-nationalist battle with the Redmondites, who had loyally supported the imperial war effort and were now facing political oblivion, were suddenly resuscitated during the near anarchy of the military escalation by the IRA in the so-called 'winter offensive' of 1920. Had the crop from this 'Last Land War'* been allowed to grow and ripen, the outcome of the Anglo-Irish conflict might have been quite different.

This resurrection of the hungry – an inconvenient smallholder revolt – flowed from a variety of tributary sources, and a number of factors inspired its resurgence. While actively opposed from early 1920 by the Sinn Féin leadership in Dublin – most notably by Arthur Griffith – it was often vigorously stoked by grass-roots Sinn Féin militants, in defiance of central authority.

Of less consequence, but more irksome for the Dáil cabinet, was the ironic Machiavellian and counter-intuitive involvement

* Thus characterised by Judge Kevin O'Shiel in a series of articles for the *Irish Times* in 1966. 'The Last Land War', *Irish Times*, 22 November 1966.

of the hostile apparatchiks of the proudly sectarian Ancient Order of Hibernians (AOH). This was a pietistic Roman Catholic association still affiliated to the largely moribund IPP. The gamekeepers of 1918 became the poachers of 1920.

Given that the grazier class, when its members were not vehemently loyal to the Union, tended to be Redmondite in its sympathies, this particular brand of AOH subversion was impudently opportunistic rather than measured and principled. It was based on that fundamental axiom of conflict from the battlefield to the schoolyard, 'the enemy of my enemy is my friend'. Particularly prominent in the new border counties created by the 1920 Government of Ireland Act, the Hibernians were more than happy to foster antagonism towards Sinn Féin.*

Even four years of a wartime agricultural boom had done little or nothing to solve the endemic problem of 'congestion' in the west of Ireland. This was a bureaucratic euphemism for too many farmers tilling far too constricted an acreage. The suspension of land redistribution, a suspension that had begun under the terms of the 1903 (Wyndham) Land Purchase Act, left more than a hundred thousand frustrated citizens waiting to access a farm of their own or to increase the size of their insubstantial holdings.[5] This arithmetical reality had been exacerbated by the understandable unwillingness of most smallholders to oblige the colonial authorities and reduce the Irish agricultural population by dying for King and Country in the trenches of Picardy and Flanders.

* Graham Sennett of the Roscommon Land Commission to Art O'Connor, Minister for Agriculture, 20 May 1920, on the involvement of the AOH in land seizures: 'The most vile hooligans that did the dirty work against us in the General Election ... are marching, with the tricolour, to commandeer lands.' Quoted in Kevin O'Shiel, Bureau of Military History, Witness Statement #1770, 975.

A further frustration was the wartime sealing of the customary outlet of emigration to Britain and beyond. In 1920, one-third of all farmers in the west of Ireland still occupied uneconomic holdings. Prosperity for the few – food prices had almost trebled during the Great War – had served only to supercharge the rise in land values, putting those vital additional acres out of reach of the smallholder.

But now, thanks to the activities of the IRA in the winter and spring of 1920, there were no longer any policemen around to prevent the forcible acquisition of grazier land. So if the 'boys' could be persuaded to turn a blind eye, *cothrom na féinne* (fair play) was at hand.[6]

The land agitation of 1920, which easily eclipsed its wartime predecessor in savagery, threatened to destabilise much of rural Ireland. Whole areas of the countryside had now been largely unpoliced since the hasty withdrawal of the Royal Irish Constabulary from small rural barracks to larger towns in the early months of the year. The flight of the 'Peelers' was a boon to the IRA, but the resurgence of the turmoil of the 1880s prompted by the withdrawal of Crown policing was inconvenient and unwelcome to the new custodians of law and order. By 1920, Sinn Féin was trying on a new outfit for size. The party was 'already on the way to becoming a new political establishment in their own right'.[7]

What happened to the party in some of the more disturbed districts of rural Ireland – the *Sligo Champion* might even have styled them 'bolshie' – was a harbinger of how the newly minted power bloc that was Sinn Féin would ultimately melt down into its constituent parts. Sinn Féin was always a coalition of competing interests, of 'landed and landless, propertied and unpropertied, farmers and agricultural labourers, shopkeepers and shop assistants'.[8] These factions, in order to capture the moment, had fused in their opposition to conscription and in the decisive 1918 general election. Fission always loomed as a distinct possibility. If the Sinn Féin leadership failed to come to terms with the renewed radical agrarianism of rural Ireland, it could lead to a debilitating chain reaction and the fragile coalition could fall apart.

And the turmoil didn't stop at cattle-driving either. Whether it marked a return to the tactics of the Land War, or was inspired by the prevailing environment of assault and reprisal – by then a feature of daily life – the appropriation of 'underused', 'surplus' or 'untenanted' land was on the rise, accompanied by a degree of aggression that mirrored the violence of the overarching colonial military conflict.

On 4 March 1920, Frank Shawe-Taylor from Ardrahan, County Galway, a land agent and relative of Lady Gregory, was murdered in a supposed IRA attack that probably had more to do with local animosities over land tenure than with the independence struggle.[9] Then a north Galway grazier was shot dead, and in June and July three herdsmen (employed by graziers) were murdered.

More typical was the experience, the following month, of Godfrey Hardy of Crusheen, County Clare, who was accosted and beaten by a gang of fifteen to twenty men demanding that he sign over his land to them. When he refused to do so, he was blindfolded, his hands and legs were bound, and revolvers were pointed at his head. When his sister attempted to come to his rescue, she was driven off (thankfully uninjured) by a fusillade of bullets. Hardy's employees later had their homes fired on, and boycott notices were placed on the family's land.

Hardy was one of a number of Protestant landowners who later had recourse to the Republican land courts (see below), and he thus managed to retain his holding – to the fury of his neighbours – because of the intervention of the Dáil in the growing chaos.[10] It was episodes such as this that prompted even a populist IRA commander like Michael Brennan in east Clare to warn against any tolerance of agrarian agitation.[11]

Hardy was more fortunate than a number of loyalist land-owners in west Cork – among them Justice of the Peace Thomas Kingston of Rosscarbery – who were suspected of passing information to the authorities. In some instances, their houses were burned and their land 'confiscated to the government of the country'. However, attempts to divide the land among local activists were frustrated by west Cork IRA commander Tom Barry, who would not permit the arbitrary reassignment of seized property. He ordered the sale of the farms and the retention of the profits in trust. After the Truce, Barry recorded that he was 'at present awaiting instructions as to where to send the money'.[12]

In 1920, Cahir Davitt, son of Land League founder Michael Davitt, was a young barrister who would go on to become a justice of the High Court in the 1950s. As a judge of the Republican courts, Davitt was witness to antagonisms and feuds that had their origins in the waning decades of the nineteenth century. In his thousand-page Bureau of Military History Witness Statement in the 1950s, Davitt referred, for example, to a case in Midleton, County Cork, a throwback to the agrarian turmoil of the late Victorian era. He was required to pass judgement in a dispute involving two County Cork families whom he calls the McCarthys and the O'Sullivans.

In 1920, the O'Sullivans owned a farm from which the McCarthys had been evicted a generation before. The O'Sullivan family had thus earned itself the unenviable 'land grabbers' epithet. At the outset of the Anglo-Irish War, one of the dispossessed McCarthys returned to Midleton and joined the local IRA. The

O'Sullivans – two middle-aged sisters and a brother still *in situ* on what had been the McCarthy farm – began receiving threatening letters demanding the restoration of the property to McCarthy. When the brother was shot and wounded, the family capitulated (under additional pressure from a local Roman Catholic priest) and signed over their farm to the McCarthys.

Later, alleging that they had been forced to convey the property under extreme duress, the O'Sullivans sought to regain possession of their land through the auspices of a Republican court presided over by Davitt. He found in their favour. His decision did not go down well with the people from Midleton in attendance.

The priest who had brokered the land transfer intervened, informing Davitt in open court that his judgement 'would not conduce to the peace of the parish'. There then followed a disturbance involving one of the O'Sullivan sisters, who was physically abused by an onlooker. Half-a-dozen Republican police stood at the back of the court, and Davitt called upon them to restore order. His instructions were ignored and he was, as he put it, subjected to 'muttered observations casting doubt upon my paternity'. Davitt was forced to adjourn the court sitting, with no expectation that his decree would ever be executed.

This assumption proved to be correct. Some years later Davitt discovered that 'the O'Sullivans had been given a holding in a different neighbourhood by the Land Commission' and the McCarthys were 'left in undisputed possession of their ancestral acres'.[13]

It could reasonably be argued that an old injustice had been rectified. That was certainly the viewpoint of the McCarthys, the local curate and the members of the Republican police who declined to enforce Davitt's decision. However, were that outcome to have been replicated across the country in similar cases, it would have led to countless local internecine disputes that would have done little to advance the cause of the nascent Irish republic.

Enter Judge Kevin O'Shiel.

2.

In 1920, when his moment arrived, O'Shiel was an accomplished Tyrone-born barrister with Sinn Féin sympathies. He was approached to become a judge in the embryonic Republican court system. The new structures were largely based on the notion of a parish court – the closest equivalent was the Crown administration's petty sessions – which did not require judges with legal experience. However, the higher echelons – the Circuit and Supreme courts – were far more professionalised. O'Shiel found himself acting largely as a mediator in civil land disputes conducted in arbitration courts tolerated even by the Crown authorities.* Based on principles of conciliation, these courts quickly began to assume a more confrontational character as petty boundary clashes gave way to outright expropriation. When Arthur

---

* In June 1919 a decree of Dáil Éireann had established a system of National Arbitration Courts, created to deal with civil legal disputes, mostly over land. A year later the Arbitration Court system was supplemented by criminal courts, known as Dáil Courts. One of the ironies of the Anglo-Irish conflict is that Finance Minister Michael Collins, who exercised control over the rather threadbare purse strings of the Republican administration, was at least as enthusiastic as Justice Minister Austin Stack when it came to the establishment of an alternative legal system (and a parallel apparatus of local government). He once told fellow IRB chief Seán Boylan: 'It is more important to get our people to refuse to recognise British Local Government than to attack their armed forces.' (Boylan, BMH-WS, #1715)

Griffith became concerned with the dogs of agrarian war being let slip across rural Ireland, he sent for O'Shiel.

Among the objections to the creation of full-blooded Dáil land arbitration courts was the fear that disappointed litigants would have an incentive to become informers for the British forces. An unintended and embarrassing consequence of the establishment of a separate system of Republican justice was the gratitude, all too fervently expressed at times, of astonished unionist landowners whose usurped properties were regularly restored to them by the decisions of Republican judges like O'Shiel – decisions required to be enforced by (often reluctant) Republican police.

When Griffith summoned O'Shiel to that meeting in Dublin in early 1920, there were still over 170,000 tenants on the land of doggedly intractable Irish landlords. Their lordships were unwilling to sully their heritage by selling their properties, despite years of land purchase legislation, even on the relatively generous terms on offer from the Estates Commission and the Congested Districts Board. These holdings consisted of more than five million acres, 36 percent of the value of Irish agricultural land, often rented on a short-term basis to graziers to avoid the threat of compulsory purchase. Impoverished smallholders were taking matters into their own hands and resorting to intimidation and outright violence to bring the eleven-month practice to an enforced conclusion. The Arthur Griffith encountered by O'Shiel – a Home Affairs minister about to pass the tyro judge an exacting assignment – appeared to be a very troubled man:

> Griffith, in my interview with him, made it very clear to me that he took the gravest possible view of the outbreak and was definitely of opinion that if it was not speedily and effectively dealt with it, it might well engulf the great Sinn Féin movement

that had been built up with so much toil and sweat, and sweep it away, together with its major creation, the very Dáil itself.[14]

In his Bureau of Military History Witness Statement, and a series of articles written for the *Irish Times* in 1966, O'Shiel catalogued some of the attempts by agrarian egalitarians to capitalise upon, and make their own contribution to, the prevailing anomie.

He was, for example, called upon to adjudicate on a number of lucrative land seizures around the village of Creggs* in County Galway. The area's 'by no means indigent citizens' had formed a Land Committee which had managed to appropriate 4,000 acres 'by the simple process of driving their neighbours' cattle off their owners' lands, seizing those lands and using them for their own, or other cattle, as they thought fit'.[15] The members of the committee – O'Shiel described them as 'Commissars'; perhaps he was a *Sligo Champion* reader – had rewarded themselves for their efforts by patronising the Galway Races, where they 'put up at a good hotel ... and dined and wined well, the wine, need I say, being invariably the finest champagne, and plenty of it, too'.[16]

When O'Shiel demanded access to the committee's records, his able district registrar, one Eamon Casey seconded from the Clare IRA, threatened to shoot some of the 'Commissars' unless the documents were forthcoming. O'Shiel concluded his account with the laconic observation that 'in due course the Creggs Land Committee was wound up and its ill-gotten lands restored to their rightful owners'. His decisions in the case, which went

---

* The village appeared, to O'Shiel at any rate, to take great pride in its signal contribution to the life of Charles Stewart Parnell, viz. the taking of it. He had been soaked to the skin in a persistent shower in Creggs while making his last speech in September 1891, and died of pneumonia some weeks later.

against the appropriators, were not calculated to improve the local standing of Sinn Féin.

In a similar case, in County Roscommon – a county much enamoured of ad hoc land seizures – O'Shiel noted that the defendant's solicitor waved aloft a 'properly executed indenture' (a deed of transfer of ownership) and insisted to the court that 'we are not confiscators'. However, when O'Shiel sought clarification from the plaintiff's attorney, he was informed that:

> My client had but to glance at that precious deed to see that it involved the surrender to these so-called purchasers of a substantial proportion of his property for an absurdly trivial price. He naturally declined to sign, whereupon two of these brigands, standing on either side of him, drew revolvers and presented them at his head, whilst others began to dig a grave on the lawn in front of him.[17]

In May 1920, O'Shiel adjudicated in his first land dispute in a Republican court and found in favour of two plaintiffs, Hyland and Murphy, whose land in Kilmaine, County Mayo had been seized. The defendants, however, simply ignored the court's verdict and continued their occupation of the farms. O'Shiel sought some remedy from an unsympathetic Minister for Defence, Cathal Brugha, who was intolerant of any diversion of IRA resources or energies. It was only after the intervention of Arthur Griffith that action was taken to enforce O'Shiel's judgement. A week after O'Shiel's intervention, armed men arrested the culprits in the Hyland and Murphy case in the middle of the night and carried them off to an 'unknown destination'. This, as it happened, was an island in the middle of Lough Corrib, where the defiant offenders remained until they had had second thoughts.[18]

Is it any wonder that, as O'Shiel pointed out in his 1950s' witness statement, there was method in the apparent madness of the Crown authorities in allowing the Republican court system to continue untrammelled until the autumn of 1920? The wily Dublin Castle administration was hopeful that unpopular judicial decisions by the likes of O'Shiel or Davitt, often handed down in favour of entrenched unionist landowners, would undermine support for the IRA campaign.[19]

This, however, does not appear to have happened. O'Shiel wrote in 1966, 'On hundreds of occasions we could have been betrayed to the British, with comparatively little risk, but that, in my experience, never occurred.'[20] It is possible, though, that this had more to do with the mortal fear engendered in aspirant informers by the deadly sanctions of the IRA.

3.

Meath smallholders (such beings did exist) were far less militant than their counterparts in Roscommon and the west. But they were not entirely behind the door when it came to driving cattle off land that they wanted. One branch of activists in the village of Culmullin, for example, called themselves the Culmullin Vigilance Committee. How exactly their vigilance was made manifest is unclear. What is certain, however, is that the nocturnal activities of the 'drivers' often complemented those of their diurnal cousins in the Back to the Land movement.

Back to the Land was an organisation that, at its most constructive, offered solutions to rampant agrarian inequity. But while the movement's leadership cadre often included patently law-abiding citizens, priests among them, there was a recognition

even within its own ranks that it was also 'a ruffianly movement…
responsible for burnings and so on'.[21] This clandestine element
could be highly persuasive in offering landlords something more
than a simple cash incentive for selling up.

Underlining the affinity between the shadowy mavens of cattle-
driving and their more conspicuous partners in Back to the Land,
in May 1920 a huge herd of 500 cattle was surreptitiously removed
from an estate at Curraha, between Ashbourne and Ratoath. The
beleaguered Royal Irish Constabulary managed to stir itself to
investigate, resulting in three members of the Navan Back to the
Land branch spending a month in Mountjoy Gaol. The organisation was restructured shortly afterwards with the avowed intention
of ending 'irresponsible actions on the part of individuals'.[22] It is
doubtful that this lofty ambition was ever fully realised.

The *Meath Chronicle* of the first half of 1920 teems with reports
of cattle-driving. The first of these can be seen as a softening-
up exercise designed to expedite the sale of the Liscarton estate
north of Navan. The *Chronicle* reported on 10 January 1920 that
the grazing cattle of the estate 'were driven on to the public road.
Gates and piers were broken down'. The report concluded with
the news that all the cattle were duly returned (albeit by the civil
authorities) 'little the worse of their midnight ramble'. Two months
later, negotiations were taking place for the purchase of the estate
by the Navan Back to the Land branch. *Post hoc ergo propter hoc?*

In March 1920, a 'drive' on the Fitzherbert estate at Proudstown,
north-east of Navan, included a more sinister element than the mere
dispersal of livestock. The *Meath Chronicle* reported that 'as a sort
of silent threat of further depredations of a more intimate personal
nature a grave was dug on the lands and a cross placed over it'.[23]

Clearly the practice of cattle-driving, like its older brother, the
timeworn art of boycotting, had not withered with the ending of

that passage of Irish history with which it was most associated, the 1906–09 Ranch War. As with the *Meath Chronicle*'s reassurance that the cattle of the Liscarton estate were 'little the worse of their midnight ramble', it was difficult for ordinary citizens to take cattle-driving all that seriously. To most *Chronicle* readers, the bewildered cattle were being taken for a pleasant evening stroll.

Granted, their sale value might have diminished, but that would have been of no concern to the beasts themselves, forced to stumble terrified through the darkness. The inherent cruelty of the practice would have made little impression on a nation of carnivores, and there was precious little sympathy in rural Ireland for their owners. They were 'land grabbers', 'gombeen men', 'land sharks' or, worse, unionist grandees.

A sense of moral outrage and cultural disgust at the ubiquity of self-satisfied ranchers, and their effective subversion of the gospel of the Land League in their triumph over the small farmer, afforded legitimacy to the activities of the Robin Hood figures pledged to reverse the slide into agrarian consolidation. But by late 1920, thanks to the interventions of the Republican courts, the noise was beginning to abate. If the cattle-driver did not fall foul of a newly censorious IRA, he was vulnerable to the even less sympathetic Black and Tans. This proliferation of gamekeepers meant that the poaching season was closed.

But the closure came too late for twenty-three-year-old IRA Volunteer and Meath farmer Mark Clinton.

4.

Cormeen, Relagh Mór, Relagh Beg, Cloggagh, Finternagh, Agh-naclue, Lenanavragh, Greaghnadarran, Srahan, Carriga.

It reads like the poetic monologue from Brian Friel's *Faith Healer*, with the Welsh villages of Abergorlech, Abergynolwyn, Llandefeilog, Llanerchymedd, Aberhosan, Aberporth relocated to rural Meath. The Celticism and the landscapes are not dissimilar. They are villages or townlands – an Irish village often being merely a townland with notions – within a few kilometres of each other. Back in the dying months of the political entity known as the United Kingdom of Great Britain and Ireland, they would have been a few miles apart and would have accounted for a picturesque, but not enthrallingly so, thousand-odd acres of patchwork fields of rural County Meath.*

The townland of Cormeen is less than a kilometre from the Cavan-Meath border. That frontier lies to the west. Bizarrely, six kilometres due east is another Meath village named Cormeen. There is a further community of the same name in County Cavan itself, in the western barony of Tullyhunco. Cormeen (Cor Mín) translates from Irish as 'smooth round hill'. In drumlin country there is no shortage of smooth round hills, hence the popularity of the place-name.

The nearest towns of any consequence are Mullagh to the south and the tautological Baileborough (*baile* is 'town' in Irish, and borough is 'town' in English) to the north. Both lie in County Cavan. Cormeen, and the land around it, is one of many salients along the Cavan-Meath border. If you drive on the main road between Mullagh and Baileborough – terms such as 'main' being relative – for about a kilometre and a half after you pass Cormeen, you will, unbeknownst to yourself, enter the purlieu of Relagh Beg and the adjoining Relagh Mór. In England they might

---

* It wasn't until the late twentieth century that Ireland abandoned imperial measurements, just as it had forsaken the empire itself decades before.

bear more imposing Latinate names like Relagh Magna and Relagh Parva.

Just before you reach Relagh Beg, there is a minor road to your left. This takes you across Cloggagh Bridge and offers a view to your right of Cloggagh Lake, the name a transliteration of the Irish word *clocha*, 'a stony place'. Unpromising.

The Clintons of Cloggagh (sometimes written Clogga or Clugga) were originally a Norman family. The first of them, Simon de Clinton, arrived in Ireland in the late twelfth century, a few years after the invasion spearheaded by Richard de Clare, aka Strongbow, the second Earl of Pembroke. The Clintons originally settled in County Louth, but in the mid-eighteenth century one James Clinton migrated to the farthest reaches of the neighbouring county of Meath. There he found work as a stone mason building a cornmill on the Borora river at Cloggagh. The Borora, also known as the Owenroe (*abhainn rua* – 'red river') rises near Baileborough and flows into the larger Leinster Blackwater near Kells. River water goes through some interesting pigmentary modifications in the north midlands.

James Clinton married wisely to his employer's daughter, Anne Smith. His own heirs would succeed to the land and establish the Clinton family in Cloggagh/Cormeen for the better part of two centuries. When Patrick Clinton inherited the family acres in 1852 on the death of his father – another James, a century removed from his namesake – the farm still included the mill and a number of outhouses, and extended for a hundred acres.

Three years after it came into his possession, Patrick Clinton's relatively prosperous holding was assigned a valuation by the surveyors of Sir Richard Griffith. The so-called Griffith's Valuation was a series of surveys of land and buildings, conducted across the country in the 1850s to assess liability for Poor

Law taxation. The valuation was based on the productivity of the land.

The survey for County Meath was completed in the summer of 1855.²⁴ Patrick Clinton's property was valued at £70, lagging locally behind only that of his neighbour Patrick Smith, whose farm of 147 acres, named Rosemount in the anglicised fashion of the day, was assessed at £91. Included on Patrick Clinton's holding were four houses and small gardens occupied by agricultural labourers. Clinton himself was listed as their 'immediate lessor'.²⁵

At that time, most of Cormeen and its environs belonged to one James Kemp Sturgeon. The townland had been a gift to his ancestors from a grateful Lord Protector of the Commonwealth of England, Scotland and Ireland, the unloved (in Ireland at least) Oliver Cromwell. At a time when 'landlord' was a term of abuse, Sturgeon was one of the most unpopular examples of the breed, an absentee. While he wintered and summered in his native England, he relied on a local agent to collect his rents and keep him in the manner to which he and his ancestors had been long accustomed.

That agent was the Clintons' neighbour, Patrick 'Poragon' Smith. As a consequence of his exalted position, he exercised an element of power and authority in the community that belied his own 147 statute acres. Power, authority and enthusiastic detestation. Never one to shy away from ejecting tenants in default of rent, Smith was noted for his habit of acquiring for himself the property of his evicted neighbours. Inevitably, when allied to his duties as Sturgeon's agent, this greatly enhanced local antipathy towards him. Such was the antagonism he excited that his reputation was long dogged by allegations of indulgence in the medieval sexual practice of *droit de seigneur* with local women before their wedding nights, a reputational hanging offence in nineteenth-century Ireland.

In similar fashion to the ancestral stonemason James Clinton, progenitor of the Cloggagh line of Clintons, Patrick Clinton married well. Rose Smith, daughter of Poragon, became the mother of his ten children.[26]

As already noted, Joseph Clinton inherited the land on the death of his father Patrick in 1892, returning from the United States to take over the family farm. John Clinton, five years older than his brother, could probably have chosen to do so instead, but opted to remain in America. Had he returned to take possession of those hundred acres on the Ulster-Leinster border, he might have lived beyond 1915. However, given the turbulence of the revolutionary years, perhaps his lifespan would not have been greatly extended.

Shortly after his return from the US, Joseph Clinton, gangly and monkishly ascetic in appearance, married Kate Osborne of Corryrourke, near Mullagh. Not long thereafter, his mother Rose decided to join her family in Colorado and later Arizona, rather than remain on the Cloggagh farm.

The newly installed Clintons of Cloggagh went on to have eight children of their own. Our focus is on the first five siblings, Patrick (b.1893), Peter (b.1894), Rose (b.1895), Mark (b.1897) and Bridget (b.1900), all of whom would figure prominently and tragically in the struggle for Irish independence.

By 1920, Joe Clinton's eldest son Patrick had already moved out of the family home. In 1915, at the age of twenty-two, he left Ireland and settled in Glasgow. That he did not coalesce with the rest of the extended clan in the United States suggests that he always intended to return to Ireland. In Scotland he joined B Company of the Glasgow battalion of the Irish Volunteers, the militia set up to defend Home Rule which became the main force behind the 1916 Rising and later formed the core of the IRA.

He was involved in the training of that small and exposed force of Irish Glaswegians, and in the purchase and smuggling of arms.

Tasked once with carrying a bagful of weapons on the ferry from Stranraer to Larne, Clinton was told to expect a welcoming guard of Irish Volunteers on his arrival in the County Antrim port. Instead, he became a victim of Murphy's Law ('anything that can go wrong will go wrong') and found himself on the wharf dressed in the uniform of an officer of the British army, with not a Volunteer in sight.

Puzzling out what to do, he spotted an army vehicle nearby with a driver in attendance. Pulling rank and feigning the nonchalant arrogance of the British officer class, he summarily ordered the soldier to drive him to Belfast. His chutzpah convinced the driver that he was dealing with a superior officer, and although he pre-sumably had an entirely different reason for being in Larne, he obeyed his new orders.

Despite his apparent access to an officer's uniform, Patrick Clinton managed to avoid being drafted into the British army during the First World War. His return to Ireland in 1918, after a relatively short stint in Scotland, may well have been occasioned by the threat of an imminent call-up. He settled in Dunboyne, County Meath, befriended local IRB strongman Seán Boylan and, in his own words, 'became a full-time officer of the Meath Brigade'.[27]

After an IRA reorganisation in early 1921, the Meath Brigade was assimilated into the 1st Eastern Division, with Boylan as O/C and Clinton as adjutant; he also retained his position as divisional intelligence officer (I/O). In a campaign notable principally for a sequence of near misses and aborted raids, Pat Clinton was one of the commanders of the operation that marked the nadir of Meath IRA activities, the spectacularly unsuccessful attempt to derail a British troop train near Celbridge, County Kildare, on the night of 2 July 1921, shortly before the truce that brought hostilities to an end.

The entire operation was compromised when the hundred-man IRA unit was detected and intercepted by British forces. One participant, Matthew Barry of the 2nd Meath Brigade, who was in a platoon under the command of Pat Clinton, was unimpressed by the quality of the operational planning that night, though he made no specific complaint about the role played by Clinton himself. 'It was, as far as I know,' Barry recalled, 'the first operation carried out by the divisional staff, which had not long been formed, and a very poor job they made of it. Looking back on it now, the whole thing seems to have been badly planned and badly controlled.'[28]

After the July 1921 Truce, when the prevailing wisdom among the ranks of the IRA was that it would not be long before the resumption of hostilities, Pat Clinton came under intense pressure and scrutiny. Against his wishes and his own better judgement, he continued to operate as divisional adjutant and I/O. By his own admission, in a 1921 letter to GHQ, he did neither job particularly well.

IRA Deputy Chief of Staff Eoin O'Duffy – future leader of the fascist Blueshirt organisation – agreed wholeheartedly with Clinton's self-evaluation. In a report on the Eastern Division dated 21 October 1921, by which time negotiations on a putative Anglo-Irish treaty had begun in London, O'Duffy offered a stinging assessment of Patrick Clinton's capabilities. 'I do not believe Clinton is fit either for the position of Divisional I.O. or Divisional Adjutant and I recommend he be reduced... he is only of mediocre ability.'[29]

In a report submitted the following month, Pat Clinton candidly and ruefully acknowledged his own shortcomings. After a rundown on the performance of all the brigade IOs (including his cousin Raphael McKenna), he sought the appointment of a full-time divisional intelligence officer 'as I cannot devote the necessary time to the work. At present I am acting as Adjutant and I/O and to judge from results neither job is being done as it should be... I respectfully suggest that someone more competent than I be placed in charge of this department.'[30] The signing of the Treaty four weeks later ended the contretemps between Clinton and the increasingly powerful O'Duffy.

In fact, that was by no means the end of their professional relationship. In September 1922, Eoin O'Duffy became the second commissioner of the newly established Garda Síochána. At around that time Pat Clinton resigned from the National Army, in which he held the rank of colonel commandant,[31] and joined the new police force. His previous history with O'Duffy does not appear to have hindered his upward progress: by 1926 he was a superintendent based in Tralee, County Kerry.

Pat Clinton's spirited sister Rose was also living away from home in 1920, but for entirely different reasons. When you consult the 1901 and 1911 census returns, Rose Clinton is conspicuous by her absence from her father's farms. Instead, she lived with her mother's family, the Osbornes, in Corryrourke near Mullagh. Later, in a move that would greatly convenience members of the Meath IRA who were on the run, Rose would live in the townland of Fegat, near the village of Carnaross, five kilometres to the west of Kells, the home of two of her uncles. Their farmhouse, and the land around, might have been chosen by a capable general to make a stand against a superior enemy. It was adjacent to extensive and impenetrable bogland on one side and reachable only via a long narrow lane. Anyone venturing down that boreen other than by stealth would announce their presence minutes before reaching the farmhouse.

This remoteness made it an exceptionally secure safe house for IRA Volunteers with compelling reasons not to return to their own homes, and they were fed, watered, washed and housed there. Rose acted as a willing and vigilant hostess. The Bureau of Military History Witness Statement of Meath Brigade second-in-command Séamus Finn of Athboy reads like a latter-day TripAdvisor recommendation: 'Always open to us and where we received wonderful hospitality.'[32]

So secure was the Osborne demesne that in early 1920 it became a temporary IRA headquarters, presided over by Commandant Eamon Cullen – later an assistant Garda commissioner – with Rose Clinton alternating between domestic chores and scouting duty.[33] Frequent visitors included Séamus Finn and Rose's brother Patrick.

If wandering Black and Tans posed little threat to the house's regular visitors, the IRA arms dump in a nearby barn certainly did. It was less mobile than the fugitive Volunteers. Black and Tan best practice after discovering such an arsenal involved the immediate arrest of the landowner, often preceded by a severe beating and the burning of the adjacent farmhouse. The Osbornes of Fegat managed to avoid all the above.

Rose joined Cumann na mBan in 1917 and became captain of the Mullagh branch in 1920. This meant that for four years she took part in all the standard activities of the sister organisation of the Irish Volunteers, collecting funds, election canvassing – she worked on the pivotal East Cavan by-election of 1918 which saw Arthur Griffith defeat the IPP candidate, J.F. O'Hanlon, in the final straw poll before the December general election – carrying despatches and learning first aid.

Of course, Cumann na mBan was a close blood relative of the IRA and among the less compassionate activities in which Rose Clinton participated was the transport of guns. The recipient on each occasion was her Mullagh cousin John McKenna. At least one purpose to which those weapons may have been put will be discussed in Chapter 8.

Towards the end of the conflict, Rose Clinton also supplied food to the newly formed east Cavan/north Meath IRA active service unit, which trained on Mullagh Hill under the watchful eye of another of her McKenna cousins, T.P. Junior.[34] By the spring of 1920, so many Meath Volunteers were on the run that the time had come to put together a flying column. Rose Clinton's level of engagement reinforces the judgement of the compilers of the British army's *Record of the Rebellion in Ireland* that 'mistaken chivalry' had allowed too many women to get away with too much subversive activity.[35]

Peter and Mark Clinton, who worked on their father's farm, were both members of the Gaelic League. As well as being a cultural nationalist, Mark Clinton was a political militant and an IRA Volunteer. His brother Peter, dark and with the ranginess of his father Joe, would follow Mark into the ranks of the Meath Brigade in June 1920, his motivation dictated by the events about to be described.

Their fiery sister Bridget was also a Cumann na mBan member, training as a nurse when the War of Independence broke out. Unlike her siblings, who either remained neutral during the Civil War or, as in the case of Patrick Clinton, joined the National Army and fought against the new Republican insurgency, Bridget remained a committed Republican and a supporter of Sinn Féin until her death on New Year's Eve 1983.

5.

'As the twig is bent so grows the tree.' A more colloquial version is that hoary old cliché 'a chip off the old block'. Fifty-year-old Philip Smith had been Poragon's twig; now he was his own tree.

Phil Smith was one of the reasons the Back to the Land movement had emerged in the first place. As a magistrate and the owner of two substantial farming establishments,[36] he was hardly unique in early twentieth-century Ireland. The 'rancher' had already begun to assume the mantle of the landlord, not least as a bête noire. The 'cattle jobber', 'dealer', 'grazier', 'land shark' or 'rancher' – he came with as many tags as there were native cattle breeds – was part cartoon villain, part postulant aristocrat.

How you defined a rancher, of course, depended on your circumstances. You did not have to populate hundreds of acres of arable land with beef cattle to qualify. To the subsistence smallholder, any neighbour capable of producing a modest surplus might earn the label (as the luckless Mayomen Murphy and Hyland discovered). To the landless labourer, even the subsistence smallholder might look like a grazier.

But Phil Smith was clearly entitled to the designation. On one level, he was an enterprising agricultural capitalist who had done well for himself. Viewed from the cramped confines of a smallholding or labourer's cottage, however, he was a stereotypical land shark who had inherited most of his wealth, and whose property portfolio contributed directly to the scarcity of available land in County Meath and elsewhere. In addition to the 150 or so acres of the original Rosemount 'home farm' at Cormeen – at least some of which, it was claimed locally, had been acquired after a Land War eviction[37] – Smith also owned an extensive farm about six miles away in Coole, near Kilmainhamwood.

In the 1911 census, this is listed as including five stables and six additional outhouses.

Smith lived on the Coole farmstead with his eighty-year-old mother Margaret and his widowed sister Rose Payne, in a farm building with nine rooms and an ostentatious five windows (showy by the lights of the 1920s) at the front of the house. The Smiths employed a female domestic servant and two male farm labourers. With the proceeds of the Coole establishment and the rent from Cormeen, let out on the eleven-month system, Phil Smith was more than comfortably off.

The Smith properties had once exceeded the Clinton land by a factor of less than one-third. By 1920, Joe Clinton's holdings of around 100 acres had been soundly eclipsed by those of his first cousin, and the Clintons were now the poor relations of the extended family.

But the Clintons themselves were also objects of jealousy and animosity. Memories, actual and mythical, were long and bitter in rural Ireland. Ownership of ninety-four statute acres of County Meath almost axiomatically provoked assumptions on the part of many less land-endowed neighbours that the land had not been acquired ethically. An altercation in 1919 involving Joe Clinton's brother James is a case in point – an atavistic encounter between the retired Inland Revenue officer living temporarily on the Cloggagh farm and an aggrieved neighbour, John Finnegan of Carriga, which began with a bad joke.

James Clinton passed by at the February fair in the centre of Mullagh while Finnegan was getting into a cart along with two others, and jocularly remarked, 'Don't overload the cart.' Finnegan took exception to the pleasantry, but it was the nature of his splenetic response that was most revealing. It was a vicious primer in recent Irish agrarian history and mythology. Finnegan descended from the cart and began to berate Clinton. 'You are one of the grabbers,' he roared, 'and you come from a breed of grabbers and your grandmother made many a hearthstone cold.'

Because James Clinton was the grandson of Poragon Smith, this was presumably a reference to the late agent's wife. But Finnegan wasn't finished. His next line of attack culpably misrepresented the reality behind the murder of John Clinton in Arizona. 'It is no wonder,' he sneered, 'your brother was shot dead in America for grabbing land.'

John Finnegan was obviously unfamiliar with the subtleties of the Homestead Act, given that his gibe was hardly intended as a defence of the rights of dispossessed Chiricahua Apache. Having concluded his diatribe, Finnegan launched into a brutal physical assault on James Clinton, knocking him down, kicking him and jumping on his chest. For this attack, he was sentenced to a month's imprisonment by the magistrates at the next Mullagh Petty sessions. Finnegan had previous – in September 1914, he had assaulted an RIC constable.[38]

Phil Smith, unsurprisingly, had long since come to the attention of the night raiders of rural Meath. The return of 'outrage' to grazier lands in 1917/18 had not bypassed the county. As the owner of untenanted land, Smith was subjected to acts of intimidation in 1918. The pattern was familiar. Damage was caused to his property. Graves were dug in his fields as a warning. A manned RIC hut had been allocated to the Smiths, who claimed a sum of money from the county rates on foot of the malicious damage.

Then, in 1919, the auction at which Smith's Cormeen acres would have been rented for eleven months was boycotted. 'At the auction people bid a ridiculous figure' was how he put it.[39] Unable to find a serious bidder for the land, rather than leave the fields fallow, he rented four acres to Joe Clinton at £2 an acre, around a third of the market rate.

Had the Back to the Land movement been a factor in Cormeen, things might have turned out differently. Despite its own tangential association with 'outrage', Back to the Land was noted for an ability to restrain local smallholders' violent resentment whenever there was some prospect of a negotiated settlement over untenanted or surplus land. But there was no local branch of the organisation in Cormeen to moderate the demands of the smallholders or labourers of this isolated corner of north-west Meath. What there was, however, was a resourceful lawless element that had already begun to terrorise the locality by the time the Anglo-Irish conflict slipped past the phony war stage.

These were no ordinary outlaws. Rather than relieve their neighbours of random valuables by force or stealth, the shock troops of this faction struck at the very core of rural materiality. It was a conscious conspiracy, its zealots intent on acquiring their neighbours' land by force majeure while offering the pretext that they were merely rectifying the injustices of expropriation from the previous century by seizing the property of land-grabbers.

The middle months of the War of Independence were the season of the Cormeen Gang.

The Black Hand Gang of Cormeen was an ad hoc creation in the Irish Ribbon or Whiteboy tradition. Whiteboys and Ribbonmen, members of oathbound secret societies, were the marginalised, alienated and disruptive sons of rural Ireland. They were pledged to little more than secrecy and their own unique brand of agrarian anarchy. Immiserated, landless and radicalised, this shadowy legion of the dispossessed would have been classified by the eminent Marxist historian Eric Hobsbawm as 'primitive rebels'. Wolfe Tone would have recognised them as the 'men of no property' whom he hoped to recruit into the ranks of his eighteenth-century republican insurrection. Denied access to the higher echelons of the bourgeois leadership of the United Irishmen, they still carried their pikes at Vinegar Hill and were hanged in their hundreds by the yeomanry in the bloody aftermath of the 1798 rebellion. In 1920, however, they were seizing a unique opportunity, afforded by the prevailing anarchy, to bear arms on their own behalf.

In the highly stratified rural Irish society of the 1900s, where the poet Francis Ledwidge, whose people owned only a kitchen garden, was deemed unworthy of the hand of his beloved Ellie Vaughey because the Vaugheys were a cut above – a family of landowners near the Hill of Slane – the Cormeen Gang were the Ledwidges, and the Smiths and the Clintons were the Vaugheys. There was little doubt which interest the 'conservative revolutionaries' of Sinn Féin would ultimately support when forced to make a choice. Once push came to shove, the neo-Whiteboy faction of Cormeen 'must wait', as Éamon de Valera is supposed to have told the Labour Party – and by implication the entire Irish working class – before the 1918 general election.

Sinn Féin and the IRA, while including the odd agrarian socialist like Peadar O'Donnell in its ranks, would end up bedding down with the twentieth-century 'Gombeen men', predatory capitalists waiting in the wings to mould the nascent Irish Free State. Chaos and anomie in rural Ireland was all very well as long as they discommoded loyalist grandees and the RIC, but not when they distracted attention and diverted resources from harassment of the Crown forces, or threatened the financial interests of the more bourgeois supporters of Irish Republicanism.

In north Meath, the endemic land hunger that threatened to derail the entire IRA campaign reached a level of intensity that eclipsed the tentative efforts of the local Volunteers at deterrence.

It went far beyond digging mock graves, cattle-driving or intimidating graziers who refused to share their bounty. The boycott,
such as the one of the auction of Smith's Cormeen land, was the
least lethal weapon in their arsenal.

The Black Hand Gang of Cormeen originally came together
ostensibly to 'protect the land interests of ex-servicemen in the
area'.[40] It was an intriguing reinterpretation of the notion of
'homes fit for heroes', and indeed at least three members of the
gang had seen service in the British armed forces.[41] They certainly
went about their task with a martial remorselessness.

One of the most active IRA Volunteers in the county, Seán
Farrelly of Carnaross – his brother Patrick was commander of the
Fourth Battalion of the Meath Brigade – offered a detailed account
of the campaign of terror centred on Cormeen to the Bureau of
Military History in the 1940s. A born storyteller, he described the
virtual anarchy that prevailed in parts of the county once the phony
war of 1919 had given way to the winter offensive of 1920:

> With the withdrawal of the RIC from the small barracks all
> over the country and the state of turmoil in the country at the
> time, gangs of blackguards got together here and there all over
> the country to loot, rob and work their will on the people. One
> such gang calling themselves 'The Black Hand Gang' operated
> in the Newcastle and Tierworker areas. It was composed of men
> from every organisation in the districts including the AOH, Sinn
> Féin, ex-British soldiers, and even members of the IRA. Their
> aim was to get established on the land by brutally hunting people
> from their homes. Composed as they were, it can be seen how
> dangerous an organisation it was and how hard it was to track
> them down. When outrages being committed by them were being
> investigated by the IRA it was quite easy for their touts to pass on

the news and they would make their arrangements accordingly. Their activities included the wounding of people with shotguns, shooting into houses, as well as robberies. In one case they placed a landmine in a labourer's cottage and blew it to bits.[42]

Clearly the Cormeen Black Hand Gang, around a dozen-strong, meant business. Their approach smacked of the tactics of the ad hoc agrarian secret societies of the late nineteenth century, with explosives added to the mix. The RIC was either powerless to intervene or devious in opting for a policy of passivity. By withdrawing in early 1920 from most of the small rural barracks of the county, the police had surrendered the military initiative in rural Meath to the IRA. However, it quickly became apparent that it was not just the IRA taking advantage of this capitulation.

In theory, the RIC retrenchment did not mean the country-side went unpoliced. Mobile patrols were supposed to replace the static sitting targets that RIC barracks had become. The arrival of the more nomadic Black and Tans in the early summer of 1920 delivered on that official pledge.

In practice, however, in the interim there was little the RIC could do to prevent IRA military actions or organised criminal activity in the remoter parts of the county. The authorities managed to extract some propaganda advantage from their own temporary weakness: criminality of any kind could be, and was, blamed on the IRA.

There have even been suggestions that members of the Cormeen Gang, especially given the sprinkling of former British 'Tommies' among their ranks, were *agents provocateurs* working with the RIC and the Crown forces.[43] Certainly the havoc they caused tended to discommode active supporters of the Republican campaign, and they clearly succeeded in distracting the Meath IRA from military objectives. Because of the Cormeen group's activities, Seán Boylan's forces spent much of the first half of 1920 operating as a Republican sheriff's posse rather than as a military force.

And it was not as if the RIC was an entirely spent force either. Its members were leading raids, identifying suitable candidates for internment, beefing up intelligence and surprising late-night revellers in pubs right up to the Truce. Still, given a choice between stout defence of the licensing laws and dogged pursuit of the Cormeen Gang, they chose the moister option.

But if the RIC simply shrugged apologetically and deferred to the opposition, then it was up to the IRA to step in.

The Farrelly brothers, based in Carnaross, a village not far from where the worst depredations of the Black Hand were taking place, intervened after the home of local man Stephen Clarke was fired upon by members of the gang. Patrick Farrelly, according to his brother Seán, 'interviewed' several alleged members of the group and 'warned them of the consequences if a similar incident happened again'.[44]

The warning was not heeded. Terrance Gormelly, the farm hand of a local boycotted land-owner, a Presbyterian named Roundtree, was targeted next. An attempt was made to shoot him, but in a case of mistaken identity Roundtree himself was shot and wounded.[45]

Before the Meath IRA was able to make any further progress in quelling this minor insurgency, the situation intensified to a point where intervention became *de rigueur*. Citing historical grievances dating back to the previous century – all too credible in the case of the extended family of Poragon Smith – the Black Hand Gang now fastened on the Cormeen lands of Phil Smith. A portion of the Smith property had allegedly been 'grabbed' after a nineteenth-century eviction and should be returned to its rightful owners.

Whether the gang was determined to be perceived as redistributive Robin Hoods or simply intended the disputed fields for one of their own is not entirely clear. Either way, according to Seán Farrelly, 'They boycotted the place and would not let anyone enter the lands.'[46]

One of the acknowledged leaders of these latter-day Ribbonmen was a British ex-serviceman who had seen action in the Boer War, William 'Bloomer' Rogers from Relagh Beg. He nurtured a historic grudge against the world in general and the landed classes in particular. In 1883 his late father, Michael Rogers, had been removed by bailiffs from his farm near Baileborough. Although his mother was 'reinstated in an equivalent holding on untenanted land'[47] in 1918 by the Estates Commissioners, that Land War-era eviction gave Rogers an aura of moral authority which he would exploit in the agrarian crusade that he and his collaborators unleashed on north Meath.

Joe Clinton's decision to rent four acres from his cousin may have constituted an act of pragmatic husbandry, or of hazardous solidarity. The received wisdom of the Clinton family points to the latter, but the alluring tariff of £2 an acre must also have been an incentive. Phil Smith, who had approached his first cousin and sought Joe Clinton's support against the threat of the Cormeen Gang, would have been aware of the partial immersion of the Clinton family in the Meath IRA. He must have hoped that this would help defend his Cormeen lands.

Blood being thicker than water, and with the prospect of their own property becoming a potential target, Joe Clinton and his sons Peter and Mark agreed to side with Smith. Their support, given the firepower of the Cormeen Gang, was courageous, if rather injudicious. Bloomer Rogers and his shadowy associates had plans for Smith's land. The fact that the Clintons had defied the boycott initiated at the auction was an act of defiance that would not go unnoticed. But would it be allowed to go unpunished?

The ubiquitous threatening letter had long since become a feature of Irish agrarian agitation. This visceral literary genre was apt to include a rough drawing of a coffin, a warning about future behaviour and the cheery signature of 'Rory of the Hills' or one of his site-specific lieutenants. It was the early twentieth-century equivalent of today's courageous trolling keyboard warriors, giddy in the security of their anonymity, whose interventions on social media ensure such a heady level of lucid political discourse.

The Cormeen Gang, however, had shown themselves capable of persuasive violence and had little need of menacing letters. They could safely skip the postal phase of an agrarian dispute. It may only have been the presence of two vigorous young men in the Clinton household – one of whom, Mark, was known to be an IRA Volunteer – as well as the ready availability of their even more daunting older brother Patrick, which prompted the Cormeen Ribbonmen to issue a preliminary admonition. This took the form of a chilling and specific threat. The Clintons were forewarned by mail that if they intervened on behalf of Phil Smith, they would suffer the same fate as their close relative, John Clinton in Arizona.[48]

In theory (Marxist theory at least), this was an inversion of historical reality. In Arizona, John Clinton was a struggling home-steader taking on well-resourced ranchers. In Cormeen, the Black Hand Gang were the self-styled underdogs contending with a grazier class exemplified by Phil Smith and his Clinton allies. However, such historiographical niceties were of little concern to either side. Both would have seen their own cause as morally justified. The dialectic of the Cormeen Gang, based on the distinctly un-Marxist trifecta of 'terrify, smash and grab', stretched the definition of morality to breaking point.

The Clintons ignored the written threat, though the family was well aware that their antagonists were just as capable of exacting retribution for their resistance as had been Ed Scarborough in Arizona. In the middle of April they received a rude reminder that the Cormeen Gang did not indulge in idle threats. Peter Clinton took the family's two plough horses into the disputed four-acre field adjoining their own property. As he set to work, he heard shots ring out and was hit, though not seriously injured.* His attackers waited to see what would happen next.

On 10 May, Mark Clinton entered the disputed fields with two plough horses and began to plough the land owned by his father's cousin. Accounts differ greatly as to precisely what then occurred.† Only one thing is certain: Mark Clinton did not survive the day.

Alerted to the presence of the younger Clinton in the disputed field, at least five members of the Cormeen Gang intervened. Among them was a twenty-one-year-old Presbyterian ex-serviceman, William Gordon, who lived with his widower father and two older brothers in the townland of Trohanny, near Baileborough. Gordon had been one of the five thousand or so Irish men who, safe in the knowledge that the Great War was rumbling to a favourable

---

* *Meath Chronicle*, 2 October 1920. 'Peter Clinton was shot while working on this land almost three weeks before the tragedy.'
† Some accounts have Mark Clinton and the two horses being sniped from a distance of around a hundred metres (Séamus Finn in his BMH-WS #1060 puts it at 400 metres) from a bank of trees on a small hill at the edge of the field. The inquest evidence suggests that he was shot at closer range. Clinton survived long enough to identify at least the number of his killers to his father. So, if he was shot from a distance, his killers must have approached what they presumed was his dead body.

conclusion (from an Allied point of view), joined the British air force in the final months of the conflict in order to acquire a useful and marketable skill. He was retained by the RAF as a fitter, and also received weapons training. On this day, he fully exploited that.

Gordon carried a gun into the field. The first act of the men who accompanied him was to shoot and kill the two Clinton horses. Accounts differ as to who was responsible for this, and whether the five men had originally intended to also murder Mark Clinton is a matter of conjecture. After his valuable plough horses had been slaughtered, Mark Clinton may have responded aggressively and provoked a fatal response. He may have threatened the gang members with the vengeance of the Clinton family, or worse still, with the intervention of the IRA.

Whether provoked or acting in accordance with a preordained plan, William Gordon raised his gun and shot Mark Clinton. The five men then abandoned the scene, leaving their victim for dead.

4

Retribution

'Ill fares the land, to hastening ills a prey
Where wealth accumulates and men decay'

Oliver Goldsmith, 'The Deserted Village'

I.

For much of the passage of the Borora river along the Cavan-Meath border – for some of its journey it *is* the Cavan-Meath border – there is not that much to distract the eye and little enough by way of human habitation. It is a locale of isolated farmhouses in pleasant but unremarkable countryside. In that respect, it has changed little in a century. Today, the farmhouses are bigger and better appointed. Some are built over the ghosts of dwellings that would have been categorised in the 1911 census as third- or fourth-class. The air is clear, the soil is rich, the sporadic woodland is lush in summer and bare in winter, the scenery is appealing rather than breathtaking.

Oliver Goldsmith would have recognised it. When in 1770 he penned his long poem of rural decline, 'The Deserted Village', the model for the fictional Auburn was forty miles or so south-west. Some of the existential problems he identified in the poem had been superseded by 1920, but Goldsmith might as well have had the Cormeen Gang in mind when he wrote:

> Even now the devastation is begun,
> And half the business of destruction done;
> Even now, methinks, as pondering here I stand,
> I see the rural virtues leave the land.

Today, the land that once comprised the Rosemount farm – it has long since changed hands – lies just off the R191 between Mullagh and Bailieborough. The Cloggagh lands, once owned by the Clinton family, are nearby, close enough for Joseph Clinton to have heard half-a-dozen gunshots on the afternoon of 10 May 1920.

At around nine o'clock that morning, Mark left the Clinton

farm with two plough horses to work the disputed Rosemount fields. Joe Clinton accompanied his son to Rosemount and 'helped him tackle the horses to the harrow'.[1] Shortly after midday, one of Mark's sisters called over with her brother's dinner – those were the days when lunch was a meal consumed by 'the quality'. Irish farmers ate their dinner in the middle of the day.

Gunfire in such a rural area was not unusual, then as now; foxes and other predators have to be kept at bay. The remote fusillade would have been susceptible to an entirely innocent explanation. The distance was too great for Joe Clinton to tell the difference between the alien report of a rifle and the mundane blast of a shotgun, and he took no notice of the shots. At around six o'clock, day's end, he later said, 'I went up to the field where my son was working to help him home with the horses.'

But as he approached Rosemount, nothing was visible above the level of the hedge marking the perimeter of the field. Where were the horses? Where was Mark?

Joe had his answer soon enough. He saw the bulk of the dead plough horses first, lying about thirty feet apart. That was when he realised the shots had been anything but innocent. They had killed his horses.

But where was his son? He ran into the field shouting for Mark. That was when he noticed the recumbent and bleeding body. Mark Clinton was alive but barely conscious. 'The first thing I saw of him was the poor fellow's hand waving,' he told his son's inquest. 'He was lying on the broad of his back about a perch [c. five metres] from the small horse. He had no coat on. I noticed blood on his shirt.'

Mark Clinton was able to have a whispered conversation with his father before slipping into unconsciousness in his arms. When he offered to fetch a priest – there was no mention of a doctor, so Joe Clinton may have guessed that his son was beyond medical help – Mark checked him. 'Don't leave me till I die, no priest would overtake me,' he gasped, aware he had little time left. The father took off his own coat and waistcoat and created a pillow for the young man. Joe Clinton later bitterly recalled their final conversation:

> I asked him was it English soldiers shot him, and he said, 'No; I wish it was. It was your own neighbours...' I then asked him was it from behind they shot him. He said it was. Then I said, 'You could not see them?' And he said he could, that God gave him the strength to turn round and look them in the face. 'Then I fell,' he said, 'to rise no more.' 'Well you know them?' I said. He paused a while, and then he said he did. 'Name them for me,' I said. He said, 'For what? Would you hang them?' I said I would not. He then said he would tell me no names. I implored him and I commanded him to give the names, and he refused. I asked him how many were in it, and he said 'Five'... He asked me to pray for them that shot him and I did not. He said he would and that he forgave them.

Joe Clinton related this dramatic account to the statutory inquest on 12 May. And there was much more. He had a few axes to grind before he left the witness box. A small dwelling owned by the family of a neighbour, James McMahon, had lain a few yards distant. If there had been anyone inside, they had made no shift to help his stricken son. Joe Clinton had run towards the cottage to fetch the water his son had requested:

> Mrs McMahon met me at the door. She shouted, 'What do you want?' I said I wanted a drop of water for a wounded man. She told

me I could not come in. I took the water. I asked for a porringer and she refused. I saw two little girls. I asked Mrs McMahon would she send one of them down to Mickey McMahon's [a neighbour] to tell him to go for a priest. She said, 'No.' She appeared out of her mind with terror and wanted to get me from about the place. I took the water down to my son and had to give it to him out of my hand. I saw my son growing weaker.

Whether the behaviour of the farmer's wife was dictated by abject fear or lofty disapproval of the dying IRA Volunteer, there were further instances of the influence of the Cormeen Gang when Joe Clinton attempted to attract the attention of James McMahon himself. He was sowing oats little more than a hundred yards away from the scene of the shooting – he had probably witnessed the entire episode – but he did not respond to Joe Clinton's cries for help. He simply carried on with what he was doing and pretended not to hear, as did another neighbour, named only as Smith. Both men, according to Joe Clinton, turned their backs on him. Whether they were terrified of reprisals from the Black Hand Gang or believed that Mark Clinton had received his just deserts for aiding and abetting the son of Poragon Smith, neither man came to his aid.

After a few minutes, Joe Clinton's shouts drew a more supportive cohort of neighbours, including Peter Clinton, who carried the unconscious body of his mortally wounded brother to the Rosemount farmhouse. There Mark clung to life for less than an hour. Medical help, in the form of a Dr Patrick Gavin from Moynalty, arrived too late.[2]

Despite the pathos of Joe Clinton's account of his son's brutal death, there must be some doubt as to what actually transpired in Mark's final moments. Did he really tell his father that five men had been involved in his murder, and then refuse to identify them? Or did he actually name his killers? The balance of probability suggests the latter.

Joseph Clinton's poignant evocation of his son's last hour was related to a coroner's jury. Although coroners' courts were viewed in a generally positive light by Republicans and often exploited for their own ends* – so much so that they were later largely abandoned by the authorities and replaced by military courts of inquiry – Joe Clinton was unlikely to have revealed the names of his son's killers in such a public forum. Although afforded legal protection had he chosen to avail of it, he would not have wanted to make his son's killers aware that they had been identified. He might well have had his own reasons to lull them into a complacent sense of safety.

He knew that the IRA itself would deal with Mark Clinton's killers. His son Patrick, a Meath Brigade intelligence officer, and Seán Boylan, the Meath IRA O/C, would take matters in hand. On 1 June 1920, Peter became the third Clinton son to join the IRA. The search for his brother's killers was a major motivating factor.

Mark Clinton's was one of hundreds of violent deaths that year. There were still more in the first half of 1921. But his death, while not unique, was exceptional. He had not been killed by the IRA. He *was* the IRA. He had not been murdered in a random reprisal by Crown forces, though the diffusion of such a fiction would have suited his killers. He was the victim of a criminal enterprise, a conspiracy that placed little value on human life.

Mark Clinton was a casualty of that other war, the one that

* The inquest into the murder of Cork Lord Mayor Tomás MacCurtain in March 1920 is the most obvious case in point. But in County Meath, the inquest into the death of Oldcastle IRA commander Séamus Cogan was exploited by Sinn Féin for its own propaganda purposes.

placed the acquisition of agricultural land over the achievement of political independence. In keeping with the often tawdry nature of that parallel conflict, he had, according to contemporary sources, been shot dead in exchange for the payment of two pounds.

Many of the Bureau of Military History Witness Statements of County Meath IRA veterans refer to the episode. This is unsurprising, as it became something of a national cause célèbre and dozens of Meath IRA Volunteers were involved in the punitive operation that followed. Their memories, extracted in interviews mostly conducted more than three decades after the murder, differ greatly and, furthermore, are the testimonies of men who were not themselves witnesses to Mark Clinton's death. Some may be based on information exacted from members of the Cormeen Gang while in IRA custody. None is completely reliable.

The most authoritative figure, as is generally the case in this narrative, is the Meath IRA O/C Seán Boylan, like his even more famous son,* a herbal healer from Dunboyne. In an extensive interview conducted in 1957, Boylan told the Bureau, 'The two horses with which he [Mark Clinton] was ploughing had been shot dead by a man named McGovern. Gordon received the sum of £2 for the shooting from a William Rogers, an ex-South African policeman, who had organised a band of terrorists to seize the land.'[3]

Other accounts have Gordon killing the horses himself.[4] A third version has a member of the gang named Carolan – the name comes up frequently in a variety of statements – shooting the horses before Gordon intervened to kill Clinton.[5]

---

* Seán Boylan Jr. managed four Meath All-Ireland Senior Football Championship-winning teams (1987, 1988, 1996, 1999) and coached the Meath team for twenty-three years.

The killer of the two unfortunate plough horses was of little relevance to the Clinton family as they gathered at the Cloggagh farmhouse to mourn their dead son and brother. Peter Clinton was especially distraught, blaming himself for the death of his younger sibling. According to the son he named for his slain brother, Mark Clinton of Sutton Coldfield in England: 'My father never recovered from his grief. He felt that somehow he should have been able to convince his younger brother to cease. My father had a slight bullet wound from his involvement on 9 May. He was unable to discuss this sad affair with me or other members of the family.'[6]

But those were vile times. Less than a year later Peter Clinton himself would be required, by the organisation he joined in order to assuage his guilt over his brother's murder, to participate in ending the life of another young man. Given the fate of his sibling, he must have acquiesced, acting on a direct order, with the greatest of reluctance.

Mark Clinton was buried on 13 May in Moybologue cemetery a few miles across the border in County Cavan. As a Volunteer, he was accorded full military honours by a number of local IRA companies.[7] The Last Post was sounded and shots were fired over his grave.[8]

2.

The inquest into Clinton's death took place under the watchful eye of the North Meath coroner, Dr John Brangan, two days after the murder. Proceedings were conducted under the auspices of the Crown administration. It would be some time yet before coroners' courts became subsumed into the burgeoning Republican judicial structures.

The first to give evidence was Dr Patrick Gavin, who had written the death certificate. This read 'wounds inflicted by shots fired maliciously – internal haemorrhage – sudden'. Gavin offered the coroner's jury some more detail. As reported in the *Meath Chronicle* of 15 May 1920, 'He found a small punctured wound on the right side of the chest wall. There was a small piece of metal at the entrance of the wound like the casing of a bullet. There was a second wound on the back, at the left side, about one and a half inches from the spinal column.'[9]

Gavin testified that the second bullet hole was an exit wound and that the shot had been fired 'from some distance from in front of the deceased'. Dr William Parsons Lappin, scion of a medical dynasty in the nearby town of Kells,* had performed an autopsy on Mark Clinton's body and confirmed Gavin's observations. The bulk of the evidence came from Joseph Clinton, as described above.

There was a footnote to Joe Clinton's outburst quoted above, concerning the McMahons. On 22 May, the *Meath Chronicle* published a denial from Mrs McMahon that her family had refused to assist. 'On the contrary,' wrote the offended neighbour, 'I at once gave him half a gallon of water which was in the house, and I also gave him a blanket.'[10]

The murder of Mark Clinton was not just of local interest; it was treated as an event of national significance. The homicide was covered by the Dublin and Cork dailies,[11] as were the inquest and the subsequent compensation claim of Joseph Clinton for £3,100†† under the Malicious Injuries Act in October 1920.[12]

---

* Grandfather of film producer Arthur Lappin (*My Left Foot*, *In the Name of the Father*), whose family still runs a chemist's dispensary in the town. The medical side of the family currently stretches to three generations.
† Joe Clinton was awarded compensation of £400 for the murder of his son and £125 for the shooting of his horses.

The *Drogheda Independent* of 22 May 1920 editorialised not just about the murder, but about its context. The newspaper expressed its horror at the circumstances of Clinton's death but could 'understand the motives that caused it. Townsmen or city folk cannot understand the land hunger. There are those in Meath who hold land dearer than gold, dearer than their parents, dearer than their families and is it to be that land is to be set as now dearer than God's commandments?'

Personal reactions to the killing were on the one hand discreet and methodical, and on the other bellicose and episcopal. From Dunboyne in east Meath, Commandant Seán Boylan set in train the IRA investigation that would lead to the apprehension of the group that killed their comrade. The intervention of the Roman Catholic Bishop of Meath, the Most Rev Dr Gaughran, was more explicit. On 14 May he sent a letter to the parish priest of Moynalty, Father John Brogan, which was intended to be read out at Mass the following Sunday.

After some fire and brimstone biblical preliminaries invoking Cain and Abel, the blood of Ahab and Naboth, and the certainty of 'God's vengeance' on the perpetrators, the bishop informed the faithful of the diocese that 'Murder is at all times a most evil thing, but the circumstances of this murder, as revealed at the inquest, filled me with horror.' The *Meath Chronicle*, in publishing the philippic, chose to delete Gaughran's reference to the alleged callousness of the McMahons 'in view of the contradiction below', i.e. the letter of Mrs McMahon carried in the same issue.

Gaughran went further in his own sermon at early Mass in Navan on the Sunday after the murder. With God's vengeance still uppermost in his mind, he trained his rhetorical arsenal on the wider 'question of the acquisition of land', which was:

So acute that people seemed inclined to stop at nothing to appease it. People seemed to think that they could gain possession of land by threats and violence, and by knocking down gates and fences, but when persons using such methods came to die, it was God help them. He would like to see the people on the land, and see the land properly cultivated, but he would also like to see the land secured for the people by means in consonance with the Ten Commandments, for it would be better for a man to go to bed supperless than to be the owner of one hundred acres secured by means which had not the sanction of God.

Gaughran's solution was 'the enthronement of the Sacred Heart in every Catholic home'. He offered no advice to Protestants, presumably on the basis that they were more than likely to be the owners of the land. Yet while Seán Boylan bowed to none in his veneration of God, the Sacred Heart and the other divinities invoked by his bishop, he had more pragmatic and violent resolutions to offer. Vengeance, when it came – and it descended swiftly – would not be God's. It would be Seán Boylan's.

3.

Boylan had an embarrassment of reasons to finally lower the boom on the Cormeen Gang. They had murdered one of his Volunteers, the younger brother of an able and valued friend and intelligence officer. In an unsentimental era of tit-for-tat killing, there could be no immunity for such an egregious crime. Furthermore, they had defied all efforts to curtail their capacity for mayhem. These had been too half-hearted, he felt, and Boylan did not countenance timorousness among the leadership of his outlying battalions.

However, what concerned him most of all was the possibility that, encouraged by the absence of IRA retribution, this agrarian wrecking ball might turn into a *de facto* and volatile parallel insurgency that could be exploited, directly or obliquely, by the Crown forces. The Dunboyne IRA chief did not want anyone compromising his control of his bailiwick. Michael Collins, his overlord in the Irish Republican Brotherhood, would not appreciate it either. The last thing Boylan needed was a tongue-lashing from his good friend, the Dáil Minister for Finance and IRA Director of Intelligence.

The Meath IRA O/C was aware that much of the dynamism of the Black Hand operation was generated by a small corps of ex-servicemen. Republican militants had at best an ambiguous attitude towards men who had 'answered the call' between 1914 and 1918. There was a small number of Great War veterans in the ranks of the IRA, the most prominent being west Cork flying column commander Tom Barry. The number of Irish ex-servicemen murdered (around a hundred) or wounded by the IRA during the War of Independence was about the same as the number who opted to join the IRA instead.[13]

IRA units were generally wary of, or overtly hostile towards, former Irish 'Tommies'. In Meath, for example, this was formally recognised post-Truce in a communication from Pat Clinton, 1st Eastern Division intelligence officer, to his brigade IOs in September 1921. Seeking their assistance in 'getting to the roots of the enemy system', he observed that 'ex-policemen, ex-soldiers and persons of this class are used extensively by the enemy intelligence system and therefore need special watching'.[14]

Boylan was reluctant to divert resources from the harassment

of Crown forces into a punitive operation against a criminal gang
that had now emphatically shed any Rob Roy mantle it might have
sought to assume. The first IRA officers to whom he delegated
the task of apprehending Mark Clinton's killers came up empty-
handed. Only when he tapped two senior IRA figures in the
county, Patrick Farrelly and Phil Tevlin from Carnaross, and threw
the resources of the entire brigade behind the enterprise were any
meaningful results achieved.

The IRA, when required, could be even more intimidating
than the Cormeen Gang. Patrick Farrelly's brother Seán offered
a vivid account of the identification of the culprits in his statement to the Bureau of Military History:

It was a long tedious undertaking. No one in the area would
give information and many of those who could were, apparently,
afraid to do so. It was as a result of information supplied by a
Tom Tevlin and Stephen Clarke (whose house had been fired
into) that we were able to make a start. Eventually Pat and his
men located the gang in George Gartland's public house in
Baileborough one day. They were located in a room off the bar
and Pat actually overheard them plotting to drive a man named
Patrick Carolan off his farm. One of the gang, a man known as
'The Rabbit' Carolan, saw Pat and closed the door of the room;
he knew he had been detected and went on the run there and
then and did not return until the whole affair was over.[15]

It took the Meath IRA a month to track down the Cormeen
band, and gradually the identities of the members emerged. The
Carolan with the unenviable sobriquet of 'The Rabbit' might have
made himself scarce, but there was a second man of that surname
involved in the gang. This emerged from a report in the *Meath*

Chronicle of 12 June 1920. The eye-catching front-page headline read 'The Cormeen tragedy – Sensational development – Irish Volunteers take Action'. Under the byline of 'our East Cavan reporter' and probably relying on information supplied by IRA member Seán Hayes, a staffer, the *Chronicle* went on to detail how the IRA had 'arrested' four men.* The detainees were named as 'Carolan of Newcastle; Smith, Carriga; William Rogers, Relagh Beg; and Ward, Srahan'. All were townlands close to or contiguous with Cormeen. Carolan, clearly a force to be reckoned with, was known locally as 'Kill-man' Carolan:[16]

> It will not be out of place to recall that the deceased was a prominent Gael and a member of the Volunteers, so that his tragic death attracted the serious attention and investigation of his officers and comrades. The result of these activities was Thursday night's swoop, and in less than an hour the suspected parties were arrested, blindfolded, handcuffed and deposited in a lorry, which conveyed them to an unknown destination. Having done their work, the Volunteers dispersed as speedily and as mysteriously as they came, a small guard only accompanying the prisoners. The prisoners were treated very humanely. Arriving at their destination 'somewhere in Ireland', the prisoners were placed in separate rooms, the handcuffs being removed as well as the covering over their eyes. They enjoyed a hearty breakfast and next day one of the men went on hunger strike.

---

* The *Drogheda Independent*, generally less supportive of Sinn Féin, ran a far less detailed account. It asserted that two of the prisoners had implicated themselves in the shooting (*Drogheda Independent*, 12 June 1920).

The defiant Cormeen *bandito*, however, lacked the resolve of a Terence MacSwiney or a Thomas Ashe and succumbed to temptation not long after his stomach began to rumble. The hunger strike ended ignominiously. The *Chronicle*'s 'East Cavan reporter' claimed that the prisoners were being 'well treated, every solicitude being shown and endeavours made to make them quite comfortable'.

The phrase 'unknown destination' was already becoming a cliché by the middle of 1920. It was a euphemism for an IRA safe house where prisoners were held and interrogated, often none too gently. The well-informed *Meath Chronicle* reporter advised the newspaper's readers that the prisoners had already appeared before a 'courtmartial constituted by six or seven officers. Certain statements were made by some of the prisoners. The Court having concluded, the prisoners were again conducted to their place of detention.'

As an afterthought, and an indication that the deity himself was on the side of the IRA, the report concluded with the observation that 'Rev Fr Brogan, PP, Moynalty, speaking at Mass on Sunday, prayed that God might enlighten and enable the Volunteers to bring everyone connected with the murder to justice'.[17]

It all sounded somewhat innocuous, like a particularly capable sheepdog herding his charges into a convenient pen. And in fact, once the intelligence identifying all the members of the gang had been gathered, the task of rounding them up had been handled by Boylan and his men with military efficiency. Not everyone in the district, however, was supportive of this IRA swoop. The following week the *Chronicle* reported, 'It is stated that a crowd of neighbours collected and planted crops for one of the prisoners.'

Thirteen men were arrested; three were subsequently released. It was the work of just two nights. Boylan took personal charge of the operation, assisted by the highly capable Phil Tevlin. Among those rounded up on the first night was McGovern, the man named by Boylan as having shot the two horses. The Meath commandant enlisted the aid of a prominent member of the IRA's Fingal (north County Dublin) Brigade, Joe Lawless, brother of one of Michael Collins's secretaries, Eveleen Lawless.

Lawless was the owner of a sizeable truck and made himself very useful over the two nights. He also left an extremely detailed account of the operation in his statement to the Bureau of Military History in December 1954. The abduction of the offenders was carried out by a cohort of around a dozen IRA Volunteers:

> Seán Boylan sat beside me in the driver's cab and directed me where to go in his laconic mode of speech. 'Right', 'Left' or 'Straight on' when we reached a crossroads and 'Pull up here' when we arrived, was almost the only conversation between us during the drive, and occasionally he rapped out a sharp command to those behind in the body to be silent. Having left Trim far behind us I had no idea where we were when we stopped at Boylan's command near some houses, where some two or three men were quickly placed under arrest, loaded into the truck and we sped on further north.

Their route took them through the village of Moynalty, or so Lawless was informed by Boylan as he drove through a settlement he did not recognise. From there, Lawless found himself driving along narrow country roads. When they reached their destination, Boylan ordered him to turn the truck about:

> This was much easier said than done, however, as the road was very little wider than the width of the truck and there was no convenient gateway, but I managed somehow to get turned before the party could be seen in the clouded moonlight returning with another prisoner. This prisoner seemed to be tall and walked erect and square-shouldered, while he alternately cursed his captors and vowed vengeance on others. Clearly this man was of a different mettle from those we had taken earlier in the night. Arriving at the rear of the truck he refused to get into it, and had to be lifted while he struggled and was thrown with more force than courtesy into it.[18]

Lawless identified the intractable prisoner as 'a man named Smith', but it is more likely that he was a tempestuous IRA Volunteer named Bryan Finnegan. In April of that year Finnegan had been involved in the burning of the abandoned RIC barracks in Mullagh, County Cavan. Through either native recklessness or temporary over-enthusiasm, he had found himself upstairs in the burning building, with no safe route down the stairs. His only option was to jump from the first-floor window onto the street below.

This feat of derring-do obviously impressed Seán Farrelly, who described Finnegan as 'the greatest daredevil I ever met'. In his BMH witness statement, Farrelly offered a graphic description of Finnegan's boisterous resistance that night:

> We found him in his little house fully armed with a rifle. He threatened to shoot anyone who came near and we knew he

was capable of doing so and meant to do what he said. He was
captured, however, after a hole was bored in the back of the
house. He struggled violently but Pat [Farrelly] managed to get
a chain around his body. He then gave in and we marched him
to the lorry.[19]

'Rabbit' Carolan, forewarned, managed to make a clean getaway;
otherwise, the abductions of the Cormeen Gang proceeded without a hitch.

One man not picked up on either night was William Gordon,
soon to be identified by the IRA as the killer of Mark Clinton.
Gordon was already residing at the pleasure of His Majesty, awaiting
trial on charges not specifically related to the Cormeen murder.
His respite was temporary, but his arrest by the RIC the night
before the IRA swoop seems fortuitous in the extreme. The *Meath
Chronicle* reported that 'masks and arms were found in his house'.

Gordon's arrest, on dubious charges of which he would later be
acquitted, prevented his capture in the IRA trawl and served to
add to the suspicion that he was an *agent provocateur* being taken
into protective custody by the RIC. His Presbyterianism and his
service in the Great War enhanced such suspicions.

The prisoners were taken to Boltown Hall near the village of
Kilskyre, a few miles from Kells. This was the large and elegant
residence of the late Henry Dyas, who would not have approved of
his uninvited IRA guests any more than he would have esteemed
their prisoners. A successful racehorse trainer whose most famous
charge, Manifesto, won the Aintree Grand National in 1897 and
1899, he had died in 1915 and the house had been unoccupied for
some time.

4.

The IRA were not the only occupants of Boltown Hall on the day they arrived with their prisoners. A house lying vacant for the better part of five years can attract some intriguing visitors. One of the men assigned as a prison guard, Peter O'Connell, arrived in Kilskyre before Boylan materialised with the detainees. He was obliged to break up an illegal cock-fight:

> I knew that mansion was unoccupied. I got there before 6 a.m. Several Model 10 Ford cars, a crowd of more than 100 people. Took courage and moved in among them. Everybody in a hurry. Fighting game cocks both alive and dead being loaded into cars. All gone in about 20 minutes. Wondered if someone fooling me. Went down to the back yard. Saw the stable of 'Manifesto' lined with marble. Saw two motor vehicles come up the avenue.[20]

The prisoners and their guards were all present and correct, but no one had house keys, so the Cormeen Gang spent their first hours of captivity in the stable once occupied by the illustrious Manifesto. A major irritant for Boylan, as for other IRA commandants with prisoners to cater for, was the provision of food for his temporary charges. O'Connell's version of events suggests that the *Meath Chronicle* report of the relative comfort in which the members of the gang were being held was either propaganda or wishful thinking. 'Food and money scarce, went out in our turn on a bike scrounging,' was his terse observation.

O'Connell was also the only IRA veteran to make reference to the visit of two men whose presence gave the Cormeen affair a wider significance. 'The [third] day we had visitors: Gen Boylan, Gen Mick Collins, Mick Noyek (a barrister) and another bloke that I cannot place. Noyek interested in legal aspects of the case. Interviewed prisoners separately and later in a bunch. Retired to banqueting hall with Noyek to confer. I did doorman.'[21]

The 'Noyek' in question was actually prominent Dublin solicitor and Sinn Féin sympathiser Michael Noyk, who appeared for the defence in many courts martial of IRA and Sinn Féin prisoners of the Crown. Instrumental in the deliberate legal prevarication that helped save the life of one of Collins's influential intelligence assets, the renegade DMP Sergeant Eamon 'Ned' Broy, he was a legal adviser to the cabinet.

While Boylan might well have been expected to visit the Kilskyre prisoners on a regular basis, the presence of Collins and Noyk – assuming O'Connell's account is not fanciful – emphasises the significance of the Clinton murder case for the embryonic civil administration being put in place by Dáil Éireann. Noyk was central to the establishment of the Sinn Féin/Dáil court system. He makes no reference to a visit to Meath, or indeed to the Clinton murder, in his own extensive (106 pages) statement to the BMH, but as the most prominent legal consultant to the Dáil cabinet, he would have been a logical expert to accompany Collins to interrogate the prisoners or – less likely – ensure that they were being properly treated.

The involvement of Collins is noteworthy. Although the Minister for Finance and IRA Director of Intelligence did have other official responsibilities, this was not a finance or intelligence matter. So what was he doing in Kilskyre with Noyk? If any senior cabinet minister had an obligation to run the rule over Boylan's operation, it was Austin Stack as Minister for Home Affairs.

The fact that Boylan approached Collins rather than Stack, or even Defence Minister Cathal Brugha, indicates a dedicated IRB man's assessment of the real chain of command in the Dáil administration. An IRB member's loyalty to Dáil Éireann, or even to the Irish Republican Army, was often of less consequence than his affiliation to the Brotherhood. Boylan's was a calculation dictated by his personal loyalty to Collins and to the shadowy IRB (to which he would cleave during the Civil War as well), and by the antipathy of both Stack and Brugha to that organisation.[22] But the actual presence of Collins, as attested to by Peter O'Connell, can be seen as indicative of his growing awareness of the importance of the parallel system of law and justice being created by Sinn Féin, even though the prosecution of the Cormeen Gang would not be taking place under the auspices of any Dáil court.

Boltown Hall was only briefly a prison. The RIC, backed up by elements of the South Wales Borderers stationed in Meath, soon got wind that the IRA and the Cormeen Gang were sharing accommodation somewhere near Kells. House-to-house searches began, making the guarding of the prisoners even more problematic. Boylan's deputy, Séamus Finn of Athboy, in his own statement to the Bureau of Military History, recalled how Boltown Hall had to be abandoned as a safe house:

> The hunt was up and it became hot. The enemy forces got some inkling of the location of this 'Unknown' [unknown destination] and one morning, some weeks after our men had made the arrests, the enemy surrounded a big slice of country inside which this place was and after a house to house search came on it, only to find that our lads and prisoners had got away.[23]

The prisoners were then moved to an interim 'unknown destination' near Bohermeen, then transferred to a safe house owned by the O'Connor family of Salestown, Boylan's own stomping ground. Their final destination was the basement of an old rectory. According to Boylan, it 'had barred windows and made an excellent prison'.[24]

5.

'If you want to have a rabbit stew, first catch the rabbit' is an axiom of uncertain provenance. While Seán Boylan had allowed 'The Rabbit' to slip out of his hands, he still had the makings of a stew incarcerated in the basement of a safe house in his own backyard. What to do next was the question. Was there ever a temptation to send for Cahir Davitt and put these latter-day Ribbonmen on trial in a Dáil court in a quasi-public setting? If there was, neither Boylan nor any other prominent member of the Meath IRA leadership made reference to the notion when questioned by the Bureau of Military History.

Dáil courts, which mostly involved the resolution of civil cases and petty criminality, were highly vulnerable. Court proceedings involved a lot of coming and going that was difficult to conceal. They were frequently raided by the Crown forces. Any advance leakage of the timing of a Cormeen trial, and the RIC (now augmented by the Black and Tans and the Auxiliaries) would be in a position to round up the leadership cadre of the Meath IRA and release the probable killers of Mark Clinton. And (as we shall see later) the Meath Brigade had a problem with the sequestration of information.

Instead of being tried by a judge and jury, the prisoners faced the paramilitary equivalent of a 'drumhead' court martial, of the kind familiar from the Great War and normally used by the IRA for alleged spies and informers. The Cormeen Gang was tried by members of the military fraternity who had captured, guarded and interrogated them for weeks. Bear in mind that the accused would have been tried as conspirators and accessories, and that many of those on trial were, in theory at least, liable to the death penalty. Séamus Finn offered a bald account of what happened next:

> We went ahead and held a preliminary trial at which we produced all the evidence in our possession. Some of the prisoners broke down and the whole plot was revealed. We made a fuller report to GHQ and asked them to supply officers to constitute a court. After some delay and much parleying they eventually sent us down an officer who was to act as senior court officer along with two of our brigade officers. This court sat at O'Connor's and tried the prisoners. All the evidence was heard and they were given every facility to prove their innocence but all of them, with one exception, a man who was the real ringleader, admitted their guilt and implicated the killer [William Gordon – then in RIC custody] as the one who fired the shot. The leader eventually admitted his part in the affair too and the court passed sentence on them.[25]

A more vibrant and highly critical narrative of the trial of the 'Cormeen Ten' comes from Seán Dowling, a staff commandant in the Dublin Brigade of the IRA, who was then, like so many senior IRA officers, in his mid-twenties. Dowling, himself directly involved in the later trial of William Gordon, was singularly unimpressed with what he perceived to be the injustice of it all. Some years later, in an interview with the oral historian Uinseann MacEoin for the book that would become *Survivors*, he made no attempt to curtail his spleen:

They were given sentences that would make your hair stand on end. They were banished from the country. What kind of men were they? They were questioned by this bloody fool Kelly.*

> *You're a farmer?*
> *Yes sir.*
> *How many acres have you?*
> *Four acres.*
> *Have you any children?*
> *I have six.*

And this bloody bastard gave them sentences of three to fifteen years banishment. And they had to go, oh yes they had. They went to England... Our vice commandant Peadar Ó Broin was clerk of the court. He was walking up and down during these proceedings.

> *I think it is a bloody shame, I said afterwards, to hand out such sentences to those unfortunate men.*
> *Oh,* said Kelly, *we have to show these people that the IRA are determined to deal out even-handed justice.*

Peadar was still walking up and down. *Aye, he said, justice and heaps of it.*[26]

However, we must be cautious of Dowling's comments, perhaps not entirely recollected in tranquillity. He took the anti-Treaty side in the Civil War and had deeply personal reasons to be critical of the justice meted out in the fiefdom of Seán Boylan,

---

* Dr Ted Kelly, O/C 4th Dublin battalion, one of the three judges.

one of the closest associates of Michael Collins and a general in the National Army.

Bureau of Military History Witness Statements vary as to the length of the sentences of exile imposed on the ten men found guilty (three others, Thomas Finnegan, Patrick McGovern and Patrick Ward, had already been released). Some put the range at five to forty years, the latter amounting to exile for life. Once again we must assume that the most authoritative account comes from Boylan himself:

> All of them were sentenced to from three to fifteen years and ordered to be deported; their cases to be reviewed when the occupying forces had left the country. John Kelly, brigade police officer, with the help of other Volunteers, had them deported in batches of three and four from Dublin, Dundalk and Drogheda. In Dublin at the time the Great Northern Hotel, North Wall, was occupied by British military. The prisoners were taken to the South Wall and rowed across the river in time to place them on a boat for Liverpool.[27]

Despite the fulminations of Seán Dowling, the prisoners might have suffered a worse fate – they could have also been flogged. Boylan was a stern disciplinarian and on at least one recorded occasion had ordered the flogging of a number of insubordinate officers and men who refused to accept orders to stage more attacks on Crown forces in Meath. The reluctant Volunteers argued that they were inadequately armed and would not be able to protect their company districts from inevitable British reprisals.

Boylan had raised the cry of mutiny, stripped the local company commanders of their rank and had a number of them ritually flogged.[28] Given the offences of the Cormeen Gang, they could probably consider themselves fortunate to have landed in Liverpool without some more painful mementoes of their crimes.

Only the infamous 'Rabbit' Carolan escaped IRA justice. As Seán Farrelly testified ruefully in his witness statement, 'When all was over, the "Rabbit", whom we could not secure, returned to the area.'[29]

Like a lot that happened during the revolutionary period and, more particularly, its immediate aftermath, there was an enduring legacy of bitterness surrounding the arrest and exile of the members of the Cormeen Gang. Peter Clinton's son, named after his uncle Mark, was a schoolboy in north Meath in the 1940s. He recalled, 'As children [my brother and I] were often attacked at school by members of the gang's children who blamed my brother and me for their family members' deportation. When we complained to my father his only advice was: "Keep away from them. Do not get involved."'

In the main, however – outside of Cormeen and environs at least – opinion seems to have concluded that the interests of justice had been well served by Boylan and the Meath IRA. As Mark Clinton Jr. put it, 'My neighbours always treated my father with great respect and used to refer to my Uncle Mark with admiration.'[30]

Whether the story is true or apocryphal, there appears to have been one final flourish from the Cormeen Gang. Some years after his enforced deportation, one of the members who had not yet served his full term of exile is said to have returned to the Carnaross-Moynalty area and gone into a local public house. He ordered a drink and settled down to enjoy his first Irish pint in a decade or more. However, his pleasure at the tang of the cool draught was short-lived. He was tapped on the shoulder and advised by a (not unfriendly) fellow drinker that it might be advisable to leave the premises. Two of the patrons drinking in another quiet corner of the bar were relatives of Mark Clinton. The man quickly downed his drink, withdrew and was never seen in the area again.

With the Cormeen Gang removed from the east Cavan-north Meath border region, attacks on local landowners ceased. A relieved Phil Smith, whose cousin Joe had lost a son in the struggle over property rights, magnanimously raised Joseph Clinton's rent on the four-acre field in Cormeen from two pounds to six pounds an acre.[31]

5

The Third Killing

'Just because we were an army didn't mean we had
to go round shooting people all the time. We could
get our way by other means. We didn't want
to kill anyone.'[1]

Peter O'Connell, Stonefield Company,
5th Battalion, Meath Brigade

I.

In early 1920, some Irish survivors of the Great War spent a cold January evening together in the town of Kells. Here was a group of men who had seen sights no human being should ever be required to witness. They had come through a conflict where, if you were born in Scotland, there was a one in four chance that you would not survive the trenches. If you were Irish, the odds of survival were slightly higher: your prospects of being vaporised, riddled by bullets or gassed to death were a far healthier one in six.

The assembled members of the Kells branch of the Ex-Soldiers Federation had seen the worst that humankind could unleash, but when they gathered for that meeting in January 1920 they were worried. So much so that they were inclining towards vigilantism, announcing their intention to form a Vigilance Committee. Their concerns were not for themselves, but for law and order in their neighbourhood. The putative committee was not intended for their own personal protection, or for that of fellow ex-soldiers, sailors and airmen, it was 'for the purpose of combatting the existing orgy of robberies in the district'.[2]

'Where there's muck there's brass', and where there is chaos there is possibility. There was no shortage of actors willing to capitalise on the opportunities afforded by the heightened civil unrest of the War of Independence. Granted, some of the criminality that concerned the ex-servicemen gathered in Kells that winter night was due to the intensifying military conflict – still a mere 'police action' in the eyes of the British government. But the IRA was not entirely responsible for the spate of robberies and burglaries plaguing Meath and many of the counties around it. This was mostly the work of enterprising local burglars.[3]

The IRA raided private houses for arms and ammunition, not to raise money for the cause. Legendary East Clare IRA commander Michael Brennan, for example, was removed from his command by GHQ for a raid on the general post office in Limerick which netted a tidy £1,500, though the Clare IRA was allowed to retain the funds.[4] The IRA prided itself on being a disciplined army. Its members did not steal or loot. They appropriated, confiscated or commandeered. That was the theory, at least.

The *Meath Chronicle* reported multiple burglaries and four mail robberies between January and April 1920.[5] The RIC did not seem to be able to curtail this spate of lawlessness; it had its hands full trying, and largely failing, to contend with the IRA. In certain instances the RIC was even disposed to hold Republican militants responsible for some of the more serious robberies. When the Duc de Stacpoole's Tobertynan House, halfway between Trim and Enfield, was raided and looted, accompanied by the firing of six gunshots through the house's ornate ceilings, the RIC immediately blamed the IRA. The proceeds of the raid would buy a lot of guns, and de Stacpoole was an unrepentant unionist. Cui bono?

Not the IRA, it turned out, but four local thieves (ironically, one was an ex-serviceman named Fitzsimons). Seán Boylan ordered an investigation, the Trim IRA assumed constabulary mode, the guilty parties were identified, and the stolen goods were returned.

When Boylan initially approached de Stacpoole offering to try and locate the loot, the landowner was scornful. Why would he require any help from an insurgent militia, pray tell, when the RIC was already investigating the crime? Because, suggested Boylan, 'They will do nothing, they are in collusion with the robbers. They are more concerned with arresting us than restoring your property.'[6]

In addition to recovering de Stacpoole's valuables, Boylan also managed to exact a statement from one of the thieves (a man named Malone) that he had been advised by an RIC sergeant where to get the best price for the stolen goods!

When the booty was restored to de Stacpoole, he was handed a copy of Malone's statement. The original had already been sent to Michael Collins. All the stolen property was restored to its astonished owner, bar a silver horseshoe that the *ex officio* IRA constabulary had been unable to trace. The delighted grandee offered Boylan five pounds for his troubles. The IRA O/C declined this largesse.

The thieves received summary justice. They were 'stripped and flogged ... and compelled to work on a farm for three weeks'.[7] A grateful de Stacpoole wrote a letter to the *Irish Times* recounting his positive experience of retributive IRA justice, and the propaganda coup for Boylan was worth well in excess of the meagre five-pound reward. The encomium to the revolutionary constabulary was predictably carried by Sinn Féin's *Irish Bulletin*, the *samizdat* publicity sheet edited by Desmond Fitzgerald and Frank Gallagher (and typed by Kathleen Napoli McKenna from Oldcastle, County Meath).

2.

William Gordon was an ex-serviceman, but he is unlikely to have attended the January meeting of the Kells branch of the Ex-Soldiers Federation. He would have been more comfortable with the burglar and ex-serviceman Fitzsimons than with the would-be vigilantes anxious about the spate of crime in their district. Not that theft from 'big houses' was Gordon's forte. He was more preoccupied with what surrounded the houses, large and modest alike, of rural County Meath.

Billy Gordon was a leading member of the Cormeen Black Hand Gang. His interest was in impromptu land acquisition.

The Gordons were a Presbyterian family from the townland of Killagriffe near Trohanny, and worked a twenty-acre farm. The nearest town of any consequence was Bailieborough, across the border in County Cavan. The 1911 census shows sixty-four-year-old John Gordon Sr., a widower, living with his three sons, John, Henry and William, then aged sixteen, fifteen and twelve, in a modest two-room house. John Gordon's marriage had lasted six years before the death of his wife; William thus lost his mother when he was barely a year old.

The Gordons were no strangers to discord. In May 1918, Henry Gordon had been arraigned before a magistrates' court on a charge of shooting and seriously wounding a Kilagriffe farmer, George Pringle. The RIC advanced a theory that Pringle had been shot in error. Gordon's intended target, claimed the constabulary, had been a Baileborough chemist named Samuel Jones who had recently purchased a farm in Kilagriffe. The magistrate was having none of it, and after ascertaining that Jones, in the general area at the time, was not a witness to the crime, refused to allow the man to testify.[8]

By foregoing Jones's evidence, the magistrate may well have spurned an intriguing preview of the template for the murder of Mark Clinton two years later. The case was despatched to the Meath assizes in Trim in July, where Henry Gordon mysteriously managed to produce an alibi witness whose existence had not been mentioned at the petty sessions two months before, and he was acquitted.[9] The court also ordered that his gun be returned to him. This may well have been the weapon Henry Gordon's younger brother used to kill Mark Clinton on 10 May 1920.

Two months after his brother had been acquitted of the

attempted murder of Pringle, William Gordon, at the age of nineteen years and five months, enlisted in the newly established (1 April 1918) Royal Air Force.* Had he been living anywhere else in the United Kingdom, he would have become eligible for conscription in April 1917. Once drafted, he would probably have been assigned to an infantry regiment and might have completed his training just in time to die in the slaughter of Passchendaele that winter. Because he enlisted voluntarily, he was allowed the luxury of choosing his own unit. He made a savvy choice.

Gordon, coincidentally, was not alone in joining the RAF as the Great War slithered towards its conclusion. His sudden interest in a military career was in keeping with a conspicuous pattern in Irish enlistment. In September 1918, recruitment in Ireland suddenly began to increase for the first time in three years. This unexpected and perplexing Irish enthusiasm for the war coincided with the successful Allied offensive of August 1918, in which the combined British, French and US armies forced the Germans into their final ignominious retreat. The numbers of Irish recruits, on a steady downward spiral since 1915 – total recruitment in 1917 amounted to a miserable fourteen thousand, barely a division – mystifyingly began to climb.

Almost ten thousand Irishmen joined the British armed forces in what turned out to be the last four months of the war. None ever heard a shot fired in anger. Half of them opted to enlist in the Royal Air Force, where opportune training in a variety of useful vocations, not just square-bashing and physical drilling, was available.[10]

* Henry and John also joined the British armed forces and served in Mesopotamia.

William Gordon enlisted on 3 September 1918 and was re-mustered three weeks after the armistice of 11 November. He was classified as a 'rigger (aero)'.[11] His RAF file reveals a young man of average height for the time (5'6") with brown hair, blue eyes, a fresh complexion and excellent health. His nickname along the Cavan-Meath border was 'The Prop', said to have been because his physique made him capable of supporting a collapsing tunnel.[12] However, in 1920 he weighed only 137 pounds[13] – less than ten stone – so the sobriquet must have had a different basis entirely.*

If Gordon was not already familiar with the use of firearms by September 1918, his RAF training would have compensated for any deficiency. On 10 May 1920, he made his skills available to the Cormeen Gang – for a fee of two pounds, according to Seán Boylan[14] – and ended the life of Mark Clinton, thereby altering the course of his own.

3.

On 3 June 1920, William Gordon was arrested by the RIC and brought to Mountjoy Gaol. The date of his arrest seems fortuitous in the extreme, especially given the lacklustre nature of an RIC investigation into the killing of Mark Clinton which, up to that point, had produced no tangible results.

Two elements stand out. In the first place, as already mentioned, Gordon's incarceration by the RIC pre-empted his capture by the

* Historian Frank Cogan suggests that it probably derives from the fact that Gordon was a low-grade mechanic in the RAF, and one of his functions would have been to crank the engine by turning the propeller, or 'prop', while the pilot was preparing for take-off (email, 15 December 2019).

IRA. Shortly after Gordon was remanded in custody, Boylan's troops rounded up nearly all his comrades. They missed Gordon by a matter of hours.

Secondly, Gordon was not charged with the murder of Mark Clinton, but with possession of a weapon in violation of the Defence of the Realm Act. Was the intention simply to keep Gordon out of harm's way until he could be tried, acquitted and assisted out of the country for his own good? The RIC had some reason to be grateful to William Gordon, though they would no longer be collateral beneficiaries of his friends' campaign of intimidation, dispossession and violence – a crusade that had taken up much IRA time and had cost the life of an active Volunteer.

Or is it even possible that Gordon was already a collaborator, planted in Mountjoy to spy on the IRA inmates? This was a regular RIC intelligence-gathering tactic.

After his own fashion, Gordon had been serviceable to the Crown forces – there would always be a suspicion that the services rendered were more formal than ever acknowledged – but he had now outlived his usefulness.

On 23 June, Gordon was taken from Mountjoy for trial in Navan, where the matter of guilt or innocence was settled within minutes. 'We were not surprised to learn… that the proceedings at this court were not a serious matter,'[15] asserted Séamus Finn in his witness statement. The IRA was clearly not expecting William Gordon to be subjected to the full rigour of the Defence of the Realm Act. Their assumptions proved correct: the charges against the ex-serviceman were dismissed.

The degree of leniency shown towards Gordon, unless attributable to more sinister factors, must have been dictated by the arguments made on his behalf by his solicitor, P.J. Mooney. These included an emphasis on the fact that his two brothers, John and

Henry, were still serving abroad with the British armed forces. In any event, Gordon walked free from the court.[16]

Gordon now made a couple of fatal mistakes, and the IRA took advantage of the single stroke of luck it had been afforded: the reporter despatched by the *Meath Chronicle* that day to cover the proceedings of the petty sessions court was Seán Hayes, a Navan IRA Volunteer. Had Hayes not been on hand, the IRA might not even have become aware that Gordon was back in Meath before he was enabled to escape their clutches. Hayes managed to get word to Seán Boylan, also in Navan on the day, that Gordon's case had come up and Mark Clinton's alleged killer had been released from custody.

From that point on, the course of events was in part dictated by Gordon's own carelessness or misplaced sense of invulnerability. Instead of making straight for the railway station and getting far away from the town as quickly as possible, Gordon chose instead to celebrate his freedom with a visit to the Flathouse pub on Railway Street in Navan. He was accompanied by two RIC men, one of whom, Sergeant Wynne from Nobber, had been responsible for the arrest of Henry Gordon in 1918.

In what capacity they were accompanying Gordon has never been firmly established. If they were there as bodyguards, they did little to protect him. In his witness statement, one Navan IRA officer, Patrick Loughran, made the wry observation that 'as he [Gordon] left the courthouse he was handed a ten shilling note to buy himself a few drinks'.[17] The comment was indicative of the prevailing suspicion that Gordon was an RIC *agent provocateur*. But if anyone wanted William Gordon to dally that day, it was not the RIC.

Armed with the information supplied by Hayes, Seán Boylan ordered all available Volunteers to comb the town for Gordon. That seems to have involved searching every public house in Navan. Two Volunteers acquainted with Gordon, Paddy Kelly and Michael McKeon, came across their prey in the Flathouse, drinking with his RIC escort. The news was conveyed to Boylan, who in the interim had managed to lay hold of a car and a rusty .32 revolver:

> At the other end of the shop were two R.I.C. men – Sergeant Wynne from Nobber and another. I drew the gun and shouted: 'Hands up, face the wall!' They obeyed. As they did so I said: 'Anyone who leaves this house [within the] hour will be shot.' At the other end of the street were five other R.I.C. on protective duty. I pinioned Gordon and tied his hands behind his back with a piece of thin rope. I then bundled him into the car.[18]

Gordon was taken to Salestown, midway between Dunboyne and Maynooth on the Meath-Kildare border, where he was added to the complement of the Cormeen Gang already held there.

The *Meath Chronicle*, whose own reporter had precipitated the events of the day, had the inside track on the story and later gave a detailed account of what happened. The headline read 'Sensational Arrest in Navan – Acquitted by the Magistrates – Apprehended by Volunteers'. The uncredited *Chronicle* reporter, presumably Seán Hayes himself, was unsurprisingly well-informed:

> A sensational sequel to the Crimes Court held in Navan on Wednesday when a young man named William Gordon, of Kilagriffe, was acquitted of a charge under D.O.R.A. [Defence of the Realm Act] in connection with a revolver and masks found under the thatch of an outhouse adjacent to where he resided, was provided on Wednesday afternoon when some men, presumably republican police, entered a Navan public

house and took Gordon, who had been drinking there, into custody. The charge is assumed to be in connection with the murder of Mark Clinton, of Cormeen, the facts of which are well within the public memory. Seven men were arrested before this in connection with the same matter, and are still in custody. The arrest of Gordon was quietly and expeditiously carried out. He was tapped on the shoulder and told he was wanted and then taken out to a motor car in which his captors had arrived and, bound and blindfolded, he was taken away to an unknown destination.[19]

Hayes, if indeed it was he, was suitably vague about the 'unknown destination', bar a tongue-in-cheek statement that it was 'likely to be somewhere in Ireland'.

4.

Boylan had his man. The question now was, what was he going to do with him? The case was unique and complex. William Gordon, despite lurking suspicions to the contrary, had not been arrested for collaborating with the Crown forces or the RIC. He was a common apolitical murderer. What followed would be the sole example during the War of Independence of an IRA trial of a civilian suspect charged with homicide.

Boylan was determined that justice be seen to be done. A veteran of the Easter Rising, he was well aware of the conflicted interests of most of the British officers involved in the courts martial which issued almost a hundred death sentences on the insurgents in May 1916. Their attachment to the regiments that had incurred most of the British casualties meant that their judicial roles were, to say the least, of dubious legality. All should have resiled themselves from the proceedings.

That was, in effect, precisely what Boylan did. He was the brigade commander (he became divisional commander in 1921) of the murdered Volunteer Mark Clinton, and worked closely with his brother Patrick. He could take no active part in the trial of William Gordon. Boylan is clear in his witness statement: 'I wished to be impartial.'[20]

Instead, while Gordon was kept under armed guard in the house of Peter O'Connor in Salestown, Boylan took his dilemma to Dublin. There he reported to one of Collins's right-hand men, Tom Cullen, and asked to meet Collins himself. The meeting between the two IRB stalwarts took place in 35 Gardiner Street, where the IRA Director of Intelligence was asked to appoint a court to try Gordon for murder. Collins did as requested. None of the appointed judges in the case were from County Meath:

> Within a day the Court was appointed as follows; Judges – Dr Ted Kelly, John V. Joyce and Seán Dowling, all of whom were officers of the Dublin Brigade. Prosecution Counsel: Séamus O'Higgins, Captain of Trim Company, County Meath. Defending Counsel, or prisoner's advocate, Séamus Cogan, O/C. 5th Battalion, Meath Brigade.[21]

In Boylan's absence, Gordon simplified matters by confessing to his involvement in the killing of Clinton. Grilled by a team of interrogators led by Séamus Finn, he admitted his part in the murder, named the other members of the gang (already under IRA lock and key) and implicated 'Bloomer' Rogers as the leader of the enterprise.[22]

William Gordon was tried twice. His first court martial,

according to Boylan, lasted for several hours despite his candid and unapologetic admission that he had shot and killed Mark Clinton:

> The prisoner was brought before the Judges and the trial, which lasted several hours, began. He confessed to the crime and admitted attempted murder in two other cases and the burning of two homes. He was found guilty and sentenced to death. After the sitting, all the members of the Court left for their various destinations.[23]

Boylan presented the result of the trial to GHQ. After the verdict had been discussed by the Dáil cabinet, a retrial was ordered. The Sinn Féin leadership was unaccustomed to dealing with courts martial of a non-military nature, and some were uncomfortable with the verdict. According to Ernest Blythe, then Minister for Trade and Commerce, the cabinet – 'the authority vested with the prerogative of mercy' – deferred to the qualms of Countess Markievicz, Minister for Labour, who 'was disinclined to sanction the carrying out of the sentence'.[24]

We have far more detail on the second court martial and its aftermath.

The fortunes of war dictated that Gordon had a new 'prisoner's advocate' for his second trial. Séamus Cogan, Gordon's first defender and commanding officer of the Meath 5th Battalion based in Oldcastle, came to exemplify the physical perils of conducting a parallel government in time of war. In the summer of 1919, IRA chief of staff Richard Mulcahy had issued orders for the establishment of a Republican police force. This body was, theoretically at least, attached to the Department of Home Affairs under Austin Stack, and was independent of the IRA.

In fact, the distinction between the two organisations was largely mythical[25] and IRA Volunteers performed policing functions. On 22 July 1920, Cogan was one of a group of Volunteers escorting a prisoner – a common criminal convicted of stealing cattle – to an 'unknown destination'. The party was travelling by car along the main street in Oldcastle when they spotted an army cycle platoon ahead. Cogan ordered the driver to speed up and try to escape. As he did so, there was an exchange of shots between the soldiers and the IRA policemen. Cogan was killed in the fusillade and his comrades were forced to leave his body in a barn two miles outside the town before making their escape.

The poignant irony of Cogan's death – his funeral was one of the biggest ever seen in the county – was that the soldiers had merely lost their way and stopped to seek directions.[26]

The court martial itself almost had to be aborted. The arrival of a car from Dublin, and increased goings-on around Dunboyne, had not gone unnoticed. An English nurse employed in Dunboyne Castle ensured that the military was made aware of this heightened activity. The army swooped on the town and began a series of house-to-house searches. One activist resorted to cinematic cliché to elude a search party, escaping capture by lowering himself out of his back window with the aid of knotted sheets.[27]

Standing in for the ill-starred Séamus Cogan as Gordon's 'attorney' at the second court martial was Seán Dowling of the Dublin Brigade, who had railed against the exile of Gordon's associates. Dowling, a judge in the initial court martial, took his commission seriously. His line of defence was that the death of Mark Clinton had been a tragic accident. Gordon had not intended to kill the young farmer; he was merely a bad shot.

However, his arguments on behalf of his client were stymied by Gordon's adamant refusal to plead guilty to bad marksmanship.

1. Jack and Delia Clinton
c. 1910.

2. Dr P.J. McKenna and Anna
Schiebel McKenna of Salt
Lake City, Utah.

3. Ed Scarborough.

4. The field in Cloggagh,
Cormeen, County Meath where
Mark Clinton was murdered.

5. Main Street Mullagh in the early 1900s. McKenna-owned premises to the right and left of the foreground.

6. Market House, Mullagh – one of the McKenna businesses.

The Freeman's Journal

ESTD. 1763.] IRELAND'S NATIONAL NEWSPAPER. [ESTD. 1763.

DUBLIN: TUESDAY, SEPTEMBER 6, 1921.

De Valera Attends Big Aeridheacht at Navan ‖ Scenes at Skerries Race Meeting

DE VALERA WATCHES FOOTBALL MATCH ‖ NAVAN 'PIPERS' BAND MARCH TO THE AERIDHEACHT ‖ A GUARD OF HONOUR

(Above) 7. *The Freeman's Journal* front page from 6 September 1921 with Justin McKenna on the extreme right of the first picture featuring Eamon de Valera.

(Left) 8. T.P. McKenna and Sarah Clinton *c.* 1890.

(Right) 9. Sarah Clinton
c. 1890.

(Below) 10. The McKenna
family *c.* 1906 on the family
trap.

(Above) 11. The McKenna family *c.* 1906. Seated (L to R): Margaret, T.P. Jr., Una, Anna Schiebel McKenna, T.P. Sr., Ulick, Angela. Standing: Justin, Nicholas, John, Raphael, May.

(Left) 12. Raphael McKenna and T.P. McKenna Jr. – the latter in the uniform of the new National Army.

(Right) 13. Lt. Adj. T.P. McKenna Jr.

(Below) 14. John McKenna in later life, with his son Joseph.

(Above) 15. Garryard Wood, near Moynalty, County Meath, where Patrick Keelan was executed by the IRA in July 1921.

(Left) 16. The McKenna family plot, Moynalty Cemetry (probable final resting place of Patrick Keelan) with Gwyneth Williams, great-great-granddaughter of T.P. McKenna Sr. and Sarah Clinton.

'I tried to make out it was an accident, that he was a bad shot,' Dowling recalled, 'but he indignantly denied it. I did my best for the poor wretch but he was sentenced to death.'[28]

Once the court martial ended, there remained the problem of getting the court officials safely back to Dublin. The trial had taken place in Salestown, but the route to the capital went through nearby Dunboyne. Dublin Brigade driver Joe Hyland was responsible for the safe return of Dowling, an intelligence officer named Mooney and one of the three IRA judges – Dr Ted Kelly, commandant of the 4th Battalion of the Dublin Brigade. Four men driving together in a car in the autumn of 1920 were guaranteed to attract adverse attention.

Dowling recalled how they cleared their first hurdle:

> There were four of us in the car returning to Dublin, and as it entered Dunboyne, driven by a chap called Hyland, we saw this cordon of soldiers across the road ahead of us. Four men together was noteworthy enough, but we also had enough documents dealing with the damned case to hang us. However the cordon opened as we approached and we cruised through. A group of officers standing at the other end of the village, seeing this also let us through. We fanned ourselves with relief.[29]

The failure of the Crown forces to stop the car and question the occupants was because the officer in charge of the roadblock was getting an earful at the time from the parish priest about the searches in the town.

In his witness statement, Joe Hyland recalled the successful negotiation of the remaining obstacles. One of these was an armoured car with its gun trained on Dunboyne. With no angry priests to distract them, the suspicious soldiers in charge of the vehicle decided to follow the four Dublin IRA men. Fortunately, Mooney was more familiar with the countryside than Hyland. He began to direct the driver along various back roads in an attempt to shake off their pursuers, but they couldn't distance themselves from the tenacious armoured car. Outside Mulhuddart, Mooney ordered Hyland to stop. 'Give me all the papers of the courts and I will take them with me across the fields,' he told him:

> The papers, incidentally, were dealing with the court martial. He got out and went off across the fields. We got safely back into town having passed a further cordon at the Thatch near Whitehall. The patrol there held me up and asked me where I was coming from. I told them I was taking the party to the Curragh Races, which were on that day, from Drogheda. With that I was let pass through.[30]

Boylan himself waited until the military operation in Dunboyne had wound up without finding anything, and then drove to Dublin to present the second verdict to GHQ. Ernest Blythe once again participated in the cabinet discussion that followed. 'It was agreed,' he later recorded, 'that as we were acting as a government and as the man had been tried by the only sort of court possible and had undoubtedly been guilty of murder, the sentence should be confirmed.'[31]

Boylan remembers the decision somewhat differently. He claimed that the matter was referred back to him. 'I could release him or execute him as I pleased. I decided to execute him and informed GHQ to that effect.'[32]

As it transpired, Blythe, as a man of the Presbyterian faith, would play a supportive role in William Gordon's last hours. In his diaries, Home Affairs Minister Austin Stack recorded the cabinet decision on Gordon's fate. There was a proviso to the now inevitable execution. 'When I brought the matter up again,' said Stack, 'the only stipulation imposed was that the prisoner should have the benefit of a clergyman of his own faith. (He was a Protestant.) This was done, and the execution carried out.'[33]

A week after his hazardous journey from Dunboyne, Joe Hyland was ordered to make an unwelcome return trip. He picked up Ernest Blythe and a Presbyterian clergyman, Rev. Mr Irwin – an unexpected Republican sympathiser[34] – from the Russell Hotel in Dublin, and drove north-west. As he studied his grim passengers, Hyland guessed what lay in store for William Gordon.[35]

Gordon had been moved from Salestown to nearby Baytown-park, a few miles north-west of Dunboyne. Even when confronted by a minister of his own faith he was, according to Boylan, utterly unrepentant:

Gordon … told Mr. Irwin that he was not sorry and that he would do it again. During his period of arrest he kept slips of paper with the names of those who had arrested him and kept him prisoner. Mr. Irwin subsequently spoke to me and suggested that if I would have him released he (Mr. Irwin) would have him sent by the Moore McCormack Line* to the U.S.A., saying that it was a pity to see a young life going. I replied: 'Yes, and let him come back by another line to hunt down everyone connected with his arrest and trial and have them arrested by the British.'[36]

Boylan's description of the execution of William Gordon, related to the Bureau of Military History in late 1957, almost forty years after the events he is describing, was matter-of-fact and devoid

---

* A shipping line founded in 1913.

of emotion. He made no attempt to devolve responsibility for the execution onto any of his Volunteers:[37]

> Gordon was duly executed at Castlefarm, Dunboyne. I took charge. Before his execution he wept. I said: 'We have given you more time than you gave your unfortunate victim. If you have not asked the Almighty God for forgiveness, I will give you time to do so.' I gave him time to make his peace with God.

Hyland, waiting to bring Blythe and Irwin back to Dublin, recalled hearing two shots ring out in the distance. 'I knew then that the man had been executed. I took the clergyman and Blythe back again to the Russell Hotel.'[38]

Did William Gordon receive due process? Certainly, in comparison with around two hundred victims of IRA executions and reprisals, he was well treated. Meath historian Frank Cogan pondered the issue in a 2017 *Riocht na Midhe* article on the murder of Mark Clinton:

> While the conditions of his trial and subsequent execution undoubtedly fell some way short of what would be regarded as fair and equitable in the present day, however, account must be taken of the conditions of the country at the time; moreover, it must be admitted that Boylan and the others involved in his trial were conscious of the need to be as fair and impartial as possible and took steps to ensure that he was treated fairly and humanely... Certainly, there does not seem to have been any public outcry, then or subsequently, against the manner in which the Volunteers disposed of his case or of the cases against his accomplices.[39]

A month after the murder of Mark Clinton, on 19 June 1920, Dáil Éireann finally pronounced on the rampant land seizures that were beginning to imperil the entire republican enterprise. The timing was hardly coincidental. The official Dáil decree, while not an outright deprecation of the annexations, was a warning to those with a penchant for appropriation to get their priorities right. Now was not the time:

> It has come to our knowledge that claims have been and are being made in various parts of the country to farms and holdings which are being used and worked by the occupiers as dairy, agricultural and residential holdings, and that such claims are being based on the assertion that claimants or their ancestors were formerly in occupation of the property so claimed. And whereas these claims are, for the most part, of old date, and while many of them may be well founded, others seem to be of a frivolous nature and are put forward in the hope of intimidating the present occupiers.

> Now It Is Decreed by Dáil Éireann in Session Assembled:

> 1. That the present time, when the Irish people are locked in a life-and-death struggle with their traditional enemy, is ill-chosen for stirring up strife amongst our fellow-countrymen; and that all energies must be directed towards the clearing out – not the occupier of this or that piece of land – but the foreign invader of our country.[40]

The Dáil ruled that no claims, well-founded or otherwise, would be entertained 'unless by written licence of the Minister for Home Affairs'. According to Judge Kevin O'Shiel, Austin Stack, the minister, was not inclined to distribute the licences like snuff at a wake.

If the Dáil had issued the decree a month before the murder of Mark Clinton, perhaps it would have saved his life. If the Back to the Land movement had been more in evidence in the far north-west of County Meath, perhaps wiser heads would have prevailed. That was certainly the feeling of the organisation's executive committee – 'because the people would have had a means to get justice'.[41]

Perhaps. But we are still left with two bereaved fathers and two dead sons.

Part Two

THE MCKENNAS
OF MULLAGH

6

The Merchant of Mullagh

I.

The magisterial Simon de Clinton would not have approved. And he was, after all, integral to the consolidation of the twelfth-century Angevin invasion of Ireland. A feudal Norman lord, a feared and respected warrior, he had removed himself and his family from the pastoral grandeur of Oxfordshire to become a potentate in the wilderness of the Irish north-east.

He probably shared the views of his compatriot Giraldus Cambrensis, as enunciated caustically in *Topographica Hibernica*, that 'the Irish are a rude people... living themselves like beasts'. Just because Strongbow had contracted a political marriage with an Irish princess, that did not mean a de Clinton need enter into the state of holy matrimony with a backwoods member of the MacCionnaith clan, an unruly native Irish tribe very far down the food chain.

So it was just as well that Simon had been dead for seven centuries, and that along the way the Clintons had jettisoned their francophone prefix and generations of Anglo-Norman affectation. Over the same period, the MacCionnaiths had – mostly – managed to embrace Western civilisation, shrug off the unrulier aspects of their character and become the more acceptable McKennas.

The marriage of the imposing T.P. McKenna and the winsome Sarah Clinton, bachelor and spinster of Mullagh, County Cavan, on 23 November 1890, would never have happened in the twelfth century. But by the final decade of the nineteenth century, it was a formidable parochial alliance.

Both were descended from east Cavan royalty. Sarah, twenty-three, was the youngest daughter of John Clinton, a prosperous landowner whose impressive house and farm overlooked picturesque Mullagh Lake on the outskirts of the small east Cavan town. T.P. McKenna, ten years older, youngest son of Nicholas McKenna, came from a mercantile and landowning family. Neither bachelor nor spinster was marrying up or down, though each imperious paterfamilias might well have hinted otherwise.

The McKennas of Mullagh were comfortable rural bourgeoisie. They supplied groceries, seeds, 'ardent spirits' and other necessities to the farmers of east Cavan and north Meath from their various premises, which included a public house and a grocery, in the wide main street of the town. They also owned parcels of the Mullagh hinterland which were worked by family members or rented out to tenant farmers. The McKennas epitomised the arriviste rural Roman Catholic middle class of the late nineteenth century. Others of their ilk would soon seize the levers of national power. They have yet to relinquish them.

Nicholas McKenna, the Merchant of Mullagh, had earned the suffix that validated his upward social mobility – PLG – from his election in the politically becalmed 1850s to the Board of Poor Law Guardians for the nearby town of Kells. He was fortunate to survive the ideological Parnellite cull of the 1880s. The potent new Irish leader sought 'advanced' nationalist candidates to contest Board of Poor Law Guardian elections in the Irish Parliamentary Party interest.

Parnell's objective was to assemble an officer corps and move some of the more promising luminaries on to the House of Commons. But first the antediluvian 'nominal' nationalists had to be escorted to the meadows and put out to grass. The operation was by and large carried out with ruthless efficiency.

The Parnellites, however, did not succeed in slaying all the dinosaurs. Nicholas McKenna clung to his position, largely on the basis of strong personal support. He was permitted to tarry, despite his lack of 'advanced' nationalist credentials, on the basis that at least he wasn't a unionist. In fact, in both his politics and his personal appearance – a shock of wispy white hair with interminable sideburns on a distinctly high forehead – he was positively Gladstonian. Nicholas was an old-fashioned Whig nationalist, a fellow traveller of forgotten names from the middle decades of the reign of Queen Victoria. Who now recognises names like The O'Donoghue or William Shaw?

Nicholas McKenna's extended lease on his seat, however, was not without its detractors. In February 1883, the Parnellite newspaper *United Ireland*, scourge of unionists and mealy-mouthed nationalists alike, published a letter from a Bohermeen, County Meath resident excoriating the Mullagh representatives on the Kells Board of Guardians for their absenteeism and general lack of dynamism in the nationalist cause.

Nicholas McKenna went *mano a mano* with his anonymous decrier in a spirited response in the same newspaper. There was no breast-beating or equivocation. He took the criticism personally. Although he was not the sole Mullagh representative on the Kells Board of Guardians, the attack, he concluded, 'strikes at [me] alone for neglect of duty'.

If the cap fits…?

He demanded that his Lilliputian Bohermeen critic point to any important divisions from which he had been absent. He challenged him to cast his net well beyond the moment, and to McKenna's record over the last three decades. (This is unerringly a signal that a political career, even one as justifiably unheralded as that of Nicholas McKenna, has long since run out of steam.)

He railed against the Bohermeen caviller, who groused under the pseudonym 'More of It', saying that he, Nicholas McKenna, had never voted in a manner 'that was not on the side of the people'. He suggested that because the correspondent was from a locality 'remote from my own', he would be unaware of all the great work done by Nicholas McKenna. He then took a sly dig at 'More of It' for guarding his anonymity, and concluded his apologia with a *post scriptum* geography lesson: Bohermeen was not even in the Kells Poor Law district![1]

'More of It' was clearly abashed, because he failed to reply. But one Charles Ball, an actual resident of Mullagh, was not so easily deterred, and responded in the Letters column of *United Ireland* the following week. Ball began by agreeing with McKenna as to the value of his lengthy service. The sting, however, was in the tail. Mr Ball concluded by insisting that Nicholas McKenna was now old and feeble and should resign his position.[2]

2.

T.P. McKenna, son of Nicholas, added auctioneer and valuer to the family business portfolio as he gradually became more prominent within his father's domain. He was also more 'advanced' politically than his father, who died in 1893 at eighty-four. That T.P. McKenna himself became chairman of the Kells Board of Poor Law Guardians speaks to the rigid hereditary principle entrenched even then in Irish political life. He was also the first chairman of the Cavan County Board of the newly established Gaelic Athletic Association. His involvement was short-lived (1887–1889), and his exit may have been prompted by the infiltration of that organisation by the Irish Republican Brotherhood. T.P. McKenna was not sufficiently 'advanced' to kow-tow to Fenians. At least not yet.[3]

When it came to the ritual slaughter of the Parnellite split, McKenna took the safe, ecclesiastically sanctioned route and opposed the continued leadership of the adulterous Charles Stewart Parnell. In 1892, he supported the septuagenarian Protestant anti-Parnellite candidate, Samuel Young, in the East Cavan by-election. He accompanied Young, Michael Davitt and a few mandatory members of the clergy in a canvassing trail through the constituency.

Young trounced his unionist opponent by a factor of nearly five to one (6,024 to 1,360) to become the oldest serving member of the House of Commons. In complete defiance of logic and morbidity, he held the seat for a further twenty-six years without ever having to face the fuss and bother of another election! He was fortunate to pass away at the grand old age of ninety-six – he still retains the record as the oldest serving Member of Parliament – just in time to avoid the Sinn Féin landslide of December 1918. In fact, it was Young's timely demise that catapulted T.P. McKenna into a highly consequential political contest, the East Cavan by-election of 1918.

In the interim, T.P. became immersed in local and national politics as a fervent supporter of John Redmond and the Irish Parliamentary Party. He was a Cavan county councillor after the introduction of the 1898 Local Government Act, and became chairman of the General Council of County Councils of Ireland. In 1904, as recorded in the introductory chapter, T.P. McKenna was widowed by the death of Sarah Clinton less than two months after the birth of their tenth child, Una. His large family, initially scattered among McKenna relatives, was finally kept together only by an unexpected transatlantic intervention.

In November 1901, T.P. McKenna's cousin, Dr P.J. McKenna, died in the Salt Lake City, Utah hospital, Keogh-McKenna, that bore his name. He was the victim of a tragic accident, having tumbled from the rear platform of a moving train while returning from a trip to Park City along with fellow members of the Elks fraternity. In the morose phraseology of the *Salt Lake City Tribune*, he 'lay on the borderland of eternity' for a short while before passing across that final frontier. His obituary in the same newspaper was a glowing tribute to 'his innumerable acts of charity'.[4]

Forty-two years of age when he died, he left a widow, Anna Schiebel McKenna, but no children. Anna, originally from Providence, Rhode Island and known in Utah as Annie, was the daughter of a German father, Maurice Schiebel, and an Irish mother, Anna Gallagher. The only child of her marriage to P.J. McKenna had not survived infancy.[5]

Anna Schiebel would soon be surrounded by a plentiful supply of children.

A letter of condolence that T.P. McKenna sent to the Utah widow led to a sustained correspondence. In 1904, it was Anna's turn to sympathise on the death of McKenna's spouse. At around that time – perhaps it was fortuitous, perhaps a contrivance – she announced that she would temporarily abandon the Beehive State to undertake an extended visit to Europe, and hoped to include Ireland in her travels. She was encouraged to do so by her newly widowed in-law.

What followed was not entirely inevitable; nor did it proceed upon predictable lines. The two epistolary acquaintances met in the newly refurbished old-world surroundings of the Royal Hibernian Hotel on Dawson Street in Dublin. At this first meeting, Anna took the bull by the horns. After satisfying herself that this particular McKenna was cut from similar cloth to his Utah cousin, she offered an intriguing proposition to the Merchant of Mullagh.

He was given a few weeks, the residue of her European tour, to mull over a marriage proposal. Were he to present himself in Cork at the wharf in Queenstown – later renamed Cobh in a wave of anti-monarchist sentiment – and interdict her onward return journey to New York, she would unload her bags, return with him to Cavan, become his wife and, crucially, take on the task of being stepmother to ten orphaned children. She would forsake the high frosted mountains of Utah for the low hills of east Cavan.

Annie Schiebel McKenna would give way to Anna Schiebel McKenna. While she would adopt the version of her name favoured by her Roscommon-born mother, there would be no need to relinquish any monogrammed handkerchiefs.

Some weeks later, the relentlessly prosaic T.P. McKenna travelled from Mullagh to Queenstown and poetically intercepted his second bride before an ocean liner could convey her back to the USA. His far-flung family did not lose their prospective stepmother.[6]

Anna Schiebel was courageous to have taken on such a responsibility. It was the first decade of the twentieth century, and she would have been under few illusions as to which partner would bear the burden of childcare. Her first meeting with her ready-made Mullagh family, and their introduction to her, must have been difficult for both sides. But she would prove to be a capable, loving and excellent guardian to her new charges.*

Anna's arrival in east Cavan began with a clear demonstration to T.P. that he would not have things all his own way. On land

---

* I am unsure about the precise nature of her relationship with T.P.'s eldest daughter, my maternal grandmother May McKenna. As far as I can recall, May never referred to her stepmother in my presence. I do know, however, that Anna Schiebel was certainly a committed and ideal substitute mother to the younger children of T.P. McKenna and Sarah Clinton.

owned by the family on the northern shore of Mullagh Lake, he had extended a small lodge (Saunderson's Cottage) and fashioned a fine stone-built home for his new spouse. The setting was serenity itself. The property was tree-lined, and the fields in front of the house led down to the water's edge. The sylvan scene was as if from a Constable painting.

The formidable Anna, though charmed by the views and flattered by the gesture, was unimpressed. She came, she saw, and she insisted on moving back into the town. She wanted to get to know her neighbours, not lord it over them in a lakeside palace.[7] T.P.'s architectural white elephant would become irreverently known as The Villa.

Whatever his personal feelings about John Redmond's September 1914 exhortation to Irishmen to enlist in the British armed forces, T.P. McKenna certainly does not appear to have encouraged his own sons John and Raphael, both of military age, to heed his party leader's call. While they did eventually have short soldierly careers, their military experience did not involve the wearing of a uniform, and found expression in opposition to men clad in British khaki.

However, while sheltered from the realities of the Great War, T.P. was not immune to the suffering created by that barbarous conflict. In March 1915, he was one of the organisers of a concert staged in aid of the local Belgian Refugee Fund, and he discovered a therapeutic use for The Villa by housing a number of traumatised Belgian evacuees on the peaceful lakeshore.

At which point, had history not intervened, one can imagine the McKenna paterfamilias settling into a Redmondite stupor and waiting out the Great War to see what opportunities, political and commercial, might present themselves when some variant of

Home Rule was finally enacted after the European conflict had ground to a halt.

As is so often the case, history had other ideas.

In the Bureau of Military History Witness Statement of the indefatigable Seán Farrelly,* Mullagh and T.P. McKenna are portrayed as reactionary and royalist during the early years of the Great War:

> It was hard on the Mullagh people to look with favour on our movement. It must have been the most pro-British town in Ireland. Mr T.P. McKenna was then the leading light of the place. In his pro-British spirit of the time he was associated with a committee set up for the purpose of 'helping plucky little Belgium'. He got over a number of refugees from there and housed them in a villa in Mullagh. Sports meetings and regattas were run to make money for them. I mention those things to show the former spirit of a town that was now becoming one of the most Republican towns in the County Cavan.[8]

What Farrelly was hinting at was the startling conversion of T.P. from constitutional relic to revolutionary firebrand. The moderate nationalist of 1914 who offered at least tacit support to the Irish Parliamentary Party had by 1918 become a fervent and active supporter of Sinn Féin. It was a road travelled by enough of his fellow countrymen to bring an end to the dominance of the party of Parnell and Redmond in the seismic general election of December 1918. Longstanding IPP complacency, allied to cack-handed British governance in Ireland post-1916, conspired

---

* He actually supplied two, #1648 and #1734, numbering seventy-two pages of testimony.

to discredit and effectively obliterate the politics of stasis and moderation.

It took some serious missteps on the part of the British government to subvert the zealous moderation of T.P. McKenna, but the executions after the rebellion of 1916, the death in prison of hunger striker Thomas Ashe in 1917 and the bone-headed 1918 attempt to introduce compulsory military service to Ireland, as well as the constant morale-sapping effect of Irish casualties in Gallipoli, Picardy and Flanders, pierced the man's agnosticism when it came to extreme republicanism. By the summer of 1918, his politics were unrecognisable. After the autumn 1918 'German Plot' arrests of a number of leading Sinn Féiners on patently spurious grounds (the British government alleged a conspiracy between imperial Germany and the Irish nationalists to launch another uprising, supported by a German invasion), he became more than just an interested observer of the convulsions of the Irish body politic.

With the death of the grandfather of the House of Commons, Samuel Young – the senior citizen for whom McKenna had canvassed as far back as 1892 – a by-election was called in East Cavan, a constituency that extended into north Meath. It was to be a crucial contest. The tide that had been flowing in Sinn Féin's favour with successive by-election victories in North Roscommon, South Longford, East Clare and Kilkenny City had been staunched by three IPP wins in South Armagh, Waterford City and East Tyrone. East Cavan would be a pivotal contest.

Sinn Féin had long anticipated the demise of the stubbornly durable Samuel Young. Founder and former leader Arthur Griffith – succeeded as Sinn Féin president in 1917 by Éamon de Valera – was nominated to stand as the Sinn Féin candidate. J.F. O'Hanlon, a member of Cavan Urban District Council whose family were proprietors of the local newspaper, the *Anglo-Celt*, was chosen as Griffith's IPP opponent.

Griffith managed to campaign in person for only three weeks. In May 1918, along with many of his party colleagues, he was swept up in the dubious purge which became known as the German Plot. This was, depending on your point of view, a cynical British fabrication or a paranoid response by Dublin Castle to alleged Sinn Féin overtures towards Germany.

With Griffith in jail, T.P. McKenna, the perennial political fixer, took to the hustings with gusto. He actively canvassed the East Cavan constituency in the Sinn Féin cause, making numerous speeches on behalf of Griffith and driving all around the constituency to a number of public meetings. Many of those assemblies were a danger to life and limb. The East Cavan campaign was no electoral garden party. Irish hustings, especially by-elections, when the focus was exceptionally narrow, often suffered from a surfeit of vigour. East Cavan made some of the infamous nineteenth-century electoral faction fights look like sodality meetings.

The rivalry between the supporters of Sinn Féin and the IPP, many of the latter being bellicose members of the Ancient Order of Hibernians (frequently abetted by their traditional adversaries in the Orange Order – the word 'irony' simply cannot cope), was often extremely aggressive. Francis Connell, a Cavan Brigade IRA officer, recalled that 'while on guard duty around the platforms of the Sinn Féin speakers we were armed with revolvers and in some cases with shotguns which we carried openly'.[9]

Members of the erstwhile Ulster Volunteer Force, who had not seen fit to join their peers in the 36th Ulster Division, also offered spirited resistance to the message of nationalism and self-reliance preached by Griffith's acolytes. Not that the Sinn Féin supporters were angelic in their own deportment. O'Hanlon was the occasional target of well-aimed eggs and other bulkier missiles.

When the ballots were counted, Sinn Féin had secured almost sixty percent of the vote. T.P. McKenna, once a faithful Redmondite, had made the transition to fervent Shinner.

While T.P. McKenna's politics may have skipped tracks, business was still business. Though he worked energetically for the Sinn Féin cause until the establishment of the Irish Free State – thereafter becoming a follower of Cumann na nGaedheal, a supporter of the Treaty and the conservative settlement that followed it – McKenna did not unfailingly subscribe to the strictures of the new dispensation.

In response to anti-Catholic pogroms in Belfast, the Dáil had imposed a boycott in the summer of 1920 on goods coming south from the mainly Protestant businesses of north-east Ulster. Much of the energy of IRA Volunteers was expended in attempts to ensure that the boycott was applied effectively. By early 1921, in some jurisdictions, arguably including County Meath, enforcing the boycott became a substitute for the more hazardous task of confronting mobile and well-armed Crown forces.

That the boycott was only a sporadic success was attributable to merchants like T.P. McKenna, one of the many southern traders to assume that the Belfast embargo applied only to others. In March 1921, the highly motivated Carnaross IRA battalion, dominated by half a dozen members of the Farrelly family, diligently raided the Virginia Road railway station between Kells and Oldcastle to interdict any Belfast goods making it that far south. They managed to impound two carloads of produce. According to Seán Farrelly: 'It consisted for the most part of farm seeds which were consigned to Mr T.P. McKenna of Mullagh. We then left for home and sleep. Next morning, when one of our men went to inspect the stuff, all of it had been stolen.'[10]

It would not be entirely safe to assume that an opportunistic T.P. McKenna had descended overnight on the IRA safe house, where the contraband products were stored, and recovered his confiscated property.

Was T.P. one of those early twentieth-century gombeen archetypes described, in the elegantly jaundiced language of the playwright John Millington Synge, as 'the groggy-patriot-publican-general shop-man who is married to the priest's half-sister and is second cousin once-removed of the dispensary doctor'?[11] Despite his failure to place the national interest wholeheartedly above his own, that would be an unfair characterisation of the youngest son of the Merchant of Mullagh. But not entirely.

3.

Four of T.P. McKenna's five remaining sons – his eldest boy Nicholas had died in 1907 of basilar meningitis, aged only sixteen – would become even more actively engaged with Sinn Féin than their elderly father.

His two eldest boys, John (b.1892) and Raphael (b.1895), were quartermaster and intelligence officer respectively of the 3rd Meath Brigade, based around Kells. The youngest boy, T.P. Junior (b.1903), joined the IRA in Dublin as a young medical student. On the run after the seismic events of Bloody Sunday on 21 November 1920, he ended up spending the last six months of the conflict as a senior officer in the newly formed Meath active service unit (flying column). Solicitor Justin Charles McKenna (b.1897), not himself an IRA Volunteer, was elected unopposed as MP for Louth/ Meath in the 1921 general election and took his seat in the Second Dáil as a deputy, or Teachta Dála (TD).

Why would three of T.P. McKenna's sons – why would anybody, for that matter – risk their freedom and life by active physical engagement in a conflict as rancorous as the War of Independence?* The Civil War of 1922/23 is often cited as a poignant example of fraternal strife. However, in one sense at least, that description more accurately applies to the Anglo-Irish War of 1919–21, albeit the brothers in question were generally on the same side.

IRA enlistment tended to run in families and Meath, as we have already seen, was no exception. Three Clintons and three McKennas served in different locations as members of the Meath Brigade, and later the 1st Eastern Division. They were accompanied by an even greater number of Farrellys and a similar number of Tevlins and Dunnes. Fraternity was as compelling a motivator as liberty and equality.

The War of Independence, on the Irish side at least, was a family or neighbourhood affair. 'The decision to join was often more of a collective than an individual one.'[12] Persuasive role models were often to be found in the IRA in the form of one's older brother. It was all too reminiscent of the phenomenon of the ill-fated British 'Pals' Battalions of the Great War, but without the tragic consequences of that particular form of localised enlistment and communal slaughter.

There was also a rich vein of irony in much IRA recruitment.

---

* Ironically, although Justin McKenna was never a serving member of the IRA, he was the only member of his family to be jailed during the War of Independence.

Opposition to military conscription in April 1918 had united both moderate and extreme nationalists, but the absence of enforced enlistment in Ireland between 1914 and 1918 resulted in the continued presence of a legion of military-age males on a disproportionate scale, compared to the post-war demographics of England, Wales and especially Scotland. Many opted to enlist in a military conflict after all, but in a shadow army.

Neither had that cohort been thinned by the annual rush of young Irish men (and women) to the emigrant ships. Emigration from Ireland had practically come to a standstill during the carnage of the Great War.

In 1921, Major A.E. Percival – later responsible for the embarrassing surrender of Singapore to the Japanese army in 1942 – was a highly opinionated intelligence officer of the unpopular Essex regiment stationed in the rebellious county of Cork. He derived two single transferable lectures from his experience in mutinous Ireland. On these he would later hold forth, with just the required amount of philosophical invective, to enthusiastic audiences. A man who painted with the broadest of brushstrokes, Percival made a virtue of having had no truck whatever with the Catholic population of Ireland, who were either 'active Sinn Féins' (*sic*) or 'sympathetic to the Sinn Féin movement':

> The extent of their activity usually varied in the inverse ratio to their financial interest in the country – they were, for instance, the farmers and large shopkeepers who disliked disturbances, and the farmers' sons and corner boys, who had no stake in the country and preferred earning a living by plunder and murder than by doing an honest day's work. There were a large number of this latter class owing to the failure of the British Government to enforce conscription in Southern Ireland during the war, and they

nearly all had an exaggerated idea of their own importance. It was of these men that the Republican Army was mainly composed.[13]

Percival's 'analysis' illustrates precisely why the British were never quite able to get to grips with their enemy – they never really got to know them properly. The McKenna boys were neither farmers' sons nor corner boys. They all had a sizeable 'stake in the country', a stake jeopardised by their separate decisions to take up arms against British rule.

The McKennas, like their Clinton cousins, had also come under the influence of an increasingly nationalistic generation of Irish educators. The cultural revolution of the 1890s had permeated Irish schools by the early years of the twentieth century. Even some of their chosen leisure pursuits – membership of the Gaelic League or playing Gaelic games was 'a particular source of politicisation'[14] – were significant factors in the creation of the well-rounded extremist.

To have stayed the course, something all four of the McKennas managed to achieve, was not a given either. Only T.P. McKenna Jr. was permanently 'under arms' during the War of Independence; in offering part-time service, his brothers John and Raphael were more typical of the IRA Volunteer. 'Not every Volunteer could afford to take to the hills or leave his own house in order to fight the British Empire.'[15] The vast majority of IRA activists, as revealed in thousands of Military Service Pension application files, were nocturnal warriors only.

Indeed, many of those who had remained faithful to the far smaller Irish Volunteer movement at the time of the John Redmond-induced split in 1914 fell by the wayside when drilling and marching gave way to ambushes and executions. Although the chances of an IRA Volunteer actually being killed or wounded in County Meath were infinitesimally small compared with their counterparts in Cork or Dublin, that only became apparent with hindsight, and there was a perceptible decline in the number of willing activists. When 'things began to get very serious for the IRA', according to Seán Farrelly, 'a great many of our earlier peace-time Volunteers, especially the officers, who very often displayed two guns on parade, slunk away into oblivion and were not heard of again until the Truce was signed.'[16]

Most of those persisted in absenting themselves, despite the earnest attentions of the likes of IRA Volunteer Patrick McDonnell of the Stonefield company, who was himself to die in the conflict.* He visited a number of homes and remonstrated with the 'shirkers' while sporting an encouraging revolver in his right hand. As Farrelly suggested, some of those who never managed to find the time to spend hours in freezing damp fields, lying in wait for Black and Tan patrols that never came, made opportunistic comebacks once the Truce had been declared. This was a nationwide phenomenon that led to the coinage of a fittingly caustic neologism. Those who returned were christened 'Trucileers'.

4.

Justin McKenna, unlike his three brothers, was a fellow traveller rather than an active IRA member, though a raid on his house in November 1920 turned up an Irish Volunteers membership card. For much of the Great War he had been an apprentice solicitor attending lectures and tutorials at the National University in Dublin.[17]

---

* One of only three Meath IRA Volunteer fatalities.

As a young lawyer with a growing practice in north Meath, he became an active participant in the Republican court system. Although his livelihood depended on his engagement with this emerging parallel legal structure, Justin McKenna was well-disposed towards the Dáil courts from the outset, unlike some of his older, more conservative colleagues.

As early as September 1920, he and his father appeared as litigants before the North Meath Arbitration court, appealing a decision of Carnaross parish court in a property-related suit costing Justin McKenna £1 a week. The case had begun its serpentine course at Kells petty sessions during the period of transition when the various Dáil jurisdictional courts began to supplant their Crown equivalents. In the idiosyncratic phraseology of the *Meath Chronicle* reporter, 'As no magistrate appeared, it was adjourned until such time as they did appear, which would be never.'[18] The arbitration court agreed with the McKennas that 'the decision of the Carnaross court was irregular' and found in their favour.

While the session was in progress, two RIC men entered the 'courtroom'. They made no attempt to interfere with proceedings but took notes of the cases in progress. One of them even complied with an instruction from the court's presiding officer to remove his helmet.

As the Dáil courts became more credible and authoritative, the doffing of police headgear rapidly became a thing of the past. By the winter of 1920, the RIC was hell-bent on closing down the Republican courts. In his lengthy Bureau of Military History witness statement, Judge Cahir Davitt described a court session in east Cavan in November 1920 being interrupted by the arrival of the police. The RIC was intent on breaking up the legal proceedings, and the district inspector insisted on the session being terminated. Davitt asked the police to step outside while the participants in the Republican court considered their options:

> The solicitors in the case we had completed were James J. Lynch and Justin McKenna of Kells. I said that I did not believe the police had any intention of proceeding to extremes; and that I was prepared to continue the sitting; but that I would be guided by whatever view the others took of the probabilities. The majority were in favour of dispersing and holding the Court more circumspectly in some other venue at a later date. I accordingly informed the Inspector that we had concluded our business for the day and we broke up.[19]

It wasn't the first time the young Mullagh solicitor had experienced such an intrusion. Only the previous month he had been detained, questioned and searched after a raid by members of the RIC, led by the local head constable, Queenan, and a platoon of the South Wales Borderers, on the Meath County Council offices in Navan on the morning of 4 October.[20] Despite the mounting tensions of the period – the war would intensify the following month – the *Meath Chronicle* described the interaction between the Crown forces and the arbitrators as 'being conducted in the best of good humour, with courtesy on both sides, and indeed a certain amount of joviality'. None of the judges, plaintiffs, defendants, reporters or members of the public sought to escape, 'many regarding it really as an experience calculated to relieve the drab monotony of life'.[21]

Justin McKenna's RIC file confirmed his status as a useful ally of the Sinn Féin establishment, rather than an active Volunteer:

> [McKenna] is an active Sinn Féiner and a leader in his area as

regards propaganda work at least. His house is a regular meeting place for local Sinn Féiners. On account of his position he carries more sway with local Sinn Féiners than the average and his removal would have a good effect locally. Believed not to be a member of the IRA.[22]

Shortly after the court sitting described by Cahir Davitt, Justin was arrested during an RIC raid on Mullagh on 26 November 1920. It was a Friday, and the noise and bustle of the Mullagh fair day had migrated to the town's public houses when the RIC, backed up once again by the South Wales Borderers, swooped on the town and searched a number of houses. The McKenna family home was surrounded and thoroughly searched. Twenty-two rounds of .22 ammunition were found in a chest of drawers in Justin's room.

Now, while the IRA was generally desperate for any kind of ammunition, .22 bullets are primarily designed to inflict serious damage on squirrels and birds, not on human beings. The fact that the ammunition was found in a drawer does not suggest the McKennas were making any great shift to conceal their cache.

Justin McKenna disavowed all knowledge of the ammunition, but his denials were ignored. The raiders also secured 'documents purporting to relate to the affairs of an unlawful association'. By then Sinn Féin was a proscribed organisation. As the town's 'most popular and respected citizen'[23] was being taken away, his younger sister, Angela McKenna, twenty-two years of age, stepped forward. She approached the army tender and shouted at her brother, 'Goodbye Justin, and God save Ireland!'[24]

At around 1.30 a.m., the South Wales Borderers took their prisoner to the Whitewood House army base outside Kilmainhamwood, near the Cavan-Meath border. From there he was later

transported to Dundalk prison. On 26 January 1921, Justin was
tried by field general court martial in the North Dublin Union
barracks. In classic Sinn Féin fashion, he refused to recognise the
authority of a military tribunal, though he ably conducted his own
defence. His meticulous questioning of a number of witnesses was
entertaining but probably unnecessary, as Murphy's Law, rather
than that of the Crown or the Dáil, ultimately prevailed.

A British motorcycle despatch rider carrying the ammunition and documents found in Justin McKenna's room from
Dunshaughlin to the headquarters of the Dublin District Intelligence Department managed to lose the vital package somewhere
between Dunshaughlin and Clonee, and had doubled back in a
futile attempt to find the lost evidence. The hapless rider, described as 'a youthful witness',[25] testified however that he had
seen the name of the accused on the envelope he had contrived
to mislay. Justin asked the young man to spell 'McKenna'. The
best the addled witness could offer was 'Mecenin'. Sensing an
acquittal, Justin responded gleefully, 'I don't think you are a very
good scholar.'[26]

The charges were thrown out after a brief defence statement
by the man who would later become state solicitor for County
Meath. Even a British court martial could not convict in the face
of contradictory evidence – McKenna's cross-examination had
tied the arresting officers in knots too – and the inadequacies of
a callow military cyclist.

Justin McKenna's freedom was short-lived. He was not even
released from military custody. Heeding the proffered RIC Crime
Special advice that 'his removal would have a good effect locally',
Justin was rearrested without even the formality of new charges
against him, and interned in the Rath camp in the Curragh.
There he would spend the next six months of his life behind

barbed wire with convicted IRA inmates and other internees whose 'removal' was also held to improve the political health of their communities.

The Rath camp housed some of the best, brightest and most recalcitrant the Irish Republican movement had to offer. The accommodation was relentlessly austere. The inmates, permitted to wear their own civilian clothes, were housed in huts with leaky roofs. Escape attempts were frequent.

The prison regime included regular assaults on imported confectionery by staff. Cakes arriving for the inmates were closely examined, as knives, files, letters and money were often included in the pre-cooked doughy mix. Future British Army Brigadier F.H. Linden, who had enlisted in the Suffolk regiment as a private during the Great War, was one of the camp guards. He described the lengths to which the Republican prisoners would go to avoid continued detention at the pleasure of His Majesty:

> They dug a tunnel, which we did not detect and about 30 escaped one night. We foiled one effort in which an internee hid himself up to the neck in a swill cart and was found by the gate sentry who opened the cover. Others used to try and hide in the latrines or in the exercise cage, so that they would not be in their huts at nightfall and could attempt to cut a passage through the barbed wire fence.[27]

Rather than immersing himself in pig swill or devising an equally ingenious escape plan, Justin McKenna bided his time. His early release from the Rath camp would come in unexpected circumstances.

～

5.

The war experiences of John, Raphael and T.P. Junior, while they were all active members of the IRA, varied hugely.

For the duration of the Anglo-Irish conflict, John and Raphael McKenna were based in or near Mullagh. T.P. Junior had a very different set of experiences. He had joined the 1st Battalion of the Cavan Brigade of the Irish Volunteers in 1917, aged only fourteen, and the following year found himself guarding ballot boxes against the threat of AOH chicanery in the East Cavan by-election. He would spend the better part of six years almost exclusively devoting his time and energy to the Irish revolution and then to the ugly civil war that negated much of the euphoria of the successful conclusion of that revolution.

In 1920, he enrolled as a medical student in University College, Dublin (UCD). He had at some point contemplated taking holy orders, but clearly thought better of it. How close he ever got to a medical text at Earlsfort Terrace is a moot point, because as soon as he entered UCD, he joined the 4th Battalion of the IRA Dublin Brigade.[28] From then until the Truce – as all his senior officers noted when consulted as referees for his 1924 pension application – his medical studies suffered from his military commitments, until eventually he was forced to give up the former.

In the wake of the Bloody Sunday assassinations on the morning of 21 November 1920, when fourteen men (most but not all British intelligence agents) were shot by the IRA, T.P. 'was wanted by the British'[29] and became a young man on the run. Nothing in his pension application file suggests that he was directly involved in the carnage of Bloody Sunday, though the 'Squad' was supplemented on that occasion by members of the Dublin IRA brigades.

After an apparent hiatus of a couple of months, T.P. resurfaced in his native Cavan and was assigned to the headquarters of the newly formed 1st Eastern Division, under Seán Boylan. The reorganisation of the IRA into divisions was a controversial move that led to much wrangling in other jurisdictions but appears to have proceeded smoothly in Boylan's sphere of responsibility.

In February 1921, he was appointed adjutant to the 3rd Meath Brigade, based in the north-west of the county, and assigned the task of organising and commanding an active service unit ('flying column') to be made up of the many local men who, by the latter stages of the war, were on the run like T.P. himself. Training took place among the gorse bushes and bracken of Mullagh Hill, over-looking the picture-perfect lake. It was a place more appropriate to the quiet contemplation of the poetry of Yeats or Ledwidge than to the education of a nascent guerrilla outfit.

Mullagh Hill was hardly the most remote or inaccessible location in which to hide an active service unit as it drilled and trained, but it was as secluded as the topography of north Meath and east Cavan could provide, and the putative flying column managed to avoid detection. Its anonymity was aided by the fact that the Truce overtook the training of this newly established force. It was yet to be fully deployed by the time hostilities came to an end.

In a tribute to T.P. McKenna's organisational abilities, Third Brigade Quartermaster David Smith commented that the young medical student 'was one of our most energetic officers. On his return from Dublin he helped organise a good B[riga]de from chaos. He gave up his profession for the Volunteer movement.'[30]

Ultimately, he was to give up far more than his profession.

~

In 1971, Brigadier General Frank Kitson, veteran of uprisings in Kenya, Malaya, Cyprus and Northern Ireland – an officer who 'probably did more ... to sour relations between the Catholic community and the security forces', according to SDLP MP Paddy Devlin – published *Low Intensity Operations*, an influential primer on dealing with subversion and insurgency. Kitson proposed that a rebellion has three phases: protest, non-violent disorder and outright insurgency, the last often centred on 'large urban rabbit warrens'.[31]

Had Kitson been born fifty years earlier, he might well have been stationed in Ireland during the Anglo-Irish War, where he could have watched the template of nationalist insurgency being fashioned through trial and error. He would have categorised T.P. McKenna as a classic guerrilla, borrowing from the primer of Spanish resistance to Napoleonic rule, when the word was first coined, or the Boer struggle against British forces in South Africa.

John McKenna, however, would have been more of a *franc-tireur*, a phrase that originated in the Franco-Prussian War but whose currency was enhanced by Belgian civilian resistance to the advancing German invaders in the first months of the 1914–18 conflict. A *franc-tireur* was a sniper who lay in wait, seized his opportunity, then folded back into his community rather than bolting for the hills.

Belgium didn't have many hills into which a *franc-tireur* could bolt, and the Germans had little mercy on the communities that harboured the exasperating snipers. Neither did John McKenna ever stray too far from the fields of Mullagh and Moynalty in the various roles he played while harassing the invading Tans, Auxiliaries and South Wales Borderers, as well as their RIC allies.

Raphael McKenna was more insidious still. At least his brother John made no effort to conceal his loathing of the forces of the

Crown operating in his neighbourhood. Raphael McKenna, however, was more Machiavellian in his approach, in particular to
the Royal Irish Constabulary. During the day, he carried on his
work as an inoffensive auctioneer. In his parallel life, as a battalion
intelligence officer through the first half of 1921, his responsibility
was to acquire as much information as possible on the movements,
mentality and objectives of the forces arrayed against the IRA in
County Meath.

He did this by venturing into the belly of the beast. He didn't
formally join the IRA ranks until the summer of 1920, but before
that he made his car available to members of the Mullagh company
and supplied the local force with any information he could glean
from official sources. This mainly took the form of encouraging
policemen to gossip about men they knew to be heavily involved
in the Irish Volunteers. 'I was trying to find out what men the
police suspected,' he told his advisory committee interviewers in
1937, in support of his military service pension application.[32]

When he finally did become an IRA Volunteer, Raphael made
himself useful to the organisation not by shouldering a rifle or
pocketing a revolver, but by cultivating the officers of the RIC.[33]
'I was pretty great with the RIC, talking to them and calling to
the barrack,' he recalled.

This was a risky business. By maintaining regular contact with
the members of the Meath RIC, he invited local stigmatisation as
an unduly cooperative loyalist. Anyone unfamiliar with his covert
life – and he would certainly not have bruited about his work as an
IRA intelligence officer – might have assumed he was rather too
cosy with the local police.

Quite a few of the agents of Michael Collins, Florence
O'Donoghue and other IRA spymasters were men and women
embedded within the RIC or the British administration in Ireland.

Many had wished to abandon their posts and join the IRA or Cumann na mBan. Instead, they were instructed by GHQ to stay put. They could do far more valuable work from within the machine. Most would have preferred – and not simply on account of the stress of spying on their employers – not to have been identified with a cause they had rejected. In addition, there was always the risk of assassination by some over-eager and ill-informed IRA Volunteer.

That, however, was highly unlikely in the case of Raphael McKenna. His status as 3rd Brigade intelligence officer was well-known among north Meath IRA members, since he spent many of his evenings training local battalion and company intelligence officers in information-gathering techniques he had himself devised.

Of rather more consequence was the possibility, almost inevitability, that the RIC would become aware of his double role. Information he gathered led to at least three of the relatively sparse number of successful Meath ambushes. Such was the paucity of military activity that success was measured not in the number of casualties inflicted, but in the mere occurrence of any engagement with the Crown forces.

McKenna passed on information that led to firefights in Drumbaragh, Sylvan Park and Dervor. A number of projected ambushes based on his information failed to come off because of the reluctance of Crown forces to stick to their own preordained plans (see below). Had those attacks actually proceeded, the RIC might have been quicker to put two and two together. By his own admission, the RIC had their doubts about Raphael McKenna by the end of 1920, demonstrating their suspicions by dismantling and immobilising his car.

McKenna was not unique in making nefarious use of RIC contacts. In the neighbouring county of Longford – redoubt of the most successful rural IRA commandant outside Dublin or Munster, Seán MacEoin – the brigade intelligence officer, Michael Heslin, had invaluable sources within the county's railway stations and post offices and used his own brother to befriend the local RIC and procure information on troop and police movements.[34]

The Michael Collins Papers in the Irish Military Archives include a positive evaluation of Raphael McKenna as a 3rd Brigade IO in an assessment of all the intelligence officers of the 1st Eastern division. This unit extended well beyond Meath into Louth and north Dublin, as well as incorporating parts of Kildare and Westmeath:

> Intelligence Report for Month of October 1921. Brigade No.3 – IO Ralph McKenna. A very good and energetic man who has his own department working well. His system is very satisfactory and has only failed to give good results in Baileborough. According to his report he hopes to get ahead there before long.[35]

The oldest of the three McKenna brothers actively involved in the IRA was John, in his mid-twenties when Dan Breen, Seán Treacy and Séamus Robinson lit the fire in Tipperary that turned a tense political impasse between Irish nationalists and the British Empire into outright war. John McKenna – who supervised some of the family businesses in Mullagh as well as farming McKenna land in Walterstown, just outside the village of Moynalty – joined the Irish Volunteers in the early months of 1918, and was involved, like his much younger brother T.P. Junior, in the East Cavan by-election campaign.

Unlike his brother, when the shooting war began he was a part-time IRA Volunteer. He was quartermaster of the Mullagh-based G Company of the 1st Battalion, Meath 3rd Brigade, generally involved in the mundane guerrilla activities of raiding houses for arms – 'to get arms and use them to get more arms'[36] being an IRA obsession – destroying bridges, felling trees and cutting roads to discommode RIC and military movements. These activities were hardly a boon to the communities in which the IRA members themselves lived, but they were the bane of the Crown forces' lives.

Major Gerald Stone of the Devonshire regiment testified to the effectiveness of some of the rural IRA's demolition work:

> They would cut a trench nearly across the road just leaving room for a jaunty car to go round – that's the little Irish horse-drawn vehicle. To compete with that we used to carry planks so that we'd put these down across the trench, then they'd cut trees down across the road and they were too difficult to deal with and you would look for a gate one side of the tree leading to a field and then a gate the far side to see if you could get round the tree that way. If you couldn't then you would probably have to take another road.[37]

Like many of his IRA colleagues, John also became an accomplished arsonist as the Meath Brigade burned its way through most of the outlying RIC barracks abandoned in early 1920. His only confirmed exposure to gunfire was a raid on a mail van and the Meath IRA 3rd Brigade's swansong in July 1921, an attack on the RIC barracks in Kingscourt, County Cavan minutes before the Truce of 11 July came into effect.

Towards the end of the war, John McKenna found himself under the command of his younger brother as a member of the Mullagh Active Service Unit. This was not an unusual turn of events. The IRA was an organisation in which social hierarchies counted for little. Rank and seniority in an organisation consisting mainly of men in their teens and twenties were largely based on ability, reputation and popularity. If the local corner boy or ne'er-do-well was fearless and resourceful, he was likely to find himself outranking the primary school teacher who had given him up as a hopeless case. 'The boy might give orders to the boss.'[38]

Big brother John spent three weeks 'in camp' (a euphemism for sleeping out on Mullagh Hill and other equally inhospitable locations) under the watchful eye of T.P. Junior. He was joined by a number of IRA Volunteers who did not have the luxury of returning home after three weeks of drilling and discomfort. John McKenna was fortunate in that he was never forced to go on the run from the security forces, as were some of his colleagues in that nascent flying column.

All of which suggests that John McKenna's Anglo-Irish War passed off in relatively banal fashion, that he was engaged in only 'ordinary activities', as a carping typed note suggested in his pension application file.[39] That, however, would entail a frayed definition of banality. Aside from the painful events described in the next chapter, which John would have happily avoided, his experience was well out of the ordinary. It was not that of your average nocturnal warrior. In the words of two of his battalion commanders, 'he risked his life several times' and was 'one of the best Volunteers in Meath or Cavan'.[40]

John McKenna was an unassuming warrior, outwardly gentle and amiable, but he had a hard core. Though far away from the battlegrounds presided over by Seán MacEoin, Tom Barry, Séamus Robinson or even Eoin O'Duffy, he still contrived to have a harrowing war.

He was, for example, intimately acquainted with the auxiliary and reserve forces of the RIC, both at the point of a bayonet and because, in his own laconic phraseology, he 'got a few runs by the

Tans in lorries'. The temporary policemen of the RIC, mostly recruited from Britain (although roughly ten percent of the Tans were Irish) and earning up to seven pounds a week, liked to travel the byroads of rural Ireland with unwilling guests on board their vehicles as visible human shields. When a suspected IRA activist like John McKenna was among their number, the Crown forces felt more secure.

John was their hostage, for example, in the aftermath of an attack on a car carrying four RIC men – a sergeant, two constables and a member of the Auxiliaries – from Mullagh towards Virginia in February 1921. The attack took place at the foot of Mullagh Hill as dusk was descending. It was a routine and opportunistic ambush. The car was fired on, the RIC men returned fire and then sped off before suffering any casualties. A Dublin Castle communiqué claimed that, before this 'tactical withdrawal', the RIC had hit at least three of their attackers. Nothing in the exceptionally skimpy Brigade Activity Report covering the Mullagh company indicates that the ambush party suffered any casualties whatever. An illusory body count policy was not just a fantasy associated with the American forces in the Vietnam War.

At about 4 a.m. the following morning, a unit of the Tans and Auxiliaries descended on a sleeping Mullagh and raided a number of houses in the town. No arrests were made. Suspecting that the shots had been fired from land belonging to the Clintons of Mullagh House, who maintained a studious neutrality throughout the Anglo-Irish War, the Crown forces raided the home of Mark (brother of Sarah Clinton McKenna) and Catherine Clinton. The first the Clinton family knew of their unwelcome guests was when the front door was taken off its hinges by a Black and Tan boot.

However, before any serious damage could be inflicted, the

officer in charge of the raid spotted a large portrait of William Gladstone which had adorned the wall of the Clinton sitting room for many years. He also noted a number of photographs dotted around the house of Father Bernard Farrell, Catherine Clinton's brother, in full British military uniform; he had been an army chaplain in India. Satisfied that he was in the presence of a family of loyalists – he wasn't – the officer ordered an immediate withdrawal. As the Tans left, their commanding officer, in a display of noblesse oblige, ordered that the front door be returned to an upright position, though he did not go so far as to instruct that it be repaired and restored to its hinges.[41]

Twenty-four hours later there was a further raid by the Auxiliaries. This time the target was the McKenna business premises, managed on behalf of his father by John McKenna. He and James McCabe, owner of a local public house, were bundled into a lorry and driven in convoy towards Baileborough. The column made it about four kilometres north of Mullagh, as far as nearby Corlat Bridge, which they discovered to their chagrin had been demolished; at which point the Auxies released their hostages and took an alternative route to Baileborough.[42]

There was a certain irony in John McKenna being released at that precise location and being forced to walk home with James McCabe in the early hours of a glacial and dark February morning. It was not the first time he had been obliged to trek back from Corlat. He and that particular bridge had a history, one that marked him out as a man of considerable moral and physical courage.

Although never actually jailed for his subversive activities, the eldest McKenna was believed by the RIC to be one of the prime movers of the local IRA. Hence the occasional night-time visits from Crown forces. 'My home was continuously annoyed by raids and searches,'[43] he once observed without a hint of self-pity. In the circumstances, he could hardly have expected otherwise.

When an orgy of IRA destruction of roads and bridges in north-west Meath in November 1920 prompted the Black and Tans to round up the usual suspects, their first port of call was the McKenna household. John was taken away – 'arrested' would be a misleading description – and brought to Corlat Bridge. Like many other minor viaducts, it had been demolished by the IRA. Thomas J. O'Reilly, vice-commandant of the Mullagh battalion, takes up the story of what followed:

> [McKenna] was interrogated and abused to make him give the names of the men who demolished the bridge. He was given three days to get it built and threatened that if this was not done he would be shot and his father's house burned. An offer by Mullagh people to supply materials for this work was turned down by him and he refused to allow the work to be done.[44]

According to fellow battalion member Patrick O'Reilly, McKenna was threatened at bayonet point. His defiance of the members of a force not noted for its forbearance, or indeed self-discipline in the face of non-compliance, was as audacious as it was imprudent. The casual approach of the Black and Tans to due process, their contempt for the Irish population and their apparent licence to operate a policy of reprisal meant their threats had to be taken seriously.

In this instance, however, John McKenna was vindicated in his defiance. The Tans either had short memories, or were bluffing. No harm came to him or to his father's house. Corlat Bridge remained in ruins.

On 4 April 1921, McKenna was one of dozens of men rounded

up in what the *Meath Chronicle* of 9 April described as 'one of the most extraordinary demonstrations by the Crown Forces that have taken place in the district'. A force of up to fifteen lorries – on that scale, it was probably an RIC-Tan-Auxiliary operation, backed up by the British military – descended on Mullagh, took every adult male they could find to the Fair Green and began a house-to-house search for weapons and IRA Volunteers on the run. This continued from 11 a.m. to 6 p.m. Two machine guns were trained on the prisoners.

When the search produced practically nothing, a few bored Black and Tans decided to indulge their sense of humour. Two young men were selected from among the prisoners to paint slogans – 'God save the King', 'Up, Lloyd George', 'Up the RIC and the Black and Tans' – on the ruins of the old RIC barracks, burnt out by the IRA twelve months before. Threats were issued that the town itself would be burned to the ground unless information on weapons caches and safe houses was forthcoming.

The ordeal having already begun to stretch into the afternoon, spirits began to flag. Having two machine guns aimed at you often has that effect. When it was suggested to John McKenna that perhaps it might be a good idea to sacrifice a few IRA weapons to save the town from the same fate as Balbriggan and the city centre of Cork, his refusal to capitulate was couched in his usual laconic manner. 'Sure, wouldn't the place only be improved if it was burned to the ground,' he observed.[45] No IRA guns were given up.

Eventually the Crown forces left with nothing to show for their efforts other than the arrest, in the McKenna house, of young Seán McEvoy, a medical student and a Dublin relative of the McKenna clan. He is coyly described by the *Meath Chronicle* as having been 'on holidays there for some time'.[46] His holiday ended abruptly. Whether or not McEvoy had been the target of the extended search, he was certainly a prominent IRA Volunteer. He spent the rest of the war interned in the Curragh.*

Had that been the full extent of John McKenna's direct experience of the desolation of the Anglo-Irish War, he might have been more forthcoming in later life about his involvement in the conflict, as the Union faltered and gave way to the Irish Free State. But for John McKenna there was a greater ordeal to come, one that could not be overcome by the spirited insubordination he often displayed towards the defenders of Empire.

A polite, mild-mannered young man, albeit one with a backbone of steel, he would be instructed to take up a gun, look another fellow human being in the eye, and shoot him dead.

* During the Civil War, Seán McEvoy took the anti-Treaty side and was killed in action by Irish Free State forces. During the War of Independence he had been harboured in what later became a Free State home.

7

The Informer

'And now the British think I'm with the Irish,
and the Irish think I'm with the British. The long and
short of it is I'm walkin' around without a dog
to lick my trousers.'

Gypo Nolan in Liam O'Flaherty's *The Informer* (1935)

I.

It is a truth universally acknowledged that every futile Irish nationalist insurgency has been betrayed by traitors and informers. Failure is always a direct consequence of the duplicity of the infiltrator or the double agent. Factors such as hapless leadership, bad planning or a dearth of soldierly proficiency can automatically be discounted. Each crushing defeat/military calamity is entirely attributable to an Irish Judas Iscariot, Benedict Arnold or Wooden Horse of Troy, whose rank treachery quenched the fire of an otherwise auspicious revolt. *M'ochón agus mo bhrón.*

And sheer bad luck, of course. Random misfortune – bad weather, unsuitable terrain, an unexpected sunrise – serves as a convenient back-up defence against the charge of incompetence. And the absence of the French, or their tardy appearance in insufficient numbers.

But usually spies and informers.

The Irish even have their own private names for such treachery. They differed in the unionist and nationalist traditions. A loyalist traitor was (and still is, because that community continues to consider itself susceptible to betrayal) a Lundy, an insult that has survived since the Siege of Derry. The fact that few nationalists will recognise the expression 'a Carey' tells its own tale.

The most egregious nineteenth-century nationalist informer was James Carey, a member of the murderous Invincibles who turned 'approver' and became a state witness against his associates in the Phoenix Park murders of 1882. The word was still a term of abuse in the early 1900s because Carey had yet to be ousted by an equal or greater turncoat. It had not been supplanted by the time of the Anglo-Irish Treaty. Much of the credit for that goes to Michael Collins and his lethal counter-intelligence operations.

Turncoats failed to prosper between 1919 and 1921, at least on the Republican side.

The War of Independence saw a British government determined to win back the intelligence initiative after the excruciating failures of 1916. Accordingly, they deployed considerable resources to achieve superiority in the covert war. In essence, the Anglo-Irish conflict, despite its occasional set pieces, can be seen as primarily an intelligence war.* The IRA did not oblige its enemy by compelling its soldiers to identify themselves – an IRA man turning up for work in full military uniform would have been sent home to change his clothing. This made effective British counter-insurgency heavily dependent on reliable intelligence.

The IRA, despite the aspirations of Éamon de Valera, were never going to take on the Crown forces in open battle. The fact that they never attempted to do so – though the disastrous attack on the Custom House in May 1921, de Valera's pet project, came close – meant that, for the British to succeed, the IRA had to be pursued by other means. Their Volunteer members must be rooted out by nimble espionage. The British, while nowhere near as hapless as Irish War of Independence mythology suggests, never managed to achieve the emphatic victory required in this prosecution of the dark arts.

In fact, the British struggled and ultimately failed to defeat the IRA's own counter-intelligence campaign, though, as we shall see, in the months leading up to the Truce of July 1921 the covert tide was beginning to turn in favour of the Crown forces, met by an increasingly frantic response from an unnerved IRA.

* Although the rationale of historian Charles Townshend, who described the conflict as being primarily one of 'armed propaganda' on the part of the IRA, has considerable validity. Charles Townshend, *Political Violence in Ireland: Government and Resistance since 1848* (Oxford, 1983), p. 361.

The IRA had begun by successfully neutralising the Royal Irish Constabulary, as part of the Collins philosophy that it was essential to 'put out the eyes of the British'. This was achieved by a brutal campaign of assassination, a concerted boycott of members of the force (and, crucially, of their families) and a parallel moral crusade of persuasion which sought to provoke mass RIC resignations. The Collins credo was simple:

> Without her spies England was helpless. It was only by means of their accumulated knowledge that the British machine could operate. Without their police throughout the country, how far could they find the man they wanted? Without their criminal agents in the capital, how could they carry out that 'removal' of the leaders that they considered essential for their victory.[1]

Credit for the creation of an intelligence network on a par with, and often outstripping, that of Britain goes to Collins and his lieutenants, Liam Tobin, Frank Saurin and Tom Cullen; to undercover agents like Eamon 'Ned' Broy, Lily Mernin and David Neligan; and to an array of casual informants working in bars, hotels, cafés, restaurants, post offices and government buildings across the city of Dublin. Almost as impressive as the operation Collins ran in Dublin was that controlled in the city of Cork by Florence O'Donoghue, aided by his enterprising spy Josephine Brown (whom he married when their collaboration was at its height). The efforts of Collins, O'Donoghue and regional IRA intelligence officers (IOs) meant the DMP and the RIC were no longer bottomless sources of information to be plumbed by the authorities, but harried constabularies constantly forced to operate on the back foot.

By the end of the Anglo-Irish conflict, senior British sources acknowledged that 'Irish persons who were prepared to act as genuine secret service agents, i.e. as Sinn Féiners or as IRA, were difficult to find ... Secret Service was on the whole a failure in Ireland. For many reasons it was practically impossible to place a man in any inner circle.'[2]

However, while they never threatened to reach the heights of the infiltration of the United Irishmen in 1798, British espionage operations, particularly outside Dublin and Cork, slowly began to produce results. When it came to rural Ireland, the impact of the success of army intelligence was amplified by the onset of a sullen war weariness and a consequent decline in levels of complicity among the native population.

IRA achievement was based on the ability of Volunteers to operate with a degree of impunity among a supportive or at the very least docile population. While southern unionists might collaborate with the Crown forces or defy the IRA, moderate nationalists, often dismayed by the savagery of the Black and Tans and Auxiliaries, were either neutral, undemonstratively supportive or downright complicit. At least, that is, until the cumulative impact of overwhelming Crown force retaliation began to take its toll, and the latent fear of British military reprisals slowly wore down the nationalist population. For example, in Mullagh, subjected to numerous raids, the parish history records that some of the townspeople were 'tired of the constant disturbance, attacks like these caused confusion, and often division'.[3]

As the war went on, 'new British measures were deliberately intended to shrink the space for ambivalence'.[4] If Irish people were not going to support the Crown forces, then they would be made to suffer disproportionately for their *de facto* collusion with the IRA.

After the war came *ex post facto* protestations by Sinn Féin and IRA leaders of the undying support of the general populace – W.T.

Cosgrave's audio recording for the Military Archives, collected by
the Irish Folklore Commission in 1950, is a case in point. Cosgrave
maintained in his contribution, in his own oracular style, that 'the
success which attended the movement was due almost entirely
to the great support rendered by all classes of the people'.[5] Such
complicity, however, was never entirely unconditional. While
people might support the objectives of the IRA, many preferred
the organisation's violent activities to take place in someone else's
back yard. This often included IRA Volunteers.

Flying column raids could expose towns and villages near the
centre of the action to ruinous reprisals. The IRA's destruction
of roads and bridges would often result in the 'recruitment' of
improvised local labour details by the Black and Tans to repair
the damage. While such acts hardly endeared the Tans to the
conscripted labour force, the time spent on such restorations, and
the local inconvenience caused by road and bridge closures, did
not recommend the IRA to the reluctant labourers either.

Even in rebel County Clare, two IRA officers found their carefully constructed secret dugout destroyed by locals, petrified at
the prospect of Black and Tan retaliation were it to be discovered.[6]
The response in Oldcastle, County Meath – even that of the
local IRA battalion itself – to the prospect of an attack on the local
RIC barracks has already been described above.[7]

Sullen nationalist neutrality could easily metamorphose into
active but covert opposition. As the war intensified, so did the
activities of local informers and, correspondingly, IRA paranoia.
Some units became disproportionately preoccupied with the
detection and extirpation of spies.[8] While the Dáil courts oversaw
a process of restorative justice, the IRA administered justice of a
more retributive nature. More than seventy of the two hundred or
so IRA executions of the War of Independence took place in the

first four months of 1921. Ex-British soldiers, wandering beggars and strangers became objects of suspicion.

The East Clare IRA issued orders that 'All strangers walking or cycling through any part of the Brigade [territory] must be placed under arrest and held until they can prove who and what they are satisfactorily.'⁹ Cork No.2 Brigade contemplated the introduction of an order prohibiting any contact whatever between the general population and the police and military. The IRA in south Roscommon dressed up in military uniforms in an effort to entrap suspected local informers. Their subterfuge resulted in two executions.¹⁰ Inaccurate information was fed to alleged spies by the IRA in order to confirm suspicions of collaboration. If the ruse was effective, there almost invariably would be fatal consequences.

Not that all 'convicted' spies were executed. Even in Cork, the county that witnessed around a quarter of all IRA executions, the often neurotic No. 2 Brigade merely levied a £50 fine on a well-to-do farmer who notified the authorities that a trench had been dug in a local road. When the unit sought permission from GHQ to impose the fine, the response from IRA O/C Richard Mulcahy was 'If you think you could get £100, do so.'¹¹ Times were hard.

In theory, all IRA retributive killings of civilians were required to have the imprimatur of a GHQ which by 1921 was 'certainly worried about the escalating rate of executions'.¹² However, as the conflict continued and intensified, more and more life-and-death decisions were being made without recourse to GHQ, and in some cases by quite junior officers.

In one instance, an Offaly IRA commander failed to clear an execution with Dublin and instead sought the permission of his parish priest. The victim, a man named John Lawlor, had been 'going into houses for a glass of milk' and was 'seen in company with the military and police on two occasions'. The priest apparently inquired whether or not Lawlor had been court-martialled by the IRA. On being informed that 'due process' had been followed, he endorsed the killing.[13]

In Kerry, *pour encourager les autres*, the 2nd Brigade kidnapped and murdered a septuagenarian, Thomas O'Sullivan, nicknamed Old Tom. Two British army deserters had told the IRA that O'Sullivan was a frequent visitor to the military barracks in the town of Rathmore. O'Sullivan was executed on 4 May 1921 and his body was left at 'a place called the Bog Road near the village of Rathmore'. Fifth Battalion Captain Manus Moynihan, commander of the Rathmore company, added a refinement of his own to the summary justice inflicted on Old Tom – his corpse was used as bait to lure the RIC into an ambush. Eight Black and Tans died in the subsequent attack. The counter-retaliation led to the burning of the house of Cork IRA intelligence chief Florence O'Donoghue.[14] And so it went.

Even in the relatively tranquil north midlands, the man who would later become Ireland's premier Fascist, Eoin O'Duffy, had a short way with spies and dissidents. In O'Duffy's section, County Monaghan, eight 'civilians' were shot as informers.[15] One hapless victim of the Monaghan IRA was one of their own young 'delivery boys' who had fallen into the hands of the Crown forces, wilted under the threat of torture and divulged some of his limited store of information. When he was released from custody and voluntarily confessed to his offence, O'Duffy had him shot. Similar treatment was meted out to three members of the Ancient Order of Hibernians, an organisation noted for its almost primeval opposition to Sinn Féin in the county.

But O'Duffy's most controversial execution involved the shooting dead of a local poteen maker, Kate (Kitty) Carroll. She had been fined by the IRA for her illegal distilling operations but defiantly continued to produce her 'mountain dew'. In an injudicious attempt to eliminate some local competition, Carroll wrote to the RIC identifying other illicit distillers in the county. When this was discovered, she was shot dead by the IRA. Lest there be any doubt about her crimes, her body was adorned with the label 'Convicted spy, IRA'.[16]

And in some measure, this upsurge in the IRA response to British intelligence successes was effective. Fear of IRA retaliation – and direct warnings of impending retribution – persuaded at least some of the newly emboldened spies who had driven the British intelligence resurgence to retire while the option remained. It became too dangerous, even in areas of relatively low IRA activity, to risk being detected in the transfer of information to Crown forces. Sources of intelligence slowly began to dry up once more, especially in Munster, where IRA treatment of suspected informers was particularly brutal.[17]

3.

What of suspected or 'convicted' informers in County Meath?

As we have seen, although it is a distasteful metric based on fatality statistics, it is clear that Meath was not exactly a cockpit of the War of Independence. Three Volunteers lost their lives (one as a result of friendly fire), two RIC men were killed in action (one more died in an accident), and there was a single British military death, that of Sergeant John Herrod of the South Wales Borderers, who was kidnapped and executed as a spy. Herrod was one of the few IRA victims to be drowned rather than being shot. Four members of the Crown forces also died in what were essentially workplace accidents.[18] In contrast, executions conducted by the Meath IRA outnumbered the total number of military fatalities on both sides.

Two details stand out. Almost all verifiable extra-judicial killings took place during the final phase of the war, March–July 1921,* and most of the targets had served in the British armed forces or the police from 1914 to 1918. The Meath IRA executed six men for spying.† When William Gordon is added to the calculations, the number of executions exceeds the body count of those killed in action.[19] Only one of those executed, Patrick Keelan, had no connection with the British armed forces or the RIC/DMP. The identity of one victim is still unknown – he called himself Michael O'Brien, he may have been a British bounty hunter, and he was shot dead in Navan by future Fianna Fáil government minister Michael Hilliard on 1 March 1921.[20]

In the case of County Meath – which was hardly unique – it is apparent from a number of Bureau of Military History Witness Statements that the IRA was coming under increasing pressure in 1921 as a result of enhanced British penetration of its operations. A close examination of the records of the military units of British army battalions based in the county suggests that regiments like the South Wales Borderers did not lack for local informants to guide their searches and raids.[21]

In his witness statement, Peter O'Connell, adjutant of the 5th

* The date of the execution of Bryan Bradley (see below) is uncertain. It probably took place shortly after he was kidnapped in January 1921. However, in 1922 a probate court assigned a date for his death in April 1921.

† Bryan Bradley, 'Michael O'Brien' (still unidentified), John Donohoe, Sergeant John Herrod, John 'The Thatcher' Farrell and Patrick Keelan. A seventh man, Thomas Smyth, long assumed to have been executed as a spy, appears to have been murdered in an unsanctioned killing – essentially a local feud – by a gang that included a number of IRA volunteers.

Battalion of the Meath IRA, was under no illusions 'that the enemy had several agents in the district':

> We got two very important letters from a young man named Jack Tuite, a post office clerk at Kells, which he had intercepted. They were directed to the authorities and had been sent from the Virginia Road or Stonefield district. The letters contained the names of all Volunteers in the Stonefield and Whitegate areas. We were unable to do anything about it.[22]

When it comes to British counter-intelligence activities in the county, the most authoritative testimony of all is that of Seán Boylan. Even in the 1950s, the Meath IRA O/C was still convinced that a number of planned operations had been sabotaged by insider information coming from one of the senior members of his officer cadre. In his statement to the Bureau he even identifies his main suspect as one Thomas E. Duffy, an IRA officer from Navan:

> Time and again I tried to persuade the officers of Navan (or 6th) Battalion to drop Duffy and have nothing to do with him, but they would not take my advice. His father, with whom he lived, was an ex-R.I.C. man, and I had a suspicion then that both Duffy and his father were in constant touch with the R.I.C. in Navan and elsewhere.[23]

Boylan felt vindicated after the war when he received a detailed letter from a former RIC constable named McGarrity who had been stationed for a number of years in Navan. Boylan included the text of McGarrity's letter in his witness statement, claiming that 'it shows, if true, that Duffy was being paid by the R.I.C. for information supplied during the pre-Truce period'.

McGarrity claimed to have opened boxes belonging to RIC Sergeant Neilan and Head Constable Queenan in Navan RIC station. In Neilan's box he had discovered a typewritten letter, dated February 1921 and signed by Duffy, that 'contained information about the shooting of policemen to take place at a future date'. In Queenan's box was another typed letter bearing the initials T.D., which alerted the Navan RIC to an ambush due to take place on the Dublin Road. McGarrity added that:

> I clearly recollect Sergeant Neilon [*sic*] sending up a Constable to T.E. Duffy's father with money in bank notes for young Tom… He left the envelope on the mantelpiece in the guard room for a few minutes, and I noticed it was addressed in type to Thomas E. Duffy. I noticed this kind of an envelope going twice a week for about five months in 1920 and 1921. About one month before the Truce he was not getting much money.

In his exhaustive account of the War of Independence in Meath, Oliver Coogan addresses these allegations and, without naming Boylan's chief suspect, suggests that:

> The 'suspect', if he was a police informer, must have been an excellent actor who sustained the performance of his role over a protracted period, for in the years both before and after the Troubles, he made a large contribution not only to political but also to the cultural life of the county.[24]

Coogan does not mention, possibly for fear of betraying Duffy's identity, that Boylan might have had an ulterior motive in identifying the Navan man as an RIC informer. During the Civil War, Boylan sided with his good friend Michael Collins and became a senior officer in the National Army. Such was the degree of loyalty that Boylan had inspired in his 'troops' that he managed to persuade most of the county's senior Volunteers to join the military campaign against the anti-Treaty forces, or at the very least to remain neutral.

Duffy, however, was one of a relatively small number of Meath IRA Volunteers – future Fianna Fáil minister Michael Hilliard and most of the members of the Farrelly family of Carnaross were others – who took the Republican side in that ugly fraternal struggle. Ironically, by the 1930s Duffy was secretary of the IRA Old Comrades Association and was chivvying senior members of the organisation for comprehensive Brigade Activity Reports to assist in the identification of deserving candidates for War of Independence military pensions.[25]

Whether or not Duffy was guilty of collaboration with the RIC, the fact remains that the IRA in Meath appears to have been infiltrated. In his witness statement, Matt Govern of the Kells Battalion recorded how he was instructed by battalion O/C Pat Farrelly to go to Carnaross 'to arrest a man named Christopher Farrell, a suspected spy'.[26] Farrell was held for questioning, and the Truce may have saved his life. Later in his statement, Govern identified another suspected informer still plying his dubious trade *after* the Truce had come into effect on 11 July 1921:

I noticed a party of Tans in civilian clothes arrive in a motor car. All carried revolvers. They had a civilian named Weir with them who wore a mask. Weir was a suspected spy and was manager of the gas works in Kells. I sent word to O'Reilly* to get out of the

* Patrick O'Reilly of Moynalty, 1st Battalion, 3rd Brigade of the 1st Eastern Division.

house. He had only just done so when the Tans searched it for him. If they had caught him they would certainly have finished him off. Weir was there to identify him.[27]

Given that the Truce had already come into effect and – if the story is true – the Tan activity was therefore entirely extra-curricular, Govern is probably correct in his assessment of the treatment that would have been meted out to O'Reilly.

While aborted and abandoned ambushes were a feature of the War of Independence throughout the country, the Meath IRA seems to have been defined by its bad luck. One operation after another was abandoned because the enemy did not oblige by turning up. Convincing anecdotal evidence indicates that this was not all attributable to simple misfortune, and that the Meath IRA had been compromised. So, in 1921, Boylan and his leading subordinates went on a silent offensive.

In the first six months of 1921, the Meath IRA executed at least six men (five of them civilians) and attempted to kill three more. Only two of the executions, the first and last, are of direct relevance to this narrative, and one of those for geographical reasons only. The final killing of an alleged informer, which took place barely a week before the Truce, will be dealt with elsewhere.

4.

The first fatal victim of Meath IRA vengeance in 1921 was postman Bernard 'Bryan' Bradley, a First World War veteran demobilised in June 1919, who lived with his sister Mary Lynch in Currow, Carnaross at the time of his murder.

On 8 October 1920, Bradley had a foretaste of what was in

store for him. He was brutally assaulted, knocked down and kicked while lying on the ground by four men, all members of the Carnaross IRA.[28] Bradley initially pressed charges but thought better of that decision; when the case came before the November Kells petty sessions, neither he nor the four defendants put in an appearance.[29]

If the beating was a warning to Bradley about his future relationship with the Crown forces, it failed to work. As a postman, he was well placed to supply low-level information to the RIC and continued to do so. Two months later, the IRA took conclusive punitive action.

Sometime around 10 p.m. on the night of 2 January 1921, Mary Lynch heard a knock on her front door. At that hour, at that time of year, it was unlikely to be a social call. Her son opened the door and Mrs Lynch heard a voice demand sharply, 'Where is Bryan Bradley?' The young boy pointed to his uncle's room. With that, two men burst into the house.

Bradley was given five minutes to get dressed, then left with the two men, one of whom returned shortly thereafter to fetch his prisoner's coat. As the interloper left the house for a second time, he somewhat surreally apologised for the disturbance. That was the last Mary Lynch ever saw of her brother.

She didn't ascertain his fate, though she must have guessed, until the following year when, in response to an inquiry, the Department of Defence of the newly established government of the Irish Free State wrote to her on 8 February 1922 to confirm that Bryan Bradley had been 'arrested on a charge of espionage, court-martialled by a duly authorised authority, and executed'.[30] In response to further enquiries about the date of his execution, whether he had left a will, and the all-important question for a Roman Catholic family in 1922 – had he been attended by a priest? – there was only silence. Then, on 3 May, Mary Lynch was told in another official letter that her brother had 'died fortified by the rites of the Catholic Church'.

A probate case in December 1922 ruled that the fact of Bradley's death should be formalised and 'gave leave to state death as having taken place in April, 1921'.[31] The IRA is unlikely to have imprisoned Bradley for that length of time; it is far more likely that he was shot within hours of being taken away. Oddly, there was no reference at the time in the *Meath Chronicle*, *Drogheda Independent* or *Anglo-Celt* to the disappearance of a local postman, a highly visible figure.

The background to Bradley's execution was explained to the Bureau of Military History in the 1950s by the ever-informative Seán Farrelly. Farrelly, himself from Carnaross, recalled the Bradley killing with singular clarity but could not recall the correct first name of the victim, referring to him throughout as Nicholas, a name by which he may have been known locally. Ironically, Bradley had secured an appointment as postman in the village only after local IRA O/C Jack Tevlin found himself temporarily residing at the pleasure of His Majesty. The contrast between the recreational activities of the two postmen could not have been more stark:

Living as he was among all the boys and with his advantage as postman, he was in a position to know every active IRA man in the district. He used his opportunity and compiled a list of every IRA man in the area. In a raid on the local Post Office in the early Spring of 1921,* the list together with a letter from him were found among the mail addressed to Dublin Castle. The

* Farrelly is incorrect in his chronology. It is far more likely that by 'early spring' of 1921 Bradley was already dead.

list contained twenty-one names, every one of whom were active IRA men. He was arrested and court-martialled. He was found guilty and sentenced to death. Before his execution, Father Swan, a Kilmessan man, and a curate in Moynalty, heard his confession and administered the last rites of the Church. He was buried in Rathmaine Wood.[32]*

It was not to be Father Swan's only exposure to IRA retribution.

Bradley left behind 'wearing apparel' worth £5 and a total of £102 in cash, lodged – where else? – in the post office savings bank. The probate court allowed Mary Lynch access to her brother's estate, though she would probably have preferred to be informed of the location of his body.

One of the implications of Seán Farrelly's witness statement is that at least some of the money that ultimately accrued to Mary Lynch had come to Bradley from the RIC, earned during his brief and tragic foray into rudimentary espionage. To this day the body of Bryan Bradley has never been restored to his family. He remains one of the estimated fifty 'disappeared' of the Irish revolutionary era (1919–23) whose bodies have yet to be recovered.[33]

A few months after the killing of Bryan Bradley, another victim would be interred in a shallow grave in Walterstown a quarter of a mile away. His execution would be a family affair.

* The reference has been transcribed incorrectly. The wood in question, near Moynalty, is known locally as Rathmanoo Wood.

8

The Fourth Killing

'All … having assisted the enemy, must be shot or otherwise destroyed with the least possible delay.'

Ernest Blythe, *An tÓglach*, 15 August 1918

'They forgot for the moment their hatred of him. They forgot that this helpless, shapeless mass of humanity was a menace to their lives. They forgot that he was a viper they must crush. They only knew, at that moment, that he was a poor, weak human being like themselves, a human soul, weak and helpless in suffering, shivering in the tolls of the eternal struggle of the human soul with pain.'

Liam O'Flaherty, *The Informer*

I.

On the brow of a low hill, a few hundred metres from the tree-lined track between Moynalty (County Meath) and Kingscourt (County Cavan), stands Garryard Wood. It is actually little more than a circular thicket, taking up only a couple of acres of valuable Meath farmland. In winter, it is just about visible through the trees from the main road. In summer, it is sheltered from view and can be spied only from a winding back road just past the townland of Salford.

Where today there are trees, there used to be a castle, from which the unpretentious copse derives its name. Garryard is an Anglicised corruption of *cathaoir árd* (high seat). For generations the building atop the hill was the high seat of the Betagh family, Roman Catholic aristocracy who lost almost everything to the seventeenth-century Cromwellian invaders. You can see why the adventurers who accompanied the Lord Protector – his 'protection' did not extend as far as Ireland – would have coveted the verdant countryside around Garryard. Today the land consists of fine rolling pastures where fat, contented cattle graze placidly.

A local legend, or *piseog*, would have us believe that a long tunnel begins underneath the wood and connects to Kingsfort on the opposite (southern) side of Moynalty village. A mysterious fiddler can sometimes be heard walking underground, playing enchanting melodies as he goes. The intervening Owenroe River apparently offers no impediment to his wanderings or performance.

In 1921, the copse abutted the Walterstown fields farmed by local IRA quartermaster John McKenna.

A few hundred metres to the north-east lies Rathmanoo Wood. Here the trees are bunched more closely together and the foliage is more dense. Rathmanoo is similar in shape and scale to the neighbouring Garryard. Both have interchangeable mobile colonies of crows and ravens. In the late nineteenth century, the area between the two woods witnessed a spate of evictions by Moynalty Roman Catholic landlord John Farrell. As was frequently the practice, once the unfortunate families had been driven from their smallholdings, their houses were razed. This earned Farrell the nickname Jack the Leveller.[1]

Back in the 1970s, the two thickets and the shallow valley between were the playground of young Joe McKenna, son of John, an elderly father who had postponed matrimony until it was almost too late. Joe remembers his father with great affection as a genial soul who rarely raised his voice, and certainly never raised a hand, to any of his children. Joe and his playmates would from time to time indulge in a macabre pursuit, children having an innate sense of the Gothic: they hunted for buried bodies in Garryard and Rathmanoo woods. This game was not based only on childish fantasy, it was also predicated on local mythology – whispered folklore had it that two men had been interred in the neighbouring thickets.

One day, his interest piqued by a friend who testified to having seen a tell-tale bulge in the earth of one of the copses, Joe made the mistake of breezily enlightening his father about this innocent but ghoulish activity. Instead of expressing interest or curiosity, John McKenna rebuked his son with unfamiliar severity. Joe was warned to stay away from Garryard and Rathmanoo, and to stop playing grisly games.

John McKenna's anger had not been sparked by parental outrage at his son paying too much attention to old wives' tales about buried bodies in dark forests, or trespassing on the land of 'The Colonel' (Colonel Farrell), the descendant of Jack the Leveller. He did not have to rely on local folklore when it came to the secrets of Garryard and Rathmanoo. He knew that Bryan Bradley was still buried in a shallow grave in Rathmanoo; where precisely, he could not be sure. He was fortunate in not having been one of those selected to shoot Bradley and dispose of his body.

But Garryard was different. That was where the IRA had taken nineteen-year-old Patrick Keelan on the night of 2/3 July 1921. That was where John, his brother T.P. and his cousin Peter Clinton were among those who had shot, killed and buried Keelan.

2.

The War of Independence began as a localised insurgency. The overwhelming Sinn Féin vote in the 1918 election was far from being an explicit advance endorsement of the violent upheaval that followed. That was triggered in part by the feral impulses of a small number of militant provocateurs like Seán Treacy and Dan Breen, who undertook regional initiatives with national consequences. In 1919, the tail wagged the dog. The military campaign, foisted on the party by hardcore activists, saw Sinn Féin and Volunteer GHQ struggle to keep pace. By 1920, depending on your perspective, the dog had either taken back control or long since given up the ghost and decided to follow wherever the tail led.

A year later, it was far from clear that the Irish Republican movement had been pulled in the right direction. By early June 1921, 4,500 convicted or suspected IRA men and women (there were almost thirty of the latter) were either in jail or interned in holding facilities like the Rath camp in the Curragh or Ballykinlar in County Down. Barely 2,000 active IRA fighters, many on the run and members of flying squads, remained in the field. They were ranged against fifteen times that number of policemen – including reservists and Auxiliaries – and soldiers, equipped with weapons that the IRA guerrillas could only dream of,[2] assuming they ever had the luxury of a peaceful night's sleep.

One inventory suggested that as the Truce approached (unbeknownst, of course, to any of the participants) the IRA could count on only 569 rifles and 477 revolvers, with twenty bullets per rifle. They did have a fearsome arsenal of 220 pikes and six swords, so they could probably have organised a credible re-enactment of the 1798 Battle of Vinegar Hill, but with little hope of a more favourable outcome.[3]

Ultimately it was the counterproductive British response to militant provocation, predominantly in Munster, that allowed the IRA to survive and prevail. Nothing concentrated the mind of a previously moderate Irish nationalist like the circus of ill-discipline – encompassing vigilante homicide, arson and state terror – promoted by the UK government. The introduction of mercenary paramilitary policemen from Britain (the loathed Tans and Auxies) and the British 'nod and wink' approach to reprisals against the Irish civilian population predictably turned the IRA into a defensive militia with implied popular approval to pursue its primary interest, the achievement of political autonomy.

However, not everyone was convinced by notions of a chivalrous IRA populated by latter-day Cúchulainns. Some citizens were sullenly opposed to the disruption and destruction wrought on the civilian population by the militant pursuit of legislative independence, and still more baulked at the unheroic actions of IRA Volunteers like Patrick Kane and James Dalton from Navan, who on 31 July 1920 held two young women at gunpoint and cut off their hair. Their crime had been to 'walk out' with British soldiers.[4]

At the extremities of this resentment, a very small number, for a multiplicity of reasons, chose to supply information to the authorities about IRA Volunteers and fellow travellers. One was a young man from Thomastown in County Meath – a townland due south of Kilmainhamwood and south-west of Nobber, close to the county border with Cavan – by the name of Patrick Keelan.

Keelan was nineteen years of age at the time of his death in July 1921,* the youngest of three sons of farm labourer Patrick Keelan and Mary Clarke, a domestic servant before her marriage. According to the 1911 census, neither of the older Keelans could read, a deficit increasingly rare in a country whose formal primary education system had been in place for almost a century.† The family lived in one of four labourers' cottages on land owned, until his death in 1915, by Henry Dyas of Boltown Hall, the racehorse trainer in whose empty house the killers of Mark Clinton had been sequestered for a number of weeks in 1920.[5]

Dyas must have had frequent cause to regret the tenancy of the Keelans, and in particular the dining habits of their goats. In September 1913 he brought a complaint to a petty sessions court, citing four dates on which Patrick Keelan Sr.'s two goats had trespassed on his pastures.[6] Patrick Keelan did not appear to

---

* The 1911 census suggests otherwise. There, he is recorded as being seven years old. However, his birth details, as contained in the Kells Poor Law Union Register of Births, confirm that he was born on 29 September 1901.
† Here we encounter another anomaly in either the 1901 or 1911 census returns. Mary Keelan appears to have lost the ability to read between 1901 and 1911. The former census return records only her husband as being illiterate. By 1911, both were registered as 'cannot read'. That is not the only anomaly. Between 1901 and 1911, Patrick Keelan Sr. miraculously aged by twenty years, from thirty to fifty, while his wife advanced by fourteen years, from twenty-eight to forty-two. Their death certificates indicate that Patrick Keelan was born in 1867 and his wife in 1865!

speak in defence of his livestock. It was not the first occasion on which he or his wife had faced the local magistrates – both had previous convictions for assaulting neighbours.[7]

By 1916, one of young Patrick Keelan's older brothers, John, had already died from tuberculosis at the age of fifteen.[8] His other brother, James, had been working as an agricultural labourer since at least the age of fourteen.[9] By 1921, Patrick was in the employment of fifty-six-year-old John Gaffney, a farmer from Marvelstown, a townland in the same Roman Catholic parish (Kilbeg) as Thomastown. Gaffney, like many contemporaries, had once been a supporter of Parnell and Redmond but by 1918 had transferred his allegiance to Sinn Féin.

In March 1921, John Gaffney and Patrick Keelan had a difference of opinion that would lead to the imprisonment of the former and the death of the latter. The row (over a disputed claim for unpaid wages) was sufficiently fractious for Keelan to approach the RIC with what he claimed was information about IRA weapons being stored on Gaffney's land. The intelligence – spurious and self-serving – was taken seriously enough for an army detachment under Lieutenant R.A. Firth to be sent to Marvelstown to search Gaffney's farm.

More damning, from Keelan's point of view, is that the Marvelstown raid was one of five conducted by Firth that day. It must be assumed (certainly the IRA did) that Keelan, apparently a highly suggestible young man, was persuaded to identify additional targets for the attention of the Crown forces.

Firth was told that Gaffney had three shotguns buried on his land. When he questioned the farmer, he was led to a bank of earth near a brook. After a few minutes of digging, Gaffney produced the stock of a shotgun. He claimed that it had been discovered and discarded when the earth close to the brook had recently been excavated. Firth had the bank searched, and a second stock was found. 'My information was,' Firth wrote in his subsequent report, 'that the barrels of the guns had been hidden in a bog close by, and on my questioning, Gaffney reluctantly admitted that they might be there, but stated immediately afterwards that he knew nothing about them and could show us nothing further.'[10]

The army lieutenant decided that he would return at a later date and search the bog. Gaffney was not arrested, at least not immediately. On the same day, the British military raided and searched Keelan's own house, with the aim of providing Gaffney's aggrieved young farmhand with some credible cover. The transparent ruse did not work. The IRA moved rapidly. On 23 March, Keelan was kidnapped and brought to an 'unknown destination', in this instance a vacant house in Cormeen on land owned by Mullagh merchant P.J. McMahon, an active member of the Mullagh company of the IRA.

The British military combed north Meath and east Cavan for Keelan while he was being interrogated by the IRA in Cormeen. The operation included a raid on the Thomastown house of twenty-four-year-old Patrick Clarke, an IRA company captain. The Crown forces believed that Clarke – known locally as 'The Cock' for reasons that mercifully remain shrouded in the mists of time – had been involved in the abduction of Keelan. They were unable to question him about it, however, because Clarke had legged it, more formally expressed in the official report as '[he] broke out by a window at the back and made his escape across the fields. Two sentries posted at the rear of the house opened fire on him but missed.'[11] (On 29 March, Clarke gave himself up to the RIC in Navan.)

On 27 March, while Keelan was still being held incommunicado in Cormeen, John Gaffney was arrested and taken to Whitewood

House military barracks in Kilmainhamwood.[12] From there he was brought to Arbour Hill Prison in Dublin, where he would spend the next month.

It was as if the arrest of Gaffney acted as a trigger. On 28 March, Keelan was released, with a severe warning, by his IRA captors. In the words of Carnaross Volunteer Seán Farrelly, 'The IRA thought by giving him a fright he might realise the gravity of his behaviour… It was misplaced leniency. After his release he travelled the countryside with the Tans in their raids and brought them to the house in which he had been detained. They burned it to the ground.'[13]

The Crown forces – either Black and Tans or an Auxiliary unit temporarily based at Whitewood House – wasted no time in exacting revenge for the abduction of Patrick Keelan, now launched on a brief career as an army scout and 'identifier'. Within hours of his release, Keelan accompanied a raiding party of at least two cars and two lorries back to Cormeen. They broke into the McMahon house, searched it thoroughly with fatal consequences for most of the entirely non-combatant furniture, then attempted to burn the premises.

Fortunately, they did not tarry to admire their handiwork. After they had withdrawn, neighbours were able to extinguish the flames and save the house, though not before a hole about three metres in circumference had been burned in the roof. The damage could have been far more extensive – a number of bags containing hay were suspended from the ceiling.[14] Had those caught fire, Patrick McMahon would have been filing an application for more than the £400 damages that he claimed in Navan courthouse on 26 May 1921.*

---

* McMahon was awarded £330 in damages.

The compensation case involved a passing reference to the recent history of Cormeen, when the judge inquired, 'Are there any landless men round there?' McMahon responded euphemistically, 'Yes, there was a lot of trouble round here for land.'

Beyond that misleading hint of past transactions – the Black Hand Gang was mouldering in exile – there was no attempt made on either side to identify the raiders.[15] McMahon may well have felt it wise to gloss over the character of the would-be arsonists, for fear that the question of their motivation might invite bothersome inquiries from the bench about the recent usage of his unoccupied premises.

Patrick Keelan now dropped out of sight for three months, held in what amounted to protective custody in Whitewood House. While this was for his own safety, that end could just as easily have been achieved by affording him safe passage out of the county, or indeed the country. Instead, Keelan was made to earn his keep and accompanied Crown forces on a number of raids, as navigator and 'identifier', from April to the end of June. At which point, through frustration at his confinement, a bout of homesickness or both, he made a fatal error – he visited his family in Thomastown. Within hours, he was once again a prisoner of the IRA. This time there would be no slap on the wrist, no warning to be on good behaviour. Keelan had been only provisionally freed by the IRA. He had clearly violated his probation.

The Moynalty/Mullagh IRA now had a decision to make. Did Keelan's betrayal merit exile, a sanction familiar in an area so close to Cormeen, or was he such a threat to the Meath IRA that only execution would suffice? Given Keelan's hostile response to the IRA's initial display of clemency, one cannot imagine the local battalion command agonising for very long over their decision.

Patrick Keelan was probably dead within twenty-four hours of his second abduction.

3.

Thorough accounts of the minutiae of summary IRA executions are few and far between. Some members of the Collins hit team, known colloquially as The Squad, have left vivid and sanguinary details of their activities. The narrative dictated by Vinny Byrne to the Bureau of Military History, for example, is nauseatingly graphic in places.

An exception to IRA *omertà* is the comprehensive entry in the Leitrim IRA Brigade Activity Report detailing the shooting of John Harrison.* This reads rather like the conclusion of the Frank O'Connor short story 'Guests of the Nation', but with the humanity expunged.

Harrison, a fifty-three-year-old Methodist farmer from Drum-reilly,† died because he antagonised the Aughawillan company of the IRA's 2nd Leitrim battalion once too often. In October 1920

* Erroneously named John Harris throughout the report.
† Harrison's killing, and that of William Latimer (also a Leitrim Protestant), have been described as sectarian in nature, as have many other IRA killings, in Munster in particular. That may or may not be the case. It should however be pointed out that all the IRA executions of alleged spies in Cavan and Meath were of Roman Catholics. William Gordon, the only non-Catholic victim, was not shot for passing information to the security forces. In one instance in County Meath, for example, C.W. Chaloner, a Protestant ex-serviceman who had alerted the Crown forces to an IRA ambush, was neither shot nor exiled. His car was taken as a punishment for his infraction.

an IRA levy was imposed on farmers in the Aughawillan area, with proceeds intended for the purchase of arms and ammunition. Harrison refused to pay his £1, and when he persisted, a cow was taken from his farm by local IRA Volunteers in 'distraint'. In the process, the IRA 'bailiffs' came under fire from Harrison, who was disarmed and later agreed to pay the levy.

However, according to IRA sources, Harrison subsequently identified Volunteers of the local company in a letter to the Ballinamore RIC carried into town by his fifteen-year-old daughter Mary on 21/22 April 1921. Because the farmer and his family were being closely watched, Mary Harrison was stopped and searched by the IRA before she could complete her errand. The letter was found, and Harrison was shot dead that very night. Aughawillan Company Captain Thomas Smith left a detailed account of the murder of Harrison in a chilling section of the battalion's Brigade Activity Report.

Just before midnight on 21 April, the IRA unit surrounded Harrison's house and placed men at the front and rear entrances:

> We demanded admittance in the name of the IRA and he was so long, and making so much noise, we got suspicious of his movements. We kept banging at both doorways, when next a shot rang out and again two or three more. So I gave the order 'each man two rounds'. We smashed the windows... I called out to surrender or we would blow up his house. He surrendered, having put a short service rifle on the window, and about twenty rounds of ammunition. I asked him to open the door and he did so. John McGuire and Paddy Martin [got in] the back window at the same time. He begged us not to shoot him. I said we had to carry out our orders. We told him he had to come with us, we also told him he needed no coat. So, we brought him about

three hundred yards down towards the bog. I asked him was there any reason why he shouldn't be executed as he was both spying and informing. He never made an answer. The three men who fired the shots were Volunteer Patrick Martin... Volunteer James McTeigue... and Volunteer John McGuire. I myself, as Captain, placed a label with cord around his neck – 'Shot as spy and informer. Beware.'

Harrison was one of seventy-three IRA victims shot between January and April 1921 whose bodies were similarly adorned, as British intelligence operations began to catch up with those of their opponents and IRA paranoia intensified.[16] Even the scale of that slaughter, however, failed to match the 150 'official' reprisals carried out in the first six months of 1921 by Crown forces,[17] as the conflict entered its terminal phase.

The end of John Harrison's life was probably no different from that of most IRA execution victims (a couple were drowned rather than being shot), but the complete lack of any apparent misgivings in Smith's narrative makes his account all the more disturbing. It is hard to believe, whatever danger Harrison posed to the Leitrim IRA, that the men who killed him, and those who witnessed his execution, could have accomplished their task as callously as Smith's utter lack of contrition suggests in this unsettling narrative. They may not have been enduringly haunted by the memory of John Harrison; they may have rationalised their part in his execution. But they cannot have entirely banished him from their thoughts and nightmares.

In contrast, we have practically no information on the last day of Patrick Keelan's life. We know that his fate was sealed as rapidly as that of John Harrison. According to a British military log, he was 'taken from his home in the early hours of the morning of 2 July 1921'.[18] He was probably shot shortly after dusk that night.*

His abduction, like Harrison's, was witnessed by traumatised family members who could have had little doubt about the fate that lay in store for him. Did he, like John Harrison, offer spirited resistance? Was he armed? Or did he go quietly to his preordained fate?

Keelan's final hours were spent somewhere between a small labourer's cottage in Thomastown and Garryard Wood in Walterstown, about six kilometres as the crow flies, eight by road. Since it was barely a fortnight past midsummer, Keelan would have been kept under lock and key during the long hours of daylight on 2 July. It was not safe to begin moving him to Garryard until after sunset, at around 10 p.m. In making that journey under duress, he was brought in the direction of Carlanstown to the house of Kilbeg parish priest Father Swan. As in the case of Bryan Bradley a few months previously, he heard Keelan's final confession.

He was taken past the houses of neighbours who would have reacted to his death, in many instances, with brooding resentment. No one in Thomastown was going to argue with the IRA, but it was not as if revolutionary fervour had suddenly conferred the gift of infallibility upon the local Republican leadership. From the

---

* The military log records: 'At 02.00 a number of men visited the house of Patk. Keelan, Thomastown, Nobber and kidnapped his son who was detained for a day and subsequently released.' Sadly for Keelan, the second part of the entry was based on false information. The only source who suggested that Keelan received 'due process' in the form of an IRA court martial was Patrick O'Reilly in his BMH Witness statement (#1650), who recorded that 'he was tried by officers of the Dublin Brigade sent down from G.H.Q. He was found guilty and sentenced to be shot. The execution was duly carried out.' However, O'Reilly also attested that Keelan's re-arrest came 'within a few days' of his original abduction. The gap between the two events was three months.

perspective of many of those who had known him since child-
hood, Patrick Keelan was a harmless young man, 'slow' in one of
the many Irish euphemisms describing those of low educational
achievement. Openly visiting his family, with a Damoclean sword
suspended over his head, was either an act of bravado or the folly
of one unused to weighing consequences.

However, as far as the IRA was concerned, Keelan was fully
capable of jeopardising operations. A more disinterested court
martial, one not entirely drawn from the cadre to which he posed
a threat, might well have accepted the prevailing view that Patrick
Keelan was a simpleton and opted to exile him. But local exigencies
prevailed. He was to be shot, not 'sent away'.

The question now was: Who would be selected to perform this
unedifying task?

Did they draw lots? Did willing volunteers come forward? Or,
more likely, were three reluctant shooters, probably men unknown
to their victim, chosen from among the ranks and ordered to carry
out the repulsive task of shooting dead an unarmed youth?

One thing is clear: at least three of the men who ended the
life of Patrick Keelan had no personal axe to grind with him.
They had not been directly affected by his activities and there is
no evidence that they had played any part in his original abduction in March 1921. They were also blood relatives who, on that
inauspicious night of 2/3 July, would find themselves with blood
on their hands.

We do not know definitively, except in these three instances,
exactly who took part in the killing of Patrick Keelan in Garryard
Wood. Anecdotal evidence suggests that captain of the Carnaross
company, Patrick Clarke, who had escaped the British follow-
up raid in the wake of Keelan's initial abduction, and John 'The
Tinny' Smyth, captain of the Kilbeg company, were present or at

the very least involved in preparations for the execution.[19] They are reported to have recruited two young local boys to dig a grave in Garryard Wood.[20]

We can, however, clearly identify three of the actual participants: T.P. McKenna Jr., his brother John McKenna and their cousin Peter Clinton.

In his 1924 application for a military pension, T.P. McKenna could point to his lengthy involvement in the Volunteers, the IRA and the Civil War National Army to support his claim. His application lacks detail, however, when it comes to the specifics of that short but eventful military adventure. It is largely left to others to itemise the main features of a career that began in earnest in 1920 and ended with his demobilisation from the National Army as a colonel-commandant in March 1924. The impression one gets, based on the evidence of a number of referees – IRA officers with whom he served – is of a capable and diligent Volunteer entrusted with an unexpected level of responsibility for someone so young. From February 1921, aged only eighteen, he was Meath 3rd Brigade adjutant and commanded the Mullagh-based active service unit.

It is actually through one of T.P.'s senior IRA officers, David Smith, Meath 3rd Brigade quartermaster, that we can confirm the teenage Volunteer's involvement in the firing squad that took the life of Patrick Keelan. In a section relating to McKenna's service between 1 April and 11 July 1921, in response to the question 'What military services did the applicant render?', Smith wrote: 'Took part with ASU at Mullagh. Executed spy at Carlanstown.'

As it happens, Smith was one village out.* While Keelan was

* Though Walterstown is technically in the postal district of the more distant Carlanstown.

probably escorted to his place of execution through the village of Carlanstown, his life ended in the environs of the adjacent picture-perfect village of Moynalty. As brigade adjutant, T.P. McKenna, despite his youth – he was younger even than Keelan – was likely the highest-ranking IRA officer in Garryard Wood that night. He did not shirk his terrible responsibility.

Because it was the IRA habit to ape many of the military trappings of the Crown forces (down to organising itself into companies, battalions, brigades and, by 1921, divisions), it was not always the practice to despatch an alleged spy or informer with a single bullet to the head or heart. That was a ritual more familiar during the recent Northern Ireland 'Troubles'. To the 'Old' IRA, a firing squad was considered more appropriate and martial.

With its chronic lack of ammunition, however, Volunteer units could not afford the ten- or twelve-man firing squads of British military practice. As is clear from the execution of John Harrison, a three-man firing party was more common. So who were the other two members of the firing squad?

In the case of T.P.'s cousin Peter Clinton, it is apparent from his own military pension application that he was present at the killing of Keelan. In July 1921, he was a member of the New-castle battalion of the Meath IRA. In fleshing out his activities during the final phase of the War of Independence (April–July 1921), he wrote that he 'took part in the execution of a sentenced spy'.[21] Only one spy was killed by the IRA in north Meath during that period,* which puts Peter Clinton in Garryard

---

* John 'The Thatcher' Farrell was also killed at around this time, but that kill-ing took place near Athboy, in the southern part of the county and appears to have been an opportunistic rather than a sanctioned execution.

Wood on the night of 2/3 July 1921. His pension application, however, does not tell us if he was one of the men who fired the fatal shots.

There is no doubt whatsoever when it comes to the role played by John McKenna, Mullagh company quartermaster. While Garryard Wood was on the estate belonging to the Farrell family, it was also on the edge of the Walterstown land farmed by John McKenna. Was this the reason he was included in that sombre gathering of IRA loyalists? Or was he there in his capacity as an IRA quartermaster, one of whose functions was the squirrelling away of the weapons required for the task on hand? At least some of which had been smuggled to him by his cousin Rose, Peter Clinton's sister.

The first bald statement of John McKenna's presence in Garryard Wood on the night of 2/3 July comes in the particulars he laid out when he applied for a military pension in 1937. Here, in the slot covering the relevant time period, he points out that he was a 'member of party which executed enemy spy at Walterstown, Moynalty'. As in the case of Peter Clinton, that merely places him at the scene of the execution.

But there are two more revealing documents included in this file. Applicants under the terms of the 1934 Military Pensions Act were obliged to attend an interview before being considered for an award. They were asked a series of searching questions by representatives of an administration that, although it had expanded the scope of the 1924 Act to include female applicants and Republican veterans of the Civil War, was obliged by budgetary constraints to be as parsimonious as its predecessor. John McKenna was relatively expansive in his responses until it came to the issue of Keelan's execution. On that point, the exchanges were terse, and probably quite tense:

Q. You were in a good many ambushes that did not
   come off?
A. Yes.
Q. Execution of a spy?
A. Yes.
Q. Was it more than one?
A. Only one.
Q. Were you actually at the execution?
A. Yes.
Q. Who was he?
A. A man named Keelan.

The interviewer, displaying an unusual level of delicacy, then
passed on to matters that were not quite so raw without ascertaining precisely what part John McKenna had played in the
killing of the 'man named Keelan'.*

It is not until a full-blooded endorsement of John McKenna's
capabilities as an IRA Volunteer, in a covering letter from his
former O/C Thomas J. O'Reilly, that we finally get to the nub
of the matter. O'Reilly, in an effusive letter of reference, begins
by pointing out that 'on all occasions when specially good men
were required for IRA operations he was one of the men chosen
from the Batt[alion] to undertake the work'. He goes on to praise
McKenna's defiance at Corlat Bridge in the face of a Black and
Tan threat against his own life and his father's property, and his

* There is an interesting insight into the rationale behind the disbursement
of military pensions in John McKenna's file. A typed and unsigned memo
dated 2 June 1937, to the members of the advisory committee due to interview
McKenna later that day, directs them towards a preferred line of questioning.
The memo reads, 'This man's *best* [my italics] claim is being at the execution
of a spy … the rest is all ordinary activities.'

rebuffing of 'an offer by Mullagh people to supply materials for the work ... he refused to allow the work to be done'.

The sting is in the tail. In an effort to copper-fasten the legitimacy of John McKenna's application, O'Reilly wrote: '[John McKenna] was selected as a member of the firing squad and took his place in the execution of Keelan, an enemy spy, in 1921.'[22]

O'Reilly doesn't say whether he witnessed the killing, but as O/C of the 1st Battalion of the 3rd Meath Brigade,* whose authority extended from Mullagh in County Cavan to Nobber in County Meath, O'Reilly would have been *au fait* with all IRA activities within his section.

Even July nights can be chilly in the Irish north midlands. But in Garryard Wood on the night of 2/3 July 1921, a few hours after dusk, an altogether different chill descended on the McKenna brothers as they carried out their dismal task. At least Patrick Keelan was not required to dig his own grave, a small mercy in an often merciless conflict.

It is unlikely that either of the McKennas played any part in the decision that ended the young man's life. Both, however, played unsought-after roles in his death. Before Patrick Keelan was shot, on first sight of the upturned earth that had been dug as his grave, he begged his executioners that his body should instead be buried in consecrated ground.[23] That his wish was eventually granted had little to do with this fervent valedictory plea.

T.P. McKenna, sadly, only had a few more years left of his own life in which to come to terms with his role in the execution. John McKenna had to live with himself for more than half a century.

But first he was compelled to endure the sequel.

* Formerly the 4th Battalion, before the 1921 reorganisation.

4.

While Patrick Keelan lay undisturbed in his shallow grave in Garryard Wood, the Anglo-Irish War came to an end, a few days too late to save his life. After the Truce began, the two sides shadow-boxed, continued preparations for the inevitable resumption of hostilities, began to negotiate and then concluded a deal that did not match the expectations of a significant minority of Republicans. While Keelan's family pleaded for news about his fate and his whereabouts, Britain heaved a sigh of relief, withdrew its forces and then watched from a distance as a movement, never markedly monolithic, splintered into two unequal parts. Irishman slaughtered Irishman, something Keelan might have found ironic.

One of his executioners, T.P. McKenna, was encouraged by Seán Boylan to join him in transferring his allegiance to the newly formed army of the Irish Free State and defend the gains secured by Collins and Griffith in London. Patrick Clarke, another of the likely witnesses to Keelan's last moments, along with Meath IRA stalwarts like the Farrelly brothers (Pat and Seán) and Michael Hilliard, took the anti-Treaty side and participated in an eleven-month rearguard defence of the doomed Irish republic. Eleven months, and more than three thousand lost lives. It took three decades (1969–98) of internecine warfare during the Northern Ireland Troubles to rack up that many corpses.

John McKenna returned to the civilian life he had partially abandoned when he became an IRA Volunteer. He took no active part in the savage growing pains of the Irish Free State and was fortunate to live in a part of the country relatively untouched by civil conflict. This reprieve from barbarism was largely a consequence of a simple syllogism. Seán Boylan never wavered in his loyalty to Michael Collins. Therefore Boylan's overweening influence in the Meath IRA was used to recruit Volunteers to the pro-Treaty cause, or encourage neutrality among waverers. As a consequence, there was a relatively minor exodus of Meath Volunteers to the 'Irregulars'. Whereas nationally around two-thirds of IRA Volunteers actively opposed the Treaty, that proportion was almost inverted in Meath.*

With the end of the Civil War in May 1923, the new Irish Free State could begin to function, however hesitantly and ineffectually, as a working entity. Native trappings aside – token bilingualism being the most obvious – the template of governance simply mimicked much of that bequeathed to it by the unloved Crown administration. The afterbirth of revolution is bureaucracy. An inevitably prosaic administration replaced the lethal romantic poetry of guerrilla warfare.

The Keelan family did not allow much time for the new government to bed down before pressing its legitimate inquiries about the fate of the younger Patrick Keelan. In early January 1924, the secretary of the Ministry of Home Affairs received a letter from the family's solicitor, William Armstrong, demanding information about Keelan's fate. The letter is peppered with half-truths and inaccuracies – Armstrong was probably working off a highly subjective briefing from his clients – but still conveys the grief of the Keelan family and their desire for some finality.

Armstrong twice refers to Patrick Keelan as being fifteen years

---

* Take, for example, the 3rd Meath Brigade. Its Brigade Activity Report lists 27 companies and 765 active volunteers on 11 July 1921. By 1 July 1922, four of the companies had been disbanded (though two new companies had been created) and the number of members (i.e. anti-Treaty volunteers) had declined to 285 (Military Archives, MA/MSPC/RO/489, 1st Eastern Division, 3rd Brigade (Meath)).

old at the time of his abduction, and offers a highly client-centric narrative. In the solicitor's version of events, young Patrick Keelan was an innocent abroad ('a mere lad of fifteen years, apparently most inoffensive') who for no demonstrable reason was abducted consecutively by the IRA – 'armed men', to be precise – and the British military. Then, a few days after his return from the clutches of the army, the 'armed men' removed him from his home yet again on 2 July 1921. All this without any evident rationale.

'From that date,' wrote the solicitor plaintively, 'his father has never been able to trace his whereabouts. He fears that he has been killed in some manner but he would like to know if possible what has been the fate of his child.'[24]

The process that would end in Patrick Keelan Jr.'s final wish being granted began with a note from the office of the Home Affairs Minister to Garda Commissioner Eoin O'Duffy, request- ing that the police 'institute all possible inquiries into the matter and furnish a report'.[25] The Garda response, which painted a very different picture to that of William Armstrong's narrative of tragic teenage victimhood, came within a fortnight. After a brief outline of the circumstances of Patrick Keelan's death, there followed verification of his execution, confirmation that he was attended by a priest before his death – standard IRA operat- ing procedure – and that 'his remains have since been removed and interred in consecrated ground'. The clear implication was that the body had been exhumed and reburied shortly after his execution.

This, however, was not quite enough to satisfy the Ministry of Home Affairs. The secretary insisted on being told 'when young Keelan was disinterred and reburied and whether his father is aware this has been done & whether the facts are generally known or whether special enquiries had to be made by the police?'[26]

Those queries brought to light the story of the resurrection and removal of Patrick Keelan.

The Garda Commissioner's office did some commissioning of its own. The guardians of the peace in the nearest large town, Kells, were instructed to secure answers to the Ministry's questions. The Carnaross parish priest, Rev. Patrick Kelly, filled in some of the gaps. He was able to tell the police, because he had been recruited to legitimise the exhumation and removal, that Keelan's body had been moved on 2 January 1924, barely a week before the receipt of William Armstrong's letter. The removal had been kept secret, though one wonders at the coincidence of an exhumation followed so closely by a solicitor's inquiry. Did the Keelan family get wind of the reinterment of their son and apply for more information?

The official government response to William Armstrong, given the detailed knowledge now in the possession of the Ministry of Home Affairs, was sketchy and non-committal:

Although the information collected can only be described as very vague yet the main facts seem to be well established by local rumour. It appears that the boy was convicted as a spy in the Anglo-Irish war and executed about the 2nd or 3rd July 1921. It is also believed locally that his body has been buried in consecrated ground.[27]

And that was that. No expression of regret, no information beyond a vaguely articulated 'belief' that Keelan was now buried in a *bona fide* cemetery. The news cannot have offered much consolation to the family. The Free State government, despite shifting itself to make inquiries about the fate of Patrick Keelan, showed little compassion for the family of a 'convicted' collaborator.

In that respect, the Ministry of Home Affairs was hardly unique. In 1923 in Banagher, County Offaly, for example, locals boycotted a new cemetery designed to service the town. They demanded that a body buried there be removed, that of a man who had been 'shot as a spy'. Fuelling local animosity was the fact that he had been buried by the Black and Tans.[28] It took some time for the remains of almost one hundred 'disappeared' IRA victims of the War of Independence to be exhumed and reburied. Some bodies, for example Bryan Bradley and William Gordon in County Meath, are still missing a century after their deaths.

And there the posthumous fate of Patrick Keelan rested until 1931. By then the Ministry of Home Affairs was no more, rendered redundant by the creation of the Department of Justice in 1924. Patrick Keelan Sr., still seeking his own form of justice, had engaged a new legal representative and was in pursuit of financial compensation for the loss of his son. A letter from Patrick Mooney, a Kells solicitor ('also at Oldcastle and Clonmellon, Tuesdays'), on 23 March 1931 went on the offensive before the ink was dry on the salutation. Mooney indignantly denied the allegations made against Keelan Jr. of 'having given information to the British military. According to his father, and those who knew him best, it is asserted that he was not guilty of giving any information and in fact he had none to give.'

While the opening salvo hints at a certain level of local animus towards the IRA decision to kill Keelan, it was in reality a prelude to an application for compensation 'for the loss sustained by [Patrick Keelan Sr.] owing to the death of his son'.[29] This belated approach, almost a decade after Keelan's death and seven years after the confirmation of his execution, glossed over the fact that a successful claim had already been made by the Keelan family for their son's death, to the British government in 1925.[30] The Keelans had been awarded a meagre £175.* It is probably safe to assume that the approach for information on Patrick Keelan's fate made to the Ministry of Home Affairs in 1924 had been part of a trawl for evidence to validate that application.

The 1931 attempt by Patrick and Mary Keelan to extract some form of financial compensation from the government whose insurgent soldiers had killed their son quickly foundered. Four days after the initial approach, Mooney received a curt government response. An anonymous official advised the Kells solicitor that he had been 'directed by the Minister for Justice to express his regret that he has at his disposal no funds from which any compensation could be paid to the father of Mr. Patrick Keelan'. It was the only appearance of the word 'regret' in a correspondence stretching back over seven years.

Had he been compensated by the Free State government, Patrick Keelan Sr. would not have had very much time to enjoy the award. He died of heart failure in 1933 at the age of sixty-six. His wife Mary followed him in 1942, her death attributed to 'senile decay'; she was seventy-seven. At the time of both deaths, only one of their three sons, James, was still alive. There is no evidence that either of Patrick Keelan's parents were ever informed of his final resting place.

Where, then, was Patrick Keelan reburied?

The Garda file on his January 1924 reinterment offers no definitive information. For that, we must resort to rumour and anecdote.

---

* Contrast this with the sum of £350 granted to the father of executed British spy John Donohoe, or more than £1,800 awarded to Francis Dooner, whom the IRA attempted to kill on 26 March 1920 near Kilberry, County Meath.

5.

A few hundred metres outside the pretty village of Moynalty, County Meath, on the road to nearby Mullagh, lies the town's cemetery, a shrine dotted with tall cruciform monuments. In the midst of this garden of stone stands an impressive grave-marker reminiscent of the ancient Celtic crosses in the nearby Church of Ireland cemetery in Kells. Carved on its surface are scenes from the Bible. It is topped off with an image of the crucifixion of Christ. Like a marble sentinel, it guards an extensive plot, capable of retaining the mortal remains of a few dozen souls.

The plinth below the biblical imagery carries the names of more than twenty members of the McKenna family. Not all are buried below; some are simply memorialised there, their actual remains in many instances interred in Mullagh cemetery, a few kilometres to the west. A couple are buried much farther afield, in Argentina and the United States.

Some of those at rest in this small parcel of land are not even formally acknowledged. One corner of the plot, the south-western section, contains the remains of a number of deceased infants of the extended McKenna family.

Another unacknowledged resident, the late Patrick Keelan, may well occupy the opposite corner of the plot.

In January 1924, when Keelan's body was moved, few of those directly concerned with his execution could feasibly have been involved in his exhumation. T.P. McKenna was still serving in the National Army and was based in the Curragh. Patrick Clarke, if he was even present in Garryard Wood on the night of 2/3 July 1921, was a defeated soldier of the anti-Treaty IRA and would have been an unlikely collaborator in the gruesome reinterment.

But John McKenna had never left Walterstown. He was still farming land adjacent to Garryard Wood and must have had the location of Keelan's shallow grave etched on his consciousness, and his conscience. McKenna was an affable, decent, humane and religious man who bore no grudges and had no personal stake in the execution of Keelan. He had not been one of the young man's jailers, and had not been identified as an IRA Volunteer by Keelan during his twelve weeks of ad hoc service with the Crown forces. He had probably been chosen as an executioner for that very reason. It wasn't personal.

His Roman Catholic background and convictions might have disposed him to decline the assignment. But that would have been illogical. He had participated in numerous ambushes, albeit many of them aborted before the shooting began, where the clear intention was the taking of human life. He was a soldier and this was a war; he had his orders. The parish priest of Kilbeg had in effect given his *imprimatur* to the legitimacy of the execution. Father Swan had made his own decision when Keelan was brought to him for absolution. He may well have remonstrated with the executioners, but he did nothing to prevent the execution.

Those same Catholic beliefs made John McKenna acutely aware of the importance to his co-religionists of interment in properly consecrated ground. He may have been ordered to participate in the killing of Patrick Keelan, but he willingly volunteered to take part in the grim task of exhuming a three-year-old corpse and giving his erstwhile victim a decent, albeit covert, burial in hallowed ground.

That, at any rate, is the understanding of some of his surviving children. Although oblivious, until the October 2019 online publication of John McKenna's Military Service Pension application, of their father's role in the death of Patrick Keelan, there was some awareness among family members of his involvement in the removal of Keelan's remains to a nearby cemetery.

But where was Patrick Keelan buried after being taken from his temporary grave in Garryard Wood?

This is where anecdotal evidence and surmise take over, sprinkled with a dash of logic. The mortal remains of Patrick Keelan were surreptitiously moved in the early hours of a cold, dark January morning. While there was a priest in attendance to perform the appropriate rites, there was no hearse and no mourners. Discretion and pragmatism dictated that the body be moved as expeditiously as possible. The closest graveyard was Moynalty cemetery, less than two kilometres away.

The exhumation of a body by medical specialists, accustomed to death and decomposition, is an arduous enough task. To those unfamiliar with the sight, feel and stench of a lightly shrouded human corpse that has been in direct contact with the earth for three years, it must have been thoroughly nauseating. Nothing remained of the humanity of Patrick Keelan. The task in hand was to exhume his body, move it as quickly as possible and reinter it before daylight. Supervising the transfer of a decomposing corpse for any longer than it takes to travel the short distance from Garryard to Moynalty is unimaginable. Indirect anecdotal evidence, and common sense, indicate Moynalty cemetery as journey's end.

The involvement of John McKenna in the transfer of Patrick Keelan's body further foreshortens the identification of the specific destination. Rather than reburying him in some remote part of Moynalty cemetery where his body would inevitably be discovered sooner or later, it made far more sense to inter his remains in the McKenna family plot.

Many years later, visiting that communal grave with a companion, John McKenna was eager to point out to the visitor where precisely certain family remains were positioned. After the guided tour, his companion inquired whether anyone was buried in the north-east corner of the plot. 'That belongs to someone else,' John responded, politely shutting down any further conversation on the subject.

Without the gratuitous and intrusive use of ground-penetrating radar, which can detect bodies up to a depth of two metres, we will never know for certain if Patrick Keelan was afforded a final resting place by one of the men responsible for his death. John McKenna went to his own grave without ever speaking in any detail to his family about the unnerving and repulsive task he was asked to perform on the night of 2 January 1924.

Had he ever chosen to discuss that experience, and its tragic prelude, he would have astonished anyone who had the good fortune to know him. No one even vaguely acquainted with John McKenna would have deemed him capable of taking a human life. The same was true of his brother T.P., a would-be doctor, and their cousin Peter Clinton. That all three were involved in the death of a young man, even one whose activities had put the lives of some of their comrades in jeopardy, tells us much about the true nature of the ugly wars that traumatised and divided Ireland a century ago.

The harrowing experience of the executioners of Patrick Keelan, the indescribable suffering of his own family, the hostility of neighbours who argued that a lesser punishment was more appropriate to Keelan's crimes – all were replicated in dozens of similar slayings from Soloheadbeg to Ballyseedy between 1919 and 1923.

There is a personal footnote to the story of the exhumation and reinterment of Patrick Keelan. While researching this volume, the writer discovered that the McKenna family plot also contains the remains of his own brother and sister.

In 1941, twenty-one-year-old Máire Dungan gave birth, prematurely, to her first children, a boy and a girl. Tragically, despite receiving medical care from her own father, T.P. O'Reilly, county medical officer for Cavan, both died within days of their birth. Her mother, the Mary Theresa 'May' (McKenna) O'Reilly lionised in the prologue of this book, took over responsibility for the disposal of the remains of the two infant children from her stricken daughter. They were quietly buried in the final resting place with which she was most familiar: the McKenna family plot in Moynalty cemetery.

It is likely that they rest within a few metres of a young man who was shot dead twenty years before by two brothers of their devastated grandmother.[31]

9

Argentina

'If wars were won and lost by fighting, the Irish war,
like most others, should have been ruled a draw
by repetition of moves.'

David Fitzpatrick, *Politics and Irish Life, 1913–1921*[1]

'Cruel, humourless, hard, utterly wanting in sense
of proportion, but often full of perverted poetry and
drunk with rhetoric – a hideous, untameable breed
had been engendered… very notably among the
sullen murderous hobbledehoys in Ireland.'

McGillivray of Scotland Yard to Richard Hannay
in John Buchan's *The Three Hostages*[2]

I.

The psychological no man's land between stalemate and checkmate in the Anglo-Irish War ('a series of small localised campaigns, rather than a nationwide struggle')[3] was not unlike much of the physical topography of the so-called Great War itself. It was undulating, could slope upwards disconcertingly, was pitted with shell holes and unexploded ordnance, and even if you managed to negotiate the distance between the trenches you were faced with impenetrable barbed wire defences as you approached your objective.

Neither side in the Anglo-Irish War managed the passage successfully. With outright victory beyond the compass of either combatant, the question was what to do when the whole affair settled into a lethal stalemate. The British military leadership might have contended right up to the cessation of hostilities that, given sufficient resources, their forces had the capacity to overwhelm the IRA. While this assertion has some military validity, it has little actual relevance. In defeat or stasis, generals like to maintain that they have been obliged by politicians to fight with one hand tied behind their backs. In Ireland there were compelling reasons for restraint – if one can characterise the conduct of the Black and Tans and the Auxiliaries as restrained.

Everyone loves a David versus Goliath story, as long as they are permitted to follow the details. This means the confrontation between the giant soldier and the boy with the slingshot must be amenable to journalistic coverage. The Anglo-Irish conflict, unlike simultaneous colonial struggles being managed by British imperial forces, was but a three-hour boat journey from Liverpool. It was deprecated by an Irish-American population whose country's foreign correspondents were disinclined to accept British press releases at face value, and wanted to see what was going on for themselves.

The war was never sufficiently out of sight or mind to be conducted with gloves off. There was no prospect of Boer War-style civilian concentration camps. Croke Park on Bloody Sunday was a pale sequel to Amritsar. So if the generals (military and civil) couldn't do the job without attracting a little too much adverse publicity, then political compromise was always on the cards.

East Cork flying column commander Tom Barry was well off the mark when he wrote in his memoirs that the IRA had 'humiliated British military power', but he was a few degrees closer to the truth when he added, '[The IRA]... caused the name of Britain to stink in the nostrils of all decent peoples, and inflicted sufficient casualties on their soldiers to seriously disturb a government finding it difficult to supply reinforcements.'[4]

As the body count rose, it became more difficult for both sides to continue. For the IRA, because its potential fighting force numbered only in the hundreds, a function of the capacity to supply them with arms and ammunition. For the Liberal-Conservative coalition government, because British lives were being lost in an obscene struggle that few voters understood or much cared about, and which was causing the administration pointless embarrassment.

MILITARY FATALITIES

	Crown forces	IRA
January–June 1920	44	32
July–December 1920	171	228
January–11 July 1921	324	182
TOTAL	539	442[5]

For the IRA, a draw (despite a slight advantage in the grisly statistics above) was always a satisfactory result. Its capacity to sustain the insurrection indefinitely was waning as it continued. By the middle of 1921, 'The flying columns had become little more than fragmented bands of armed men intent on defending themselves against all outsiders.'[6] In retrospect, the militarily injudicious assault on the Custom House in Dublin on 25 May 1921 looks like a counterintuitive invitation to talks.

For the Crown forces, there was no definitive version of victory anyway. Both sides settled for stalemate, though, truth be told, most of the combatants saw the post-Truce period as merely a lull in proceedings. The safety curtain might have descended, but the second act was much anticipated.

That it never happened was partly attributable to the powerful negotiating position of the British government and partly to the exhaustion of the IRA. When Lloyd George promised 'immediate and terrible war' to a browbeaten Irish delegation in London in December 1922, the Sinn Féin plenipotentiaries knew that with an imaginative transfer of troops from the other colonial wars still in progress, the British prime minister could back up his threat. Granted, it might take a while to move sufficient military units to Ireland and to recruit more willing British mercenaries to restock the Tans and the Auxies, so 'immediate' could prove problematic, but no one doubted 'terrible'. They had already lived through it.

But while Collins, Griffith et al fumbled their way towards an agreement in London, back in Ireland both sides carried on more or less as usual, though they were no longer killing each other. The British army, the Black and Tans and the Auxiliaries stayed exactly where they were. The ranks of the IRA were swollen with new recruits, the much-maligned Trucileers – late-flowering worthies who, if hostilities were ever to recommence, would probably melt away like snow under the breath of a blowtorch.

Intelligence never sleeps, even if the troops have been (temporarily) stood down. Reports sent to GHQ from the 1st Eastern division and instructions coming in the opposite direction suggest that IRA covert surveillance, if anything, intensified during the Truce. Under observation were enemy agents, enemy post offices and railway stations (where stationmasters were classified as 'working' or 'pro-British'), as well as those highly suspect establishments: golf, tennis and cricket clubs. There, the names of active members were carefully noted in IRA intelligence reports.

The movements and transfers of individual RIC men were closely monitored and reported on in despatches to the divisional I/O, as were those of anyone who associated with members of the force, including local women. A report from Meath 4th Brigade, for example, highlighted that:

> Miss Nixon, Post Office, Ballivor, is frequently visited by Auxiliaries from Trim, entertaining them and attends dances with them in Trim. Miss Parsons entertains Auxiliaries from Trim and is seen frequently in company in public with them. Miss Gallagher, Delvin, is frequently visited by police from Castlepollard and remains in conversation with them for some time... Anna Lynch, Athboy, daughter of postman there, is keeping company with police and is very often looking for information concerning Volunteers.[7]

All four women were listed as enemy agents. Had hostilities erupted again, they might have been subjected to some form of public humiliation, as in the case of the two young Navan women whose hair was shorn for 'walking out' with members of the Crown forces (Chapter 8). Or would they have shared the fate of the more aristocratic Mrs Mary Lindsay, executed in Cork along with her chauffeur James Clarke for passing information to the Crown forces on an IRA ambush earlier that year?

Raphael McKenna was as busy as ever during the Truce. As 3rd Brigade intelligence officer, he continued to assess the reports of battalion I/Os and pass on any relevant information to his cousin the 1st (Eastern) Division spymaster, a rehabilitated Patrick Clinton who had happily surrendered his position as adjutant. On 6 December 1921, three days after the signing of the Treaty, Clinton submitted a report to GHQ in which he evaluated the capabilities of his brigade I/Os. His assessment of Raphael McKenna's performance was positive, and demonstrated that the IRA was taking advantage of the military respite to beef up intelligence resources against a renewal of hostilities.

McKenna, despite the implications of the damage to his car, appears to have mysteriously retained his ability to charm members of the Crown forces into believing he was on their side. His cousin reported that:

> This officer has built up a very fine system in his area and is in close touch with the enemy stations of Oldcastle (Military), Virginia (Military and Police) and Baileborough (Police). He has not been very successful in this respect in Kells and Nobber. The Post Offices of Kells and Oldcastle are tapped but nothing can be done in Baileborough owing to the attitude of the officials who are 'Orange'.[8]

Supplied with a detailed questionnaire which sought troop, RIC and Auxiliary numbers, as well as the identities of suspected enemy agents, Raphael McKenna proved to be a talented information gatherer. His October 1921 report is neatly typed (most others are handwritten), contains comprehensive information on the workings of the RIC, post office and local railway stations, and identifies a number of loyalist men 'drilling under the supervision of the enemy RIC and are believed to be in possession of arms'. Eight names are listed, 'all residing at Kells'. One assumes that if it became necessary to discuss their apostasy with any of the men concerned, Raphael McKenna would have had no difficulty in coming up with home addresses at which those uncomfortable interviews could take place.

Reports of the induction of sympathetic locals to the unionist cause possibly reflects a tardy effort – it began only in June 1921 – on the part of Dublin Castle to recruit a citizen militia to engage with the IRA, not unlike the notorious Special Constabulary already functioning in Northern Ireland. The failure to do so before then reflected a misapprehension that committed loyalism did not exist south of a line stretching from Sligo to Dundalk.[9] It should come as no particular surprise that there were sufficient loyalists left in the area to be of potential assistance to the RIC should the Truce be short-lived. After all, Kells had sustained a corps of the UVF in 1913–14 which drilled and engaged in rifle practice on the estate of Lord Headfort.[10]

Special mention is then made of two other men, Thomas Weir (see Chapter 7) and Patrick Reynolds. The former was 'known to have gone out with an enemy raiding party, masked and carrying a revolver'; the latter was 'known to have accompanied [an] enemy raiding party for the purpose of identifying members of the IRA and other wanted men'.[11] Given the consequences for Patrick Keelan for committing similar offences, it was only the restraint imposed by the Truce that protected Weir and Reynolds from sharing his fate. Had it broken down, both would have been top of the IRA list of execution/assassination targets.

As Raphael McKenna continued to gather worthwhile intelligence for the anticipated resumption of the shooting war, his brothers, T.P. and John McKenna, remained on alert. They continued to drill, and like most IRA activists watched and waited while treaty negotiations drifted towards their turbulent conclusion. When the agreement brought home and championed by Collins and Griffith was rejected by the bulk of the men 'under arms' but accepted by a majority of elected deputies in Dáil Éireann, all four McKenna brothers elected to side with Collins.

In doing so, they *ipso facto* 'took up arms in 1922 in an effort to disestablish the Republic', according to one of their erstwhile comrades who opposed the Treaty.[12] This, however, was literally true only in the case of T.P. McKenna, who wore the uniform of the National Army and played a part, largely at the behest of Seán Boylan, in the Civil War that followed within a few months of the crucial January 1921 Treaty vote. John and Raphael McKenna returned to farming and the family businesses in Mullagh, and took no part in the fraternal struggle that lit bonfires which would not be doused for decades.

John McKenna's final involvement in the IRA campaign came in an 'abortive attack' (his own words)[13] on the RIC barracks in Kingscourt, County Cavan. This took place minutes before the 11 July Truce came into effect and smacks of a conscious effort on the part of the Meath IRA to have the distinction of launching the final operation of the Anglo-Irish War. A car approached Kingscourt from Kilmainhamwood, took a pot shot at the nearest available Auxie and didn't bother to stop and see if the bullet had found its target. It hadn't.[14]

It was something of a metaphor for a lacklustre military

campaign that, although it had tied down a respectable number of British troops* and a significant force of Auxiliaries,† was never going to inspire any triumphalist Republican ballads.

John McKenna's subsequent demobilisation can only have exacerbated the process of coming to terms with the ghost of Patrick Keelan. Seán Boylan's deputy, Séamus Finn, recognised in his Bureau of Military History Witness Statement just how difficult it was for an ordinary farmer, postman or labourer to participate in the killing of a farmer, a postman or a labourer:

> They were the hardest operations which our men were asked to carry out and taxed their courage and discipline to the limit. For obvious reasons I cannot pay tribute in this work to these men, but they can feel sure that their efforts saved the liberty and the lives of many of their comrades.[15]

It was scant consolation for those ordered to pull the trigger.

The allegiance of John's younger brother T.P., a fellow participant in the killing of Keelan, was almost immediately transferred to the army of the Irish Free State. In his case, any unnerving

---

* Soldiers of the 1st Battalion South Wales Borderers, numbering 840 in June 1920 and down to 617 in October 1921, were stationed in Meath (Ultan Courtney, 'The War of Independence in County Meath, 1916–1921', p.675 in Arlene Crampsie and Francis Ludlow, *Meath: History and Society – Interdisciplinary Essays on the History of an Irish County* (Dublin, 2015)).

† A one hundred-strong Auxiliary unit was stationed permanently in the county from 6 August 1920 to 17 January 1922 (Ernest McCall, *The First Anti-Terrorist Unit: The Auxiliary Division, RIC*). In October 1920, nine companies of Auxiliaries were despatched to designated 'hot spots' around the country – Clare, Cork, Dublin, Galway, Kerry, Kilkenny, Limerick, Mayo… and Meath. The Meath IRA did enough to ensure that the Auxiliaries based in Trim stayed there for the duration of the conflict.

thoughts about Garryard Wood were partially subsumed in the confusion of a new and even viler conflict. John McKenna, however, accompanied by his War of Independence demons, returned to the relative banality of a shop in Mullagh and a farm in Walterstown. That he somehow managed to rationalise his experience of the night of 3 July 1921 was partly attributable to his stoicism and his phlegmatic personality.

Furthermore, the savagery and hideous brutality on both sides in the Civil War put his own actions into perspective. Measured against atrocities like the massacre of eight anti-Treaty soldiers at Ballyseedy in County Kerry in March 1923, the IRA-sanctioned killing of a persistent collaborator would have seemed much less significant.

While John McKenna managed to cope with whatever guilt he might have felt, all the while presenting a tranquil face to the outside world, others were not so fortunate.

In the commemoration – some even use the term celebration – of the centenary of the Anglo-Irish War, tales of heroism, quiet endurance and self-sacrifice are front and centre. What is often overlooked is the psychological impact on many of the young protagonists of direct association with an ugly rural guerrilla war twinned with an equally vicious urban insurgency. The psychological casualties lurking among the voluminous Military Service Pension applications often tell a story at variance with the tales of derring-do in the files of the Bureau of Military History.

Take just two examples of Volunteers who survived their tilt at the British Empire, after a fashion. They took the lives of others, but at a huge cost to themselves.

James Paul Norton was twenty years of age when he took part in the Bloody Sunday shooting of three alleged British Intelligence officers on Morehampton Road in Donnybrook, Dublin, two of whom died in the hail of bullets. The killings took place 'in the presence of their screaming wives and children'. In July 1921, Norton was jailed for fifteen years for possession of a revolver and was badly mistreated by the prison authorities in Mountjoy – where he went on hunger strike – and Dartmoor. He was released from prison in England in January 1922 under the terms of the general amnesty.

The effects of his IRA service, and the abuse suffered during his incarcerations, led to a rapid decline in his mental health and the onset of 'neurasthenia and mental debility'.[16] An unsigned statement in Norton's application for a disability pension, obviously written by a medical expert, reveals the permanent psychological damage suffered by the young IRA Volunteer:

Complete mental breakdown was reached by July 1921 when [the] applicant single-handed, and without orders, got in the middle of a roadway at the Custom House, armed with a revolver [and] attempted to capture a tender of British troops, armed and carrying full war equipment. [The] applicant was… a complete mental wreck as a result of the harsh treatment he received in Dartmoor prison.[17]

Norton passed much of the rest of his life in and out of mental institutions in Britain and Ireland, some of that time spent as a ward of court, and died in Grangegorman Mental Hospital on 15 December 1974.[18]

Also at the sharp end of the Bloody Sunday killings and many additional 'markings' on behalf of IRA Intelligence was young Charles Dalton, who had preceded his more illustrious brother Emmet into the Volunteers in 1917, at the age of fourteen. His 1950 Bureau of Military History Witness Statement[19] and his account of his brief military career in a 1929 memoir[20] are cogent, lucid and betray no frailties.

However, in a disability pension application submitted in May 1940 by his wife Theresa, we see a very different Charlie Dalton, a man whose War of Independence experience left him deeply psychologically scarred. It is clear from a covering letter sent by the medical superintendent of St Patrick's Mental Hospital, dated 3 April 1941, that Dalton was dangerously paranoid. He had been an inmate of St Patrick's since November 1938.

The letter informed the referees in his case that Dalton was 'undergoing treatment for a serious form of mental breakdown... He is acutely hallucinated – hearing voices which accuse him of murder. In my opinion the nature of Mr. Dalton's delusions and hallucinations clearly point to his experiences in the Irish War as the cause of his mental breakdown.'

Also included in the file is a letter from another mental health professional, Dr Harry Lee Parker, who is equally unambiguous in his assessment of Dalton's condition:

> Charles F. Dalton is at present completely and permanently insane. He has delusions of being shot, executed and that all around him are conspiring to kill him. He hears voices urging his destruction and his whole delusional state is definitely linked up with his previous military experiences. In my opinion such experiences this man has had during military service and particularly his own active part have preyed on his mind and conscience so that in the following years he has gradually lost his reason. I must therefore unequivocally attribute his present state to his military service and I consider him totally and permanently disabled.

Dalton's file includes an extraordinary six-page letter from future Taoiseach Seán Lemass, also a youthful participant in the carnage of Bloody Sunday. The two young men hunkered down in the same safe house on the night of 21 November 1920. In his letter to Dalton's wife, Lemass describes him as having 'become unnerved by his experiences of the morning':

> During that night he was, on occasions, inclined to be hysterical. I recollect that a tap in the dispensary was leaking and making a gurgling noise. This noise apparently reminded your husband of a similar noise he had heard when the four men were shot. He shouted to us several times to stop the noise of the tap and it was with difficulty that he was quietened.

So profound was Dalton's paranoia that when he was admitted to a Dublin nursing home in the 1930s, he would agree to occupy his room only if two friends (one of whom was former IRA intelligence officer Frank Saurin) would stand outside acting as armed guards. He even insisted on being shown their guns before he acquiesced. In March 1942, Dalton, then a resident of Grangegorman Mental Hospital, became a ward of court. In 1944, he was sufficiently recovered to be discharged from wardship and from Grangegorman. However, like Norton, he died in 1974 in a mental institution, in his case St Patrick's Hospital.

There were no screaming children in Garryard Wood in the early hours of the morning of 3 July, just Patrick Keelan's quiet despair at the sight of his final resting place. Unlike James Paul Norton and Charlie Dalton, John McKenna was a mature man, not a schoolboy engaged to do an executioner's work. He was never, as far as is known, obliged to seek professional help in coping with his demons. But he continued to live a short distance from the surviving members of the family of the man he, his brother and his cousin had killed. If he was forced to endure even a fraction of the mental torment of Norton and Dalton – and he must have been – he never showed any evidence of it. He was either reconciled or resilient.

2.

Without firing a shot, submitting an intelligence report or supervising a single active service unit training exercise, Justin McKenna had still contrived to become the only one of four activist brothers to spend any time in prison during the War of Independence. His release from the Rath camp in the Curragh, along with a dozen fellow detainees, was owed to his election (unopposed) as a Sinn Féin MP for the five-seat Louth-Meath constituency of the House of Commons of Southern Ireland, a ghostly assembly that never functioned and rapidly morphed into the Second Dáil. This was a body less circumscribed than its suppressed predecessor, and once the July Truce had taken hold, it was possible for the Dáil to meet openly and more frequently.

It did so, however, without any oratorical flourishes from Justin Charles McKenna. He certainly attended the first sitting of the Second Dáil on 16 August 1921, but is not recorded as having made a single verbal contribution to that body's proceedings in an undistinguished tenure that lasted barely a year. There have been shorter Dáil careers – he was elected on 24 May 1921 and defeated in his bid for re-election on 16 June 1922 – but few that can have been so consumed by silence.

Justin did manage, despite his reticence, to play a small but significant part in the creation of the Irish Free State. He had a bird's eye view – one not always afforded the Irish electorate, because some of the sessions were held *in camera* – of the pivotal and divisive debates on the Anglo-Irish Treaty brought back from London by the ill-designated 'plenipotentiaries'. Collins, Griffith et al had full power ('plenus' = full and 'potens' = power) to conclude a treaty, provided they referred the final document back to de Valera and the uncompromising Stack and Brugha in Dublin. It was a very Irish definition of the word.

The debates on the Anglo-Irish Treaty began on 14 December 1921 and culminated in a vote on 7 January 1922. Justin McKenna witnessed bitter exchanges in the chamber. These reflected and amplified some of the long-standing rivalries and heretofore veiled animosities between leading members of Sinn Féin. The toxic bad blood between Michael Collins and Cathal Brugha was but the most blatant example. McKenna might have blanched when Arthur Griffith snarled (to considerable applause) at Erskine Childers with the cruel jibe 'I will not reply to any Englishman in this Dáil.'[21]

Oddly, Justin would have heard little use of the Irish language, or indeed much discussion of the issue of partition. Most of the mutual antipathy revolved around Ireland's newly acquired status as a dominion, secured after the adamant refusal of the British side to engage in negotiation on the establishment of an Irish republic. The issue of the autonomy of Ulster was largely bypassed. The Anglo-Irish Treaty was narrowly accepted by a vote of 64–57, which both reflected and anticipated the visceral ruptures that lay ahead.

But before casting his vote in favour of the Treaty, Justin McKenna was forced to make a bold personal decision and abandon a long-standing friendship.

As an apprentice solicitor in Dublin during the Great War, McKenna had befriended a fellow student from Mayo named Patrick J. Ruttledge. Both had participated in Law Society apprentice debates before qualifying to practise and returning to their respective home towns of Ballina and Mullagh. Justin later established a legal practice in Kells. During the War of Independence Ruttledge was active in the Mayo IRA, and in 1921 he was elected as a TD for Mayo North and West. During Dáil sessions he renewed his old friendship with the Cavan man.

Ruttledge, an opponent of the Treaty, sought to convince Justin McKenna to oppose Collins and Griffith in the critical debates, and to support instead the approach adopted by Éamon de Valera, who led the anti-Treaty cause in the Dáil. McKenna, however, like most of his immediate and extended family,* chose to support the majority. He did so, however, under considerable duress. The pressure, physical as well as psychological, came directly from Ruttledge.

The Treaty division was an alphabetical, open roll call vote. As each TD's name was called, he or she stood and indicated their vote on the motion to adopt the deal brought back from London, calling out 'Tá' to signify approval or 'Níl' to register dissent. Just as it came to Justin McKenna's turn to vote, he felt a sharp pressure exerted on his side. He looked down to see a bulge in Ruttledge's jacket pocket pressing into his lower ribs. Ruttledge leaned in and whispered, 'Níl.'

The political decision that day was potentially transformative, but Justin McKenna was confronted with a decision that could prove personally and immediately life-changing. Was Ruttledge bluffing? Would he really carry out his threat in such a public forum, where he was unlikely to be the only TD carrying a gun? Was he even really armed? Justin stood, took a deep breath, intoned

---

* A Mullagh cousin, twenty-five-year-old John Alphonsus ('Fonsie') McKenna, took the anti-Treaty side in the Civil War.

a resonant 'Tá' and sat down. The two men never spoke again, and Justin McKenna never discovered whether Ruttledge's jacket pocket contained a gun or an index finger.

Within months of the harrowing Sinn Féin rupture over the Treaty, a fortnight before the attack on the Four Courts that began the Civil War, Justin McKenna was obliged to face the electorate in person for the first time. The Anglo-Irish Treaty called for a general election to a constituent assembly that would establish the Irish Free State. Justin McKenna, elected unopposed and *in absentia* the previous year, now went before his Louth-Meath constituents and asked them to return him to the Third Dáil.

The people of Louth-Meath, a five-seater which included Kells, where he now lived and practised law, declined the invitation. He was the only one of the six contenders to lose out in a constituency where the sole Labour candidate, Cathal O'Shannon, topped the poll with a whopping 38.3% of the vote, as against the 6% (2,135 first preferences) garnered by Justin McKenna. A member of the London delegation, Eamon Duggan, was the leading Sinn Féin pro-Treaty candidate with just under 20% of the total valid poll.

Thus ended Justin McKenna's brief, significant, eventful but unfulfilled political career. He never came within arm's length of a husting thereafter. He resumed the vocation from which many an Irish political career has been launched, as a country solicitor consoling himself with conveyancing, boundary disputes and civil litigation, leavened with occasional prosecutorial work as Meath's first state solicitor.

He died on 23 March 1950 at the hardly advanced age of fifty-three. Testifying to the status he had achieved by then, his funeral was described by the *Meath Chronicle* in a three-column front-page obituary as 'the largest seen in Meath for years'.[22] If a fraction of those who walked behind his coffin in 1950 had voted for him in 1922, he might at least have finally troubled the Leinster House stenographers.

Two years later, he was followed to the grave by would-be nemesis P.J. Ruttledge. The Mayo man had stayed the political course with which Justin McKenna had merely flirted. Wounded in Civil War fighting alongside other unappeased Republicans, Ruttledge then served as a Fianna Fáil minister in three government departments between 1932 and 1941. While serving as Minister for Justice, the man who had threatened or tricked Justin McKenna during the vote on the Treaty presided over the execution of three members of the IRA, an organisation now posing a direct threat to the administration of Éamon de Valera. Ruttledge too had clearly moved on.

3.

After July 1921, there were no more killings involving a Clinton or a McKenna. But there was one more death.

Despite the Meath Brigade's attempt at 11.55 a.m. on 11 July in Kingscourt to end the struggle with the British Empire with a belated bang rather than an undistinguished whimper, it would be ridiculous to suggest the war effort in the Royal County bears comparison with that of Cork, Clare, Tipperary or Dublin. Even the late Oliver Coogan, in his exhaustive account of the War of Independence in the county, *Politics and War in Meath 1913–23*, recognised in a scathing conclusion that:

> If some Volunteer companies had devoted as much energy and
> time to harassing enemy forces as they did towards rooting out
> and executing spies, real or imagined, then they might have taken

a lot of the pressure off some of their overworked colleagues elsewhere in the country.[23]

The Volunteer journal *An tÓglach* had counselled military caution in January 1920, a time when the phony war cycle was just ending, observing that 'it is an axiom of warfare that one must reserve one's strength in order to strike when and where one is able to do so most effectively'.[24] The Cavan-Meath IRA took that injunction a shade too literally.

Its limited potency can best be gauged by the fact that martial law, a badge of honour in Munster and other troubled regions, was not applied to Meath. There are of course extenuating circumstances. It has been suggested that the landscape of the county was too flat and featureless for the conduct of an aggressive guerrilla campaign.[25] The available woodland might have offered sufficient camouflage for the execution and burial of spies and informers, but it was not adequate for the shelter and concealment of a crack active service unit. It has also been pointed out that the Meath IRA was inadequately armed, though this was a shortcoming it shared with most other IRA brigades.

Of more concern, especially to units in the eastern part of the county, may have been the proximity of one of the major training bases of the Black and Tans in Gormanstown, a village on the small stretch of coastline within the county's borders. This offered a major deterrent to local activism. When the Gormanstown Tans were provoked into retaliatory action by the killing of two RIC men in Balbriggan in north County Dublin on 21 September 1920, their lethal response – the beating to death of two IRA Volunteers and the destruction of more than fifty buildings in the town – served as an earnest reminder of their potential for chaos. Southern parts of Meath were also dangerously close to the Curragh military base, and the entire county was only a short Crossley tender ride from the armed camp of Dublin.

Ironically, the most placid part of the county was Seán Boylan's own area around Dunboyne. There was a compelling reason for this. Because of the town's proximity to the capital, it was often visited by members of the Dublin IRA leadership in need of rest and recuperation from the strain of conducting a mutual terror campaign at close quarters with the Crown forces, in particular with the dreaded F company of the Auxiliaries, based in Dublin Castle. Boylan made sure that operations around Dunboyne were kept to a minimum, to ensure that follow-up search operations did not accidentally bring about the discovery and arrest of members of the Dublin IRA leadership cadre.[26]

Young T.P. McKenna could hardly be blamed for the relative inactivity of the Meath IRA, as one of the few Cavan-Meath IRA figures who functioned as a 'whole time active service officer'.[27] Arguably, he should also be counted among the casualties of the conflict.

Medically, he died after a long struggle against the Irish twentieth-century scourge, the so-called 'silent killer' of tuberculosis. Better known by its more graphic name, consumption, it consumed individuals, devoured families and feasted on the Irish population for generations. In the early years of the century in the crowded tenements of Dublin, it claimed thousands of victims annually.

But it did not confine its ravages to the cities; the Irish country-side was also riddled with those who succumbed to the deadly bacillus. Long exposure to the rigours of that countryside while on the run had weakened T.P.'s constitution and left him susceptible to the ravages of a disease that was no respecter of youth.

Although he was part of the first cohort of IRA Volunteers

to join the Irish Free State Army – around 7,000 in all, greatly outnumbered by 15,000 who immediately took the anti-Treaty side – it is unlikely that T.P. McKenna saw much in the way of lethal action during the Civil War. He spent most of the conflict attached to the Officers' Training Corps in the Curragh, a unit uncharitably but perhaps accurately described by one Free State bureaucrat as 'a body consisting mainly of the surplus ungazetted officers of the Army'.[28]

His recruitment was part of Seán Boylan's master plan to make sure that Meath remained loyal to Collins and the IRB. It ensured that T.P., by now an experienced and valued guerrilla fighter, was kept out of the clutches of the small but determined force of Meath IRA Volunteers who registered their antipathy towards the Treaty by joining the Republican 'Irregulars'. They attempted to turn the tables on their erstwhile allies with a number of local attacks, but with only modest success.

On 7 March 1924, having reached the rank of colonel-commandant, T.P. McKenna was demobilised from an army that had expanded in numbers to 50,000 and had itself come to pose a threat to the stability of the newly established state. The date of his exit has considerable significance. It coincided with a demand to the government from a group within the Free State force, the Irish Republican Army Organisation – led by former Deputy Director of Intelligence Liam Tobin and IRA Intelligence officer Charlie Dalton – to end the demobilisation process. The move precipitated the infamous Irish Army Mutiny, which almost brought down the fledgling administration of W.T. Cosgrave.

T.P. McKenna, however, had no stomach for mutiny, or any desire to remain in the uniform of the National Army. He wanted to resume his medical studies, interrupted in 1920 when he became a boy soldier.

Towards the end of 1925, T.P. applied for a military pension, as was his entitlement under enabling legislation passed the previous year. A Cumann na nGaedheal government that had notoriously docked a shilling from the old age pension in 1923 was nonetheless determined to emulate the governments of Europe in allocating stipends to its retired soldiers. First, however, they must prove that they had actively participated in the sharp end of the Anglo-Irish War, had not taken the Republican side in the Civil War, and were male.*

After a dismal bureaucratic struggle, T.P. was allocated an annual pension of £110 per annum, grudgingly bestowed by a Defence Department unimpressed with his Civil War record. When he eventually got his pension in April 1927, it was backdated to October 1924 and amounted to a useful lump sum of £275.

Useful, that is, had he actually been able to continue his medical studies. But by the spring of 1927 his increasingly frail health was fatally compromised, and he would spend the rest of his life on the other side of the medical profession. Like his mother, who died when he was an infant, T.P.'s constitution had been weakened by tuberculosis.† All plans for a career in University College, Dublin had to be abandoned. His destiny was a temporary banishment to Argentina, where his family hoped the warm climate would enable him to recover.

His exile proved to be permanent, however, like that of many hundreds of thousands of fellow emigrants, men and women

---

* Female combatants or active members of Cumann na mBan or the Irish Citizens' Army (1916 Rising) were not considered for the award of pensions until amending legislation introduced by de Valera's Fianna Fáil government in 1934.
† His older sister Margaret, a nurse, would also die of consumption, aged only thirty, in 1930.

let down by a 'conservative revolution' that did little more than change the hue of the status quo from royal blue to emerald green. Far from heralding societal change, Irish independence brought disillusionment in its wake. Hundreds had died on both sides in pursuit of an ideal that, though only partially realised, brought precious little change to the social and economic conditions of the Irish people.

Why South America? What prompted T.P. McKenna to venture so far afield in the hope of restoring his failing health?

Why not English-speaking Colorado, the destination of choice since the late nineteenth century of many Irish – those at least who could afford the journey – seeking relief from the horrors of tuberculosis and other debilitating conditions? Argentina had a small Irish expatriate population, but T.P. was condemning himself to working with a language alien to him and dealing with the foibles of a society of which he was wholly ignorant.

In his short biography of his great-uncle, London-based film-maker Stephen McKenna has pointed to the probability that the McKenna family had been influenced in the choice of Argentina for T.P.'s recuperation by a former inmate of the Rath prison, one befriended by his brother Justin McKenna during the latter's six-month confinement in the Curragh.

One of the oddest narratives of the 1916 Rising is that of Eamon Bulfin. Born in Argentina to Irish parents, it was Bulfin who, under orders from James Connolly, raised one of the two flags (the one bearing the words 'Irish Republic' in gold on a green background) over the GPO. Captured after the Rising, Bulfin was deported to Argentina after a brief internment in Frongoch prison camp in north Wales. When the Anglo-Irish War broke out, he was asked by de Valera to remain in South America and represent the interests of the upstart republic there.

Eamon Bulfin's uncle, Francis, shared the Rath camp with Justin. He was released at the same time as the Cavan man, and for the same reason – he too had been elected as a member of the House of Commons of Southern Ireland. Although Eamon Bulfin had finally returned to Ireland from Argentina by the time of T.P.'s departure for South America and could be of no direct practical assistance, Stephen McKenna speculates that the relationship between Justin McKenna and Francis Bulfin might have been instrumental in the choice of Argentina as a 'rest cure' destination.[29]

On 26 July 1927, T.P. boarded the RMS *Demerara* in Liverpool, bound for Buenos Aires via Oporto and Lisbon.[30] On his arrival in South America, he quickly found work in St Lucy's English school in Buenos Aires, contributed some poetry to an English-language newspaper, the *Southern Cross*, and fretted about the regular payment of his IRA pension. Otherwise, he involved himself with the small Irish community – his obituary refers to his efforts to establish an Irish Society in Buenos Aires[31] – and hoped that his health would improve.

But it was already too late for that.

Not long after his arrival in Buenos Aires, T.P. was forced to abandon the capital for the distant province of Catamarca, a mountainous, semi-arid region a thousand kilometres inland to the north-west. There is a sense of foreboding and melancholy in his final letter to the Military Pensions Board in Dublin in May 1928, informing them of his move. He describes Catamarca, unflatteringly, as 'an almost uncivilised region':

This place has never been settled by any members of the Nordic races – except invalids for short terms – and as there is a very strong racial antipathy among the Latin races against their Northern neighbours, the possibilities of work are very remote. Consequently, I will have to rely solely on my pension and you can see the horrible position I will be in if I receive a draft which I cannot negotiate.[32]

T.P.'s removal to the clear air but rugged terrain of Catamarca was short-lived. His condition continued to deteriorate and he soon found himself in a hospital in Córdoba, south-east of Catamarca. Given his own painfully brief flirtation with the practice of medicine, he must have known that he had very little time left. The prognosis for advanced consumptives, in the era before the widespread use of antibiotics, was stark.

He was fortunate in Córdoba to encounter a self-appointed hospital visitor, Isobel Day, who hailed from Fife in Scotland and was herself a TB survivor. She had also travelled to Argentina for the good of her health, in her case in 1924. Happily, her condition was not too far advanced; her body responded to the warm Argentinian climate and her health was restored. Grateful for this reprieve, she chose to devote much of her spare time to looking after less fortunate TB victims. T.P., for whom she did much before and after his death, was one of the casualties of the dreadful disease on whom she lavished her attention.[33]

T.P. McKenna died on 13 February 1929. He was twenty-six years old and virtually penniless, having been unable to earn a living for many months. His desperate missives to the Military Service Pensions Board whenever his payments were delayed or misdirected testify to the bleakness of his situation. Isobel Day made arrangements for his burial, and was, as far as we can tell, the sole mourner at his funeral. His grave in the San Vicente cemetery in the city of Córdoba is unmarked.* Like Robert Emmet, an inspiration to many young men of his generation, his epitaph is unwritten.

His father, who himself died later that same year,† was devastated by the passing of a second son. Notifying the death of T.P. McKenna to the paymasters in the Department of Defence – which was duly relieved of the burden of disbursing £110 per annum – the ageing Mullagh merchant prince was in no doubt about the actual cause of his youngest boy's death:

> Born in 1903 he was too young and frail for the work he undertook in the Volunteer IRA and as a consequence his health became broken and when he went to the Argentine for a change he found he was late – too much run down to stand the horribly hot climate over there.[34]

Isobel Day conveyed the tragic news by cable to Mullagh, and she was to do even more for the family. Later that year she made a return journey to her native Scotland. From Fife, she despatched a parcel of the dead man's effects: his writings, his watch, his fountain pen and other memorabilia of the person she described in a covering letter to his father as her 'dear boy'.[35]

Thankfully and somewhat fortuitously, the writings survive,

* As his great-nephew Stephen McKenna – the only family member to make the journey – discovered when he went in search of his grand-uncle's grave in 2019 (Stephen McKenna, *A Gallant Soldier of Ireland: The Life and Times of T.P. McKenna Jr.* (London, 2019), pp.119–137.
† By coincidence, 1929 also marked the birth of a third T.P. McKenna, a son to Raphael and his wife Mary, who thus carried the name into another generation. He went on to a distinguished career as an actor in the Abbey Theatre, before moving to London and an international career on stage, in film and on television. www.imdb.com/name/nm0571435/bio

though a lengthy prose piece was only recovered from potential destruction as recently as 2019. While living in Argentina, T.P. had taken the first faltering steps on what might have developed into a career as a writer. He wrote some (rather poor) poetry and started work on a draft of a novel based, very loosely, on his own experiences of the Anglo-Irish War. His prose, while of the Biggles/Bulldog Drummond variety, was far superior to his deeply felt but entirely unconvincing attempts at verse.

One example of the latter, 'The Call of the Lonely Curlew', is a fictionalised narrative poem derived from his brief experience of training and leading a flying column. It attempts to convey some sense of the risks and the uncertainties faced by men on the run, often compelled to sleep in the open, constantly on their guard:

> One man had been sent out to forage some grub, another on
> sentry-go crept,
> And the others curled up, each the best way he could, and in
> different octaves all slept
> No saints, scholars or supermen these, yet each in his own way
> was true
> To the land of the mists and the mountains, the home of the
> lonely curlew.[36]

The long prose piece, an unfinished handwritten manuscript of forty-four pages, is similarly fictionalised and reads as if it was intended for an Irish-American audience primed for sensational underdog narratives of the Anglo-Irish War. It begins with an idiosyncratic and superfluous account of recent Irish history, before launching into a breathless chronicle of IRA audacity and British duplicity. It opens with one of the few irrefutably auto-biographical statements in the 15,000-word piece: 'In 1919, I was studying medicine in the National University in Dublin. Like every young Irishman of any spirit I was a member of Sinn Féin and the Irish Volunteers.'

What follows is the story of Mac, a well-connected IRA recruit, brother of a TD and son of a Sinn Féin activist who 'assured the return of its candidate in his constituency'. As an IRA Volunteer in Dublin, Mac becomes enmeshed in the workings of the Michael Collins espionage network. He attracts the attention of the British spymasters of Dublin Castle, and an assassin, Wilson, is deployed to locate and murder him. An inconclusive gunfight takes place between rebel and hit man, in which a policeman is shot dead.

While T.P. himself was forced to go underground after the Bloody Sunday killings of 21 November 1920, there is no evidence that he was as closely aligned with Collins, Liam Tobin and Tom Cullen (all name-checked in the work) as his fictionalised Mac.

There is no reference in the manuscript to the most deadly IRA activity in which the author himself was personally involved. While spies, agents, assassins and informers abound, the cheerless reality of extra-judicial execution does not form part of the narrative, at least up to the point where it was interrupted by the author's own death.

The saga, provisionally entitled *A Soldier's Story*, is an uneasy mix of escapist fiction, insider experience and periodic tutorials on the progress and personalities (real and imaginary) of the Anglo-Irish War. Shorn of its didacticism, expanded in certain places and mercilessly edited in others, it might have had some potential in an era when memoirs and fictionalised accounts of the conflict were already becoming popular.[37]

The most poignant piece of ephemera that found its way from Fife to east Cavan, however, was a nostalgic two-verse poem.

Entitled 'Mullagh Hill', it is as sentimentally beguiling as it is poetically unschooled. It concludes:

> South America's grand, tis a wonderful land
> Where God's gifts are plain to be seen
> But there's only one land, made by his own hand
> That island, eternally green.
> Now most men grow old, striving daily for gold
> But it is not for wealth that I yearn
> I'll be happy when dead, if I pillow my head
> In the spot where St. Killian was born
> Sure ten times I would rather one clasp from my father
> Than handle a financier's bill
> And my mother's kind smile, than a millionaire's pile
> And I'll find them 'neath sweet Mullagh Hill.[38]

Just as the precise location of the final resting place of Patrick Keelan is uncertain, so too is that of one of the men directly responsible for his death. T.P. McKenna lies in a common grave in an Argentinian cemetery, far from the place where he had hoped to be interred.

Technically, he was not a casualty of the War of Independence, but of independence itself. He fell victim to the powerlessness of a young state to provide for the health and welfare of its citizens, even those who as ersatz soldiers had sacrificed their own health and well-being to its creation. As a victim of war, economic need and emigration, he was truly a child of the fledgling Irish Free State.

Epilogue

'An ill-favoured thing, sir, but mine own.'

Touchstone, *As You Like It*, V.4.56

How much did Mary Theresa McKenna O'Reilly know about the adventures and misadventures of her extended family in the Anglo-Irish war?

Certainly, more than she ever told her grandson. In all likelihood, nothing you have read here would have come as news to her. She was never as delicately nurtured as she liked to pretend. She did not need to be cosseted and protected. And she came from an era when family was everything. Families were held together by the glue of sentiment, geography, commerce, land or all of the above. Every branch on the tree was kept well-informed of familial transactions, either on principle or by default.

Her experience of the Anglo-Irish War was by no means exceptional. She lived in a relatively tranquil part of a locality that was itself largely dormant. Her War of Independence was experienced vicariously through rumours and stories of the vicissitudes of her kin. Even when Crown forces made their presence felt in her life, they had not come hunting for her.

And when the Crossley tenders returned to England; when the nocturnal searches and threats of arson ended; when the Free State Army uniforms were placed in mothballs after the mass demobilisation of 1924; and when the country took a deep breath and settled back to gauge exactly what had been won and what had been lost; she was content to accept the outcome. Accustomed to relative comfort, she had no reason to challenge the new order. She would remain in relative comfort.

Her thoughts must have returned to the war as she grieved for her young brother T.P. in 1929. She had ample cause to blame his death on the rigours he had faced as a fugitive rebel. She also survived her other three siblings, who had made their own contributions to the prevailing anarchy after the disheartening failure of the constitutional alternative – the Home Rule Act – to which they were more temperamentally inclined. As noted, Justin, who cast his vote in favour of 'the freedom to achieve freedom' in January 1922, died of a heart attack in Kells in 1950 at the age of fifty-three. Raphael and John were granted longer leases on life. Raphael McKenna died at the age of seventy-eight in 1973, John in 1981 at eighty-eight.

John McKenna's life stretched from the rancorous aftermath of the Parnellite split to the rise of modern neo-liberalism. When he died, two years before his sister May, Margaret Thatcher and Ronald Reagan were in their pomp and the ideas of Friedrich Hayek were dominant. John had married Marcella O'Reilly quite late in life, even for an Irish farmer, and while he was blessed with five surviving children, he also experienced the heartache of losing two infants. Both are buried in the McKenna family plot in Moynalty cemetery.

In the 1860s, Karl Marx and Friedrich Engels had high hopes of an Ireland where they reckoned the population was 'more revolutionary and exasperated than in England'.[1]

Fast forward to the 1920s. Exasperated perhaps, but revolutionary only in their resourceful conduct of a successful guerrilla war. Had the writers of *The Communist Manifesto* been around in 1926 to contrast Ireland, where vigorously conservative Minister of Justice Kevin O'Higgins was establishing the Committee on Evil Literature, with Britain, where events were dominated by the nine-day General Strike, they might have had cause to revise their essay *Ireland and the Irish Question*.

While the votes and the passive support afforded Sinn Féin and the IRA from 1917 to 1922 might have been radically separatist, there was a dearth of radicalism in evidence once that separation had been achieved. There were too many running repairs to be undertaken, too many obligations – literal and moral – to be redeemed, for matters to be otherwise. Between them, the IRA (in both its War of Independence and Civil War incarnations), the Black and Tans, the Auxiliaries, the British military and the National Army had shredded much of the country's infrastructure. The Dáil administration had largely functioned on the basis of borrowing money (loans and bond purchases) from its own citizenry; a return to more traditional forms of revenue-raising, such as direct and relentless taxation, was bound to be problematic.

And then there was the Roman Catholic church seeking repayments on its mortgage – tacit clerical support for a revolutionary crusade to which the church had, in a previous generation, responded with excommunication. The debt was repaid in full, with servile interest. Hegemony in education and health was casually surrendered to religious oligarchs by a sycophantic state.

The aftermath of the Civil War brought about the flight of many of the more radical affiliates of Sinn Féin, the men and women who found themselves on the losing side. Many of those who might have challenged the penny-pinching prurience of the new Irish elite were banished to the margins or for shifting for themselves in London, Glasgow, New York and Boston. Or, in the case of Ernie O'Malley, writing bitter and compelling memoirs in New Mexico.

The winners of the Civil War, who were allowed to keep the pietistic Free State all to themselves as their reward, slid towards the condition of the revolutionary swine in George Orwell's *Animal Farm* who rapidly adopted human characteristics. Suddenly two legs were good after all. The 'conservative revolutionaries' of Cumann na nGaedheal began to resemble the conformist Irish

Parliamentary Party members – albeit without the stratospheric levels of complacency – whose policies they had emphatically rejected less than a decade before.

There certainly wasn't much appetite for workers' councils in the new Ireland, or for gender equality. The Labour Party opposition was just that, an opposition. Whether or not it had foregone a unique political opportunity by standing aside at the 1918 election, it would take almost three decades to exert anything other than the influence of the righteously indignant.

What had been the cost in lives of this ill-favoured thing?

The acknowledged expert in the fatality statistics of the Irish revolutionary period is Professor Eunan O'Halpin of Trinity College Dublin. He estimates that 2,141 men, women and children died as a result of Irish political violence between 1917 and 1921. Three locations, Dublin, Cork and Belfast, accounted for just over half of the fatalities. A further quarter were in Limerick, Tipperary, Kerry and Clare. Forty-eight percent of those who perished, a total of 898 people, were civilians, and the other 52% were combatants. Of those, 467 were IRA, 514 were RIC (including Tans and Auxiliaries) and 262 were British military.[2]

In that context, what does the passing of three men signify? The deaths of Mark Clinton, William Gordon and Patrick Keelan were about as significant to the Anglo-Irish War as was the murder of Jack Clinton to the violent history of modern Arizona, but they are not to be dismissed for that reason.

Only three, out of more than two thousand. But those three sudden and violent deaths left three families bereft and seeking answers.

The Keelans and the Gordons are still waiting for theirs.

Timeline

1917

3 February	Count Plunkett wins the Roscommon North by-election for Sinn Féin.
9 May	Joseph McGuinness wins the Longford South by-election for Sinn Féin.
10 July	Éamon de Valera wins the East Clare by-election for Sinn Féin.
10 August	W.T. Cosgrave wins the Kilkenny City by-election for Sinn Féin.
25 September	Thomas Ashe dies on hunger strike as a result of force feeding.
25 October	Sinn Féin Árd Fheis is held in Dublin.
27 October	National Convention of Irish Volunteers takes place.

1918

2 February	The Irish Parliamentary Party wins the Armagh South by-election.
6 March	John Redmond dies.

22 March	William Archer Redmond wins the Waterford City by-election for the Irish Parliamentary Party.
16 April	The Military Service Act passes, introducing conscription to Ireland.
21 April	Anti-Conscription protests take place at Catholic churches.
23 April	The Anti-Conscription general strike brings much of the country to a standstill.
17 May	The 'German plot' arrests begin.
20 June	An incarcerated Arthur Griffith wins East Cavan by-election, with much help from T.P. McKenna Sr.
14 December	The 1918 General Election result – Sinn Féin 73, Unionist 26, Irish Parliamentary Party 6.

1919

10 January	Ian McPherson becomes Irish Secretary in Lloyd George's cabinet reshuffle.
21 January	The First Dáil meets in the Mansion House, Dublin.
	Two RIC men are killed in the Soloheadbeg, County Tipperary attack launched by Dan Breen, Seán Treacy and Séamus Robinson.
10 April	Dáil Éireann declares a boycott on all RIC policeman and their families.
13 May	Knocklong – two more RIC men killed in the rescue of Tipperary IRA man Seán Hogan.
11 June	Éamon de Valera arrives in the US on a fundraising and propaganda mission.
30 July	Detective Sergeant Patrick 'The Dog' Smyth becomes the first Dublin Metropolitan Police

	(DMP) victim of 'The Squad' – he is shot, and dies of his wounds on 8 September.
7 September	Fermoy IRA attack on a Shropshire Light Infantry detachment – one soldier is killed and the town is attacked in reprisal.
10 September	Dáil Éireann is declared an illegal assembly by the British government.
15 September	Arrest of leading Meath Volunteer John Tevlin for possession of arms and ammunition.
18 October	Meath Volunteer Patrick O'Brien is arrested for possession of ammunition and two bombs. He goes on hunger strike.
23 October	John Tevlin begins a hunger strike.
31 October	The Meath IRA attack Ballivor RIC Barracks – Constable Agar killed. Attack on Lismullin RIC Station. An RIC Sergeant is injured.
17 November	Release of Patrick O'Brien from Mountjoy Gaol.
19 December	Failed attempt to assassinate Lord French, Lord Lieutenant of Ireland, near the Phoenix Park.

1920

2 January	The first Black and Tans are recruited; 100 more follow before the end of January.
15 January	Local elections for Urban District Councils take place – Sinn Féin dominate.
21 January	Assassination in Dublin of Assistant Commissioner Redmond of DMP.
23 February	The Black and Tans arrive in Meath – ten are posted to Navan.

11 March	RIC Inspector General Joseph Byrne is relieved of his post, replaced by Major General Hugh H. Tudor.
20 March	Tomás McCurtain, Lord Mayor of Cork, is murdered. The killing is attributed to off-duty RIC officers.
26 March	The assassination of Resident Magistrate Alan Bell by members of The Squad takes place in broad daylight in Ballsbridge, Dublin.
3–4 April	350 buildings (100 Inland Revenue and 250 barracks) are destroyed by the IRA. This includes the destruction of police barracks in Carnaross, Ballivor, Bohermeen, Mountnugent, Kilmainhamwood, Moynalty and Mullagh.
10 May	Mark Clinton is murdered by members of the Cormeen Gang.
17 May	First Dáil Éireann land court sits in Ballinrobe, County Mayo.
20 May	The Irish Transport and General Workers Union organises a munitions strike by dock and rail workers, refusing to transport arms and ammunition.
2–3 June	County Council and Rural District Council elections – Sinn Féin return 20 of 21 members to Meath County Council.
19 June	A Carnaross woman has her hair cropped for 'keeping company with an objectionable party'.
21 June	The 1st Battalion South Wales Borderers arrive in Ireland. Some 800 members of the regiment are stationed in Meath.
5 July	Meath IRA Volunteer Bernard Dunne is shot and

	wounded while cycling. He later identifies a Kells RIC sergeant as one of his assailants.
21 July	IRA Volunteer commandant Séamus Cogan is killed near Oldcastle while escorting a prisoner charged with stealing cattle.
	Loyalists expel hundreds of Roman Catholic employees from the Belfast shipyards.
23 July	Recruitment begins for the RIC Auxiliary Division.
27 July	Séamus Cogan is buried after an enormous funeral; the crowd is estimated at 15,000.
9 August	Restoration of Order in Ireland Act passed; it replaces the Defence of the Realm Act.
20 September	Burning of Balbriggan by Black and Tans from Gormanstown, County Meath.
30 September	An attack on Trim barracks by the Meath IRA is followed by the burning of buildings in Trim by Crown forces.
25 October	Sinn Féin Lord Mayor of Cork Terence MacSwiney dies on hunger strike.
1 November	Eighteen-year-old Dublin IRA Volunteer Kevin Barry is hanged in Mountjoy.
21 November	Bloody Sunday in Dublin. Deadly IRA attacks on alleged British spies are followed by Crown force reprisals and the murder of civilians in Croke Park. This is followed in turn by the killing of three IRA prisoners (Peadar Clancy, Dick McKee and Conor Clune) in Dublin Castle.
28 November	Kilmichael ambush in west Cork. Seventeen Auxiliaries are killed by the West Cork IRA under Tom Barry.

11 December	Burning of Cork city centre by Crown forces.
27 December	(approx.) British policy of 'official' reprisals begins.

1921

2 January	Postman and alleged informer Bryan Bradley is kidnapped from his Carnaross home by the IRA and murdered in Rathmanoo Wood on an unknown date. His body is not recovered.
1 February	The Auxiliaries arrive in Trim. N Company, consisting of 100 men, is stationed at Trim Industrial School.
	The Clonfin ambush in Longford – four Auxiliaries are killed by a force led by Seán MacEoin.
3 February	Eleven RIC / Tans are killed in an IRA ambush in Dromkeen, County Limerick.
20 February	Twelve IRA men are killed in the Clonmult ambush. Eight more are arrested.
1 March	An unidentified man calling himself Michael O'Brien from Tipperary is shot as a suspected spy by Michael Hilliard of the Navan IRA.
19 March	The Crossbarry ambush – nine soldiers and one Auxiliary are killed.
23 March	Meath IRA Volunteer Patrick O'Donnell is killed in a raid on his Stonefield home.
26 March	An attempt on the life of alleged informer Francis Dooner by the Meath IRA is unsuccessful.
1 April	Sylvan Park, Drumbaragh ambush – Constable Fox, a Black and Tan, is seriously injured in the stomach during the attack.

1 April	The Kells and Athboy fairs and all GAA matches in the area are banned because of the failure to repair bridges destroyed by the IRA in Piercetown, Drumcree and Carlanstown.
4 April	The Black and Tans raid the village of Mullagh, County Cavan – all adult males are gathered in Fair Green and kept under surveillance while houses are searched.
25 May	The Custom House is burned in Dublin in a concerted IRA raid that leads to the capture of dozens of Dublin Volunteers.
26 May	The decomposed body of South Wales Borderer Sergeant John Herrod, missing since 16 May, is found floating in the Blackwater river near Navan.
3 June	The British policy of 'official' reprisals ends.
7 June	A Meath IRA mine blows up a Black and Tan lorry, with no fatalities. An RAF plane is used in a sweep to catch the IRA unit involved.
12 June	The IRA attempt to murder alleged informer Patrick Duke, who escapes and later joins the RIC.
13 June	John Donohoe, another alleged informer, is killed by the IRA near his Ratoath home.
18 June	A huge force of British troops arrives in Meath. They camp on land owned by Lord Headfort, Captain Bomford (Oakley Park), the Radcliffs (Maperath) and the Miss McCormacks (Williamstown House). They leave after less than twenty-four hours. No explanation for their arrival or departure is offered.
22 June	The Northern Ireland Parliament opens. King

	George V makes a conciliatory speech that paves the way for the Truce.
23 June	John 'The Thatcher' Farrell, former DMP officer, is murdered near Athboy in an alleged IRA execution.
26 June	Alleged informer Thomas Smyth goes missing. His body is found in the Boyne on 5 July.
30 June	The controversial killing by the IRA of Protestant landowners Richard and Abraham Pearson in Coolacrease, County Offaly.
2 July	Alleged Black and Tan 'identifier' Patrick Keelan is kidnapped and executed by the IRA.
11 July	Truce comes into effect at 11.30 a.m. The last Meath IRA attacks take place at Maudlin Bridge in Kells and in Kingscourt, County Cavan just before noon – Tan constable W.L. O'Reilly is wounded.
6 December	The Anglo-Irish Treaty is signed.

1922

7 January	Dáil accepts the Treaty by 64–57. Justin McKenna votes in favour.

1926

10 February	The body of IRA victim and alleged informer John 'The Thatcher' Farrell is discovered in Tullaghanstown bog between Navan and Athboy. His death certificate gives the date of death as 23 June 1921.

Bibliography

MANUSCRIPT SOURCES

MILITARY ARCHIVES

Brigade Activity Reports

MA/MSPC/A/58, 1st Eastern Division, 2nd Brigade (Meath)
MA/MSPC/RO/485, 1st Eastern Division, 2nd Brigade, 1st Battalion (Meath)
MA/MSPC/RO 489, 1st Eastern Division, 3rd Brigade (Meath)
MA/MSPC/A/60, 1st Eastern Division, 4th Brigade (Meath)

Bureau of Military History – Witness Statements

Matthew Barry	#932
Ernest Blythe	#939
Seán Boylan	#1715
Charles Conaty	#1627
Cahir Davitt	#993
Seán Farrelly	#1648, #1734
Séamus Finn	#1060
Matt Govern	#1625
Michael Hillard	#1622

Joe Hyland   #644
Joseph V. Lawless   #1043
Patrick Loughran   #1624
Manus Moynihan   #1066
Peter O'Connell   #1659
Kevin O'Shiel   #1770
Una Stack   #418

Collins Papers
IE/MA/CP/5/2/29

Military Service Pensions Collection
Patrick Clinton   24SP13263
Patrick Clinton   24C142
Peter Clinton   34REF36826
Peter Clinton   MD20258
Matthew Cogan   34SP61746
John McKenna   34REF35849
John McKenna   34SP41453
Raphael McKenna   34REF45950
Raphael McKenna   MD27001
T.P. McKenna   24D38
T.P. McKenna   24SP12899
T.P. McKenna   4648D
Rose Travers   34REF50656
Rose Travers   34E6391

Public Record Office, Kew
CO 905/15, Criminal Injuries to Private Persons (Meath)
WO 35/53/227

WO 35/91/12
WO 35/207/153

Other
Census of Ireland 1901
Census of Ireland 1911
General Register of Prisoners 1920
Griffith's Valuation Book, Parish of Moynalty, Townland of Cormeen
Irish Civil Records
Irish Church Records
Irish Petty Sessions order books
Justice Department file, JUS/2019/58/85
US Census

NEWSPAPERS

USA
Arizona Republican
Bisbee Daily Review
Colorado Springs Gazette
Lordsburg Western Liberal
Salt Lake City Tribune
Silver City Independent
Tombstone Epitaph
Tucson Citizen
Western Historical Quarterly

Ireland
An tÓglach
Anglo-Celt
Cork Examiner

Drogheda Independent
Irish Law Times
Irish Times
Meath Chronicle
Skibbereen Eagle
United Ireland
Weekly Freeman's Journal

ARTICLES

Fergus Campbell, 'The Last Land War? Kevin O'Shiel's Memoir of the Irish Revolution (1916–21)', *Archivium Hibernicum*, Vol. 57 (2003).

Mary Frances Clinton, 'Homesteading in Palominas: A Two Family Tale', privately circulated (Arizona, 2011).

Frank Cogan, 'Michael Collins and the Cormeen Murder Case', *Riocht na Midhe* – records of the Meath Archaeological and Historical Society, vol. XXVIII, 2017.

Kevin O'Shiel, 'No contempt of court', *Irish Times*, 21 November 1966.

——'Dáil courts in action', *Irish Times*, 18 November 1966.

——'The Dáil land courts', *Irish Times*, 14 November 1966.

Randolph Roth, Michael D. Maltz, Douglas L. Eckberg, 'Homicide Rates in the Old West', *Western Historical Quarterly*, summer 2011.

Tony Varley, 'A Region of Sturdy Smallholders? Western Nationalists and Agrarian Politics during the First World War', *Journal of the Galway Archaeological and Historical Society*, Vol. 55 (2003).

SECONDARY SOURCES

Christopher Andrew, *Secret Service: The Making of the British Intelligence Community* (London, 1985).

Tom Barry, *Guerrilla Days in Ireland* (Tralee, 1955).

Thomas Bartlet, Keith Jeffrey (eds), *A Military History of Ireland* (Cambridge, 1997).

J. Bowyer Bell, *The Secret Army* (London, 1997).

Katherine Benton-Cohen, *Borderline Americans: Racial Division, Labor War in the Arizona Borderlands* (Cambridge, Mass., 2009).

Andy Bielenberg and Pádraig Óg Ó Ruairc, *Shallow Graves; Documenting and Assessing IRA Disappearances during the Irish Revolution 1919–23* (forthcoming, 2021).

Gray Brechin, *Imperial San Francisco: Urban Power, Earthly Ruin* (Berkeley, 1999).

Samuel Clark, *Social Origins of the Irish Land War* (Princeton, 1979).

Marie Coleman, *The Irish Revolution 1916–1923* (London, 2014).

Oliver Coogan, *Politics and War in Meath 1913–1923* (Navan, 1983).

Ultan Courtney, *The Tin Hats: The South Wales Borderers in Meath 1920–22* (Meath, 2018).

Ultan Courtney, *Mapping the Revolution: Maps, Mayhem and Murder in Meath, 1919–1921* (Meath, 2019).

Arlene Crampsie and Francis Ludlow (eds), *Meath: History and Society – Interdisciplinary Essays on the History of an Irish County* (Dublin, 2015).

Danny Cusack, *Kilmainham of the Woody Hollow. A History of Kilmainhamwood for the Centenary of the Church 1898–1998* (Kilmainhamwood, 1998).

Danny Cusack, *Tales of an Old Fenian, Memories of Matthew Gilsenan* (unpublished).

Charles Dalton, *With the Dublin Brigade* (Dublin, 1929), reprinted by Mercier Press, with an introduction by Liz Gillis.

Robert K. DeArment, *George Scarborough: The Life and Death of a Lawman on the Closing of the Frontier* (Oklahoma, 1992).

Diarmaid Ferriter, *A Nation and not a Rabble: the Irish Revolution 1913–1923* (London, 2015).

James Fitzgerald, *A Practical Guide to the Valuation of Rent in Ireland* (Dublin, 1881).

David Fitzpatrick, *Politics and Irish Life 1913–1921, Provincial Experience of War and Revolution* (Dublin, 1977).

William H. Forbis, *The Old West: The Cowboys – Time Life* Books Series (New York, 1973).

R.F. Foster, *Vivid Faces: the Revolutionary Generation in Ireland 1890–1923* (London, 2014).

J. Evetts Haley, *Charles Goodnight: Cowman and Plainsman* (Oklahoma, 1949).

Peter Hart, *The IRA at War* (Oxford, 2003).

Michael Hopkinson, *The Irish War of Independence* (Montreal, 2004).

Frank Kitson, *Low Intensity Operations: Subversion, Insurgency, Peace-keeping* (London, 1971).

Patricia Limerick, *The Legacy of Conquest: The Unbroken Past of the American West* (New York, 1987).

Uinseann MacEoin, *Survivors* (Dublin, 1980).

Ernest McCall, *The First Anti-Terrorist Unit: The Auxiliary Division, RIC* (Newtownards, 2019).

Stephen McKenna, *A Gallant Soldier of Ireland: The Life and Times of T.P. McKenna Jr.* (London, 2019).

Paul McMahon, *British Spies and Irish Rebels: British Intelligence and Ireland, 1916–1945* (Suffolk, 2008).

Mullagh Historical Committee, *Portrait of a Parish* (Mullagh, 1988).

Jay Robert Nash, *Encyclopedia of Western Outlaws* (New York, 1994).

Pádraig Óg Ó Ruairc, *Truce: Murder, Myth and the Last Days of the Irish War of Independence* (Cork, 2016).

Ann Saddlemyer (ed.), *The Collected Letters of John Millington Synge: Volume One 1871–1907* (Oxford, 1983).

William Sheehan, *British Voices from the Irish War of Independence 1918–1921* (Cork, 2005).

Richard Slotkin, *The Fatal Environment: The Myth of the Frontier in the Age of Industrialization 1800–1890* (Oklahoma, 1985).

Barbara Lewis Solow, *The Land Question and the Irish Economy, 1870–1903* (Harvard, 1971).

Charles Townshend, *Political Violence in Ireland: Government and Resistance since 1848* (Oxford, 1983).

Charles Townshend, *The Republic: The Fight for Irish Independence 1918–1923* (London, 2013).

Maurice Walsh, *Bitter Freedom: Ireland in a Revolutionary World* (New York/London, 2015).

Notes

PART ONE: THE CLINTONS OF CLOGGAGH

Chapter 1: Arizona, 1915

1 Richard Slotkin, *The Fatal Environment: The Myth of the Frontier in the Age of Industrialization 1800–1890* (Oklahoma, 1985). Information relating to the Arizona Clintons has, in the main, come from Mary Frances Clinton and Roseanne Feeback.

2 *Bisbee Daily Review*, 26 June 1915.

3 Randolph Roth, Michael D. Maltz, Douglas L. Eckberg, 'Homicide Rates in the Old West', *Western Historical Quarterly*, Summer 2011, 184–187.

4 Katherine Benton-Cohen, *Borderline Americans: Racial Division, Labor War in the Arizona Borderlands* (Cambridge, Mass., 2009), 26.

5 Mary Frances Clinton, 'Homesteading in Palominas: A Two Family Tale', privately circulated (Arizona, 2011), 2.

6 Benton-Cohen, *Borderline Americans*, 40.

7 213 U.S. 339 (29 S.Ct. 493, 53 L.Ed. 822). Boquillas Land & Cattle Company, Appt., v. J. N. Curtis, Samuel C. Curtis, Lyman Curtis, and John Summers. No. 133. Argued and submitted: 7 April 1909. Decided: 19 April 1909.

8 Gray Brechin, *Imperial San Francisco: Urban Power, Earthly Ruin* (Berkeley, 1999), 107.

9   Record of Deaths, Bisbee, Arizona, January 1915.

10   J. Evetts Haley, *Charles Goodnight: Cowman and Plainsman* (Oklahoma, 1949), 382.

11   William H. Forbis, *The Old West: The Cowboys – Time Life* Books Series (New York, 1973), 57.

12   Haley, *Charles Goodnight*, 387.

13   Forbis, *The Old West*, 62.

14   Patricia Limerick, *The Legacy of Conquest: The Unbroken Past of the American West* (New York, 1987).

15   Slotkin, *The Fatal Environment*, 285.

Chapter 2: The First Killing

1   Mary Frances Clinton, 'Homesteading in Palominas: A Two Family Tale', privately circulated (Arizona, 2011), 10.

2   Jay Robert Nash, *Encyclopedia of Western Outlaws* (New York, 1994), 143–150.

3   Nash, *Encyclopedia of Western Outlaws*, 278.

4   Nash, *Encyclopedia of Western Outlaws*, 278.

5   Robert K. DeArment, *George Scarborough: The Life and Death of a Lawman on the Closing of the Frontier* (Oklahoma, 1992), 242.

6   *Lordsburg Western Liberal*, 18 January 1901 in DeArment, *George Scarborough*, 250.

7   DeArment, *George Scarborough*, 252.

8   DeArment, *George Scarborough*, 254.

9   DeArment, *George Scarborough*, 256.

10   *Bisbee Daily Review*, 20 June 1915.

11   *Bisbee Daily Review*, 29 June 1915.

12   *Bisbee Daily Review*, 27 June 1915.

13   *Tombstone Epitaph*, 4 July 1915.

14   *Tombstone Epitaph*, 12 December 1915.

15   *Bisbee Daily Review*, 10 December 1915.

16   *Bisbee Daily Review*, 11 December 1915.

17   *Bisbee Daily Review*, 12 December 1915.

18   *Bisbee Daily Review*, 7 July 1915.

19   *Bisbee Daily Review*, 18 December 1915.
20   *Arizona Republican*, 14 December 1915.
21   DeArment, *George Scarborough*, 259.
22   Mark Foudy Clinton (California) to Basil Foudy Clinton,
      4 September 1995. Letter in the possession of the author.
23   Britt W. Wilson, 'Death on the San Pedro: the Murder of John
      Clinton', *Bisbee Review*, 1997.

Chapter 3: The Second Killing

1   David Fitzpatrick, *Politics and Irish Life 1913–1921, Provincial
      Experience of War and Revolution* (Dublin, 1977), 3.
2   Fergus Campbell, 'The Last Land War? Kevin O'Shiel's Memoir of the
      Irish Revolution (1916–21)', *Archivium Hibernicum*, Vol. 57 (2003), 156.
3   Well-outlined in texts such as Barbara Lewis Solow, *The Land
      Question and the Irish Economy, 1870–1903* (Harvard, 1971) and Samuel
      Clark, *Social Origins of the Irish Land War* (Princeton, 1979).
4   *Meath Chronicle*, 'Martry Back to the Land offer of £22,000 not
      accepted', 17 April 1920.
5   Maurice Walsh, *Bitter Freedom: Ireland in a Revolutionary World*
      (New York and London, 2015), 176.
6   Fergus Campbell, 'The Last Land War?', 161.
7   Tony Varley, 'A Region of Sturdy Smallholders? Western Nation-
      alists and Agrarian Politics during the First World War', *Journal of
      the Galway Archaeological and Historical Society*, Vol. 55 (2003), 142.
8   Peter Hart, *The IRA at War* (Oxford, 2003), 17.
9   Kevin O'Shiel, 'The Last Land War', *Irish Times*, 22 November 1966.
10   Kevin O'Shiel, Bureau of Military History Witness Statement
      #1770, 1086–87.
11   Michael Hopkinson, *The Irish War of Independence* (Montreal, 2004), 20.
12   Charles Townshend, *The Republic: The Fight for Irish Independence
      1918–1923* (London, 2013), 265.
13   Cahir Davitt, Bureau of Military History Witness Statement, #993, 85.
14   Kevin O'Shiel, Bureau of Military History Witness Statement
      #1770, 937.

15 Kevin O'Shiel, Bureau of Military History Witness Statement #1770, 1059.

16 Kevin O'Shiel, Bureau of Military History Witness Statement #1770, 1061.

17 Kevin O'Shiel, 'No contempt of court', *Irish Times*, 21 November 1966.

18 Kevin O'Shiel, 'Dáil courts in action', *Irish Times*, 18 November 1966.

19 Kevin O'Shiel, Bureau of Military History Witness Statement #1770, 970.

20 Kevin O'Shiel, 'The Dáil land courts', *Irish Times*, 14 November 1966.

21 *Meath Chronicle*, 17 April 1920.

22 Oliver Coogan, *Politics and War in Meath* (Navan, 1983), 291.

23 *Meath Chronicle*, 13 March 1920.

24 James Fitzgerald, *A Practical Guide to the Valuation of Rent in Ireland* (Dublin, 1881), 105.

25 Griffith's Valuation Book, Parish of Moynalty, Townland of Cormeen.

26 Much of the information about the Clinton family of Cloggagh comes via Mark Clinton of Sutton Coldfield and his cousin and namesake Mark Clinton, the eminent historian and archaeologist of Sutton, County Dublin.

27 Military Service Pension application, Patrick Clinton, 24SP13263, Military Archives.

28 Matthew Barry, Bureau of Military History Witness Statement #932, 22–23.

29 Deputy Chief of Staff to Acting Director of Intelligence, 21 October 1921, IE/MA/CP/5/2/29 (LXIV) and IE/MA/CP/5/2/29 (LXV).

30 Patrick Clinton to Deputy Director of Intelligence, 9 November 1921, IE/MA/CP/5/2/29 (LXXXIX).

31 Patrick Clinton, Military Service Pensions Collection, 24SP13263.

32 Séamus Finn, Bureau of Military History Witness Statement #1060, 12.

33 Military Service Pension application, Rose Travers, MSP34REF50656, Military Archives.

34 The final signature endorsing her Military Service Pension application is that of Peace Commissioner Raphael McKenna, former IRA battalion intelligence officer and also her cousin.

35 David Fitzpatrick, *Politics and Irish Life, 1913–1921* (Dublin, 1977), 32.

36 Frank Cogan, 'Michael Collins and the Cormeen Case', *Riocht na Midhe* – records of the Meath Archaeological and Historical Society, vol. XXVIII, 2017, fn3, 370, citing Thom's Directory 1916.

37 *Meath Chronicle*, 2 October 1920.

38 *Anglo-Celt*, 25 May 1918. The report is an account of Finnegan's unsuccessful appeal against the jail sentence at Baileborough Quarter Sessions.

39 *Meath Chronicle*, 2 October 1920. Smith was giving evidence at the Malicious Damages Act hearing of Joseph Clinton.

40 Ultan Courtney, *The Tin Hats: The South Wales Borderers in Meath 1920–22* (Meath, 2018), 202.

41 Rogers (Boer War), McGovern (WWi – Army), Gordon (WWi – RAF).

42 Seán Farrelly, Bureau of Military History Witness Statement #1734, 13.

43 Ultan Courtney, *The Tin Hats*, 202.

44 Seán Farrelly, Bureau of Military History Witness Statement #1734, 14.

45 Census of Ireland, 1911, Roundtree, Trohanny, County Meath.

46 Seán Farrelly, Bureau of Military History Witness Statement #1734, 14.

47 *Meath Chronicle*, 23 November 1918.

48 Information supplied by Mark Clinton, Sutton Coldfield.

Chapter 4: Retribution

1 *Meath Chronicle*, 15 May 1920. All further quotes attributed to Joseph Clinton are from this source, the account of Mark Clinton's inquest on 12 May 1920.

2 *Meath Chronicle*, 2 October 1920.

3 Seán Boylan, Bureau of Military History Witness Statement #1715, 19.

4 Charles Conaty, Bureau of Military History Witness Statement #1627, 2. 'Gordon had been hired by the gang to shoot Clinton which he did after shooting two horses just as they were being attached to a plough by Clinton.'

5   Peter O'Connell, Bureau of Military History Witness Statement #1659, 5.

6   Mark Clinton, letter to the author, 2/4/2019.

7   Frank Cogan, 'Michael Collins and the Cormeen Case', *Riocht na Midhe* – records of the Meath Archaeological and Historical Society, vol. XXVIII, 2017, 355.

8   *Meath Chronicle*, 22 May 1920.

9   *Meath Chronicle*, 15 May 1920.

10 *Meath Chronicle*, 22 May 1920.

11 *Cork Examiner*, 14 May 1920; *Irish Independent*, 8 June 1920.

12 *Skibbereen Eagle*, 22 May 1920 and 9 October 1920.

13 *Irish Times*, 17 October 2015. This is a review by the late Professor David Fitzpatrick of Paul Taylor's book *Heroes or Traitors?: Experiences of Southern Irish Soldiers Returning from the Great War* (Liverpool, 2015) in which Taylor essentially opposes Fitzpatrick's thesis that Irish ex-servicemen suffered disproportionately at the hands of the Irish during the Anglo-Irish conflict.

14 IE_MA_CP_05_02_29, (xxxiii), Collins Papers, Military Archives online. Accessed 4/11/2019.

15 Seán Farrelly, Bureau of Military History Witness Statement #1734, 14–15.

16 Information from Frank Cogan, email 13 December 2019.

17 *Meath Chronicle*, 12 June 1920.

18 Joseph V. Lawless, Bureau of Military History Witness Statement #1043, 302–304.

19 Seán Farrelly, Bureau of Military History Witness Statement #1734, 15–16.

20 D/Defence, Military Archives, Military Service and Pension Collection; file on Matthew Cogan 34/SP/61746; MSP/34/Ref 60827; MD 20434. Letter of P. O'Connell, 4/12/79. Cited in Cogan 'Michael Collins and the Cormeen Murder Case, 1920', *Riocht na Midhe* – records of the Meath Archaeological and Historical Society, vol. XXVIII, 2017, 353–73.

21 Military Archives, Military Service and Pension Collection; Matthew Cogan 34/SP/61746; MSP/34/Ref 60827; MD 20434. Letter of Peter O'Connell, 4 December 1979.

22   Michael Hopkinson, *The Irish War of Independence* (Montreal, 2004), 17–18.
23   Séamus Finn, Bureau of Military History Witness Statement #1060, 13.
24   Seán Boylan, Bureau of Military History Witness Statement #1715, 20.
25   Séamus Finn, Bureau of Military History Witness Statement #1060, 14.
26   Seán Dowling, in Uinseann MacEoin, *Survivors* (Dublin, 1980), 400–01.
27   Seán Boylan, Bureau of Military History Witness Statement #1715, 24. Charles Conaty in his BMH-WS #1627 refers to sentences of 7–15 years. The 1st Battalion Activity Reports mentions sentences of 5–15 years.
28   Seán Farrelly, Bureau of Military History Witness Statement #1734, 36–7.
29   Seán Farrelly, Bureau of Military History Witness Statement #1734, 17.
30   Mark Clinton, letter to the author, 2 April 2019.
31   *Meath Chronicle*, 2 October 1920.

Chapter 5: The Third Killing

1   Michael Hopkinson, *The Irish War of Independence* (Montreal, 2002), 145.
2   *Meath Chronicle*, 24 January 1920.
3   *The Carnaross and Mullaghea Story* (Meath, 2017), 71.
4   Michael Hopkinson, *The Irish War of Independence* (Montreal, 2004), 130.
5   *Meath Chronicle*, Kells GNR Station 31.1.1920, Dublin – Kells Mail Robbed 20.3.1920 – Motor Mail Robbery 27.3.1920 – Robbery from Mail Car 17.4.20
6   Seán Boylan, Bureau of Military History Witness Statement #1715, 16–19.
7   Seán Boylan, Bureau of Military History Witness Statement #1715, 16–19.

8   *Drogheda Independent*, 11 May 1918.

9   *Anglo-Celt*, 6 July 1918.

10   David Fitzpatrick, 'Militarism in Ireland 1900–1922', in Thomas Bartlet, Keith Jeffrey (eds), *A Military History of Ireland* (Cambridge, 1997), 388.

11   AM 175, #292949, William Gordon. In his prison record he is described as a 'fitter'.

12   Danny Cusack, *Kilmainham of the Woody Hollow. A History of Kilmainhamwood for the Centenary of the Church 1898–1998* (Kilmainhamwood, 1998), 13.

13   General Register of Prisoners 1920, 654. The prisoner admitted along with Gordon was a neighbour from Kilagriffe, Patrick Courtney, uncle of Meath historian Ultan Courtney. From a Republican family in Kilmainhamwood, Courtney was not a member of the Meath IRA but was charged with stealing a horse's collar to the value of £2.10s. He was later acquitted of the charge.

14   Seán Boylan, Bureau of Military History Witness Statement #1715, 19.

15   Séamus Finn, Bureau of Military History Witness Statement #1060, 12.

16   *Meath Chronicle*, 26 June 1920.

17   Patrick Loughran, Bureau of Military History Witness Statement #1624, 5.

18   Seán Boylan, Bureau of Military History Witness Statement #1715, 21.

19   *Meath Chronicle*, 26 June 1920.

20   Seán Boylan, Bureau of Military History Witness Statement #1715, 21.

21   Seán Boylan, Bureau of Military History Witness Statement #1715, 21–22.

22   Séamus Finn, Bureau of Military History Witness Statement #1060, 13.

23   Seán Boylan, Bureau of Military History Witness Statement #1715, 22.

24   Ernest Blythe, Bureau of Military History Witness Statement #939, 119.

25   Michael Hopkinson, *The Irish War of Independence* (Montreal, 2004), 40.

26 Oliver Coogan, *Politics and War in Meath*, 133.
27 Seán Boylan, Bureau of Military History Witness Statement #1715, 23.
28 Uinseann MacEoin, *Survivors* (Dublin, 1980), 400.
29 Uinseann MacEoin, *Survivors* (Dublin, 1980), 401.
30 Joe Hyland, Bureau of Military History Witness Statement #644, 3.
31 Ernest Blythe, Bureau of Military History Witness Statement #939, 119.
32 Seán Boylan, Bureau of Military History Witness Statement #1715, 22.
33 Una Stack, Bureau of Military History Witness Statement #418, 25–26.
34 Marie Coleman, *The Irish Revolution 1916–1923* (London, 2014), 74.
35 Joe Hyland, Bureau of Military History Witness Statement #644, 4.
36 Seán Boylan, Bureau of Military History Witness Statement #1715, 22–23.
37 Seán Boylan, Bureau of Military History Witness Statement #1715, 23.
38 Joe Hyland, Bureau of Military History Witness Statement #644, 4.
39 Frank Cogan, 'Michael Collins and the Cormeen Case', *Riocht na Midhe* – records of the Meath Archaeological and Historical Society, vol. XXVIII, 2017, 369.
40 Kevin O'Shiel, Bureau of Military History Witness Statement #1770, 1010–12.
41 Coogan, *Politics and War in Meath*, 293.

PART TWO: THE MCKENNAS OF MULLAGH

Chapter 6: The Merchant of Mullagh

1 *United Ireland*, 10 February 1883.
2 *United Ireland*, 17 February 1883.
3 Mullagh Historical Committee, *Portrait of a Parish* (Mullagh, 1988), 82–88, 100.
4 *Salt Lake City Tribune*, 30 November 1901.

5   Stephen McKenna, *A Gallant Soldier of Ireland: The Life and Times of T.P. McKenna Jr.* (London, 2019), 18.

6   Stephen McKenna, *A Gallant Soldier of Ireland*, 15–19.

7   Stephen McKenna, *A Gallant Soldier of Ireland*, 17.

8   Seán Farrelly, Bureau of Military History Witness Statement #1734, 2.

9   Arlene Crampsie and Francis Ludlow, *Meath: History and Society – Interdisciplinary Essays on the History of an Irish County* (Dublin, 2015); Ultan Courtney, 'The War of Independence in County Meath, 1916–1921', 670.

10 Seán Farrelly, Bureau of Military History Witness Statement #1734, 37–38.

11 Ann Saddlemyer (ed.), *The Collected Letters of John Millington Synge: Volume One 1871–1907* (Oxford, 1983), 116.

12 Marie Coleman, *The Irish Revolution 1916–1923* (London, 2014), 73.

13 William Sheehan, *British Voices from the Irish War of Independence 1918–1921* (Cork, 2005), 98–99.

14 Marie Coleman, *The Irish Revolution 1916–1923* (London, 2014), 76.

15 David Fitzpatrick, *Politics and Irish Life, 1913–1921* (Dublin, 1977), 217.

16 Seán Farrelly, Bureau of Military History Witness Statement #1734, 22. The page in which Farrelly names those who decided to opt out of the conflict in this way has been deleted from the online version of his Bureau of Military History Witness Statement.

17 *Irish Law Times*, 15 May 1915.

18 *Meath Chronicle*, 18 September 1920.

19 Cahir Davitt, Bureau of Military History Witness Statement #993, 69–70.

20 WO 35/53/227.

21 *Meath Chronicle*, 9 October 1920.

22 Royal Irish Constabulary, Secret Crime Special, WO 35/207/153.

23 *Meath Chronicle*, 4 December 1920.

24 *Meath Chronicle*, 4 December 1920.

25 *Drogheda Independent*, 29 January 1921.

26 *Meath Chronicle*, 29 January 1921.

27 William Sheehan, *British Voices from the Irish War of Independence 1918–1921* (Cork, 2005), 49.

28 Except where otherwise stated, all information on the military career of T.P. McKenna Jr. comes from his Military Service Pension Collection files, MSPC 24SP12899 and 24D38.

29 David Smith, referee, MSPC 24SP12899.

30 David Smith, referee, MSPC 24SP12899.

31 Frank Kitson, *Low Intensity Operations: Subversion, Insurgency, Peacekeeping* (London, 1971), 127.

32 Military Service Pensions Application, Raphael McKenna, MSP34REF45950.

33 Military Service Pensions Application, Raphael McKenna, MSP34REF45950.

34 Marie Coleman, *The Irish Revolution 1916–1923* (London, 2014), 990.

35 Patrick Clinton to Director of Intelligence, GHQ, 11.9.1921, IE_MA_CP_05_02_29, (LXXXVIII), Collins Papers, Military Archives.

36 David Fitzpatrick, *Politics and Irish Life, 1913–1921: Provincial Experiences of War and Revolution* (Dublin, 1977), 224.

37 William Sheehan, *British Voices from the Irish War of Independence 1918–1921* (Cork, 2005), 221.

38 David Fitzpatrick, *Politics and Irish Life, 1913–1921* (Dublin, 1977), 224.

39 Military Service Pension Collection, John Francis McKenna, MSP34REF35849.

40 Seán Lynch and Patrick Riley, Military Service Pension Collection, John Francis McKenna, MSP34REF35849.

41 Information from Mark Clinton, Sutton, email 9.12.2019.

42 *Meath Chronicle*, 5 February 1921.

43 Military Service Pension Collection, John Francis McKenna, MSP34REF35849.

44 Letter from Thomas J. O'Reilly, Military Service Pension Collection, John Francis McKenna, MSP34REF35849.

45 Information from Joe McKenna.

46 *Meath Chronicle*, 9 April 1921.

Chapter 7: The Informer

1   Christopher Andrew, *Secret Service: The Making of the British Intelligence Community* (London, 1985), 262.

2   Paul McMahon, *British Spies and Irish Rebels: British Intelligence and Ireland, 1916–1945* (Suffolk, 2008), 45.

3   Mullagh Historical Committee, *Portrait of a Parish: Mullagh, County Cavan* (Cavan, 1988), 95.

4   Maurice Walsh, *Bitter Freedom: Ireland in a Revolutionary World* (New York/London, 2015), 251.

5   http://www.militaryarchives.ie/collections/online-collections/bureau-of-military-history-1913-1921/voice-recordings/.

6   Maurice Walsh, *Bitter Freedom: Ireland in a Revolutionary World* (New York/London, 2015), 251.

7   Seán Farrelly, Bureau of Military History Witness Statement #1734, 37.

8   Charles Townshend, *The Republic: The Fight for Irish Independence 1918–1923* (London, 2013), 262.

9   Maurice Walsh, *Bitter Freedom: Ireland in a Revolutionary World* (New York/London, 2015), 254.

10   Charles Townshend, *The Republic: The Fight for Irish Independence 1918–1923* (London, 2013), 262 and Maurice Walsh, *Bitter Freedom: Ireland in a Revolutionary World* (New York/London, 2015), 256.

11   Charles Townshend, *The Republic: The Fight for Irish Independence 1918–1923* (London, 2013), 263.

12   Charles Townshend, *The Republic: The Fight for Irish Independence 1918–1923* (London, 2013), 263.

13   Charles Townshend, *The Republic: The Fight for Irish Independence 1918–1923* (London, 2013), 264.

14   Manus Moynihan, Bureau of Military History Witness Statement, #1066, 5–8.

15   Ultan Courtney, *Mapping the Revolution: Maps, Mayhem and Murder in Meath, 1919–1921* (Meath, 2019), 218.

16   It is not the intention of the author to enter the historiographical debate on the allegations of 'ethnic cleansing' of Protestants or the targeting of ex-servicemen by the IRA. This is simply because he

has nothing worthwhile to add to the discussion. Those interested in these controversies can consult the works of Peter Hart, Paul Taylor, Jane Leonard, David Fitzpatrick and others. On the issue of alleged ethnic cleansing, however, it may be pertinent to quote a small section of Pádraig Óg Ó Ruairc's *Truce: Murder, Myth and the Last Days of the Irish War of Independence* (Cork, 2016), in which he asserts that 'The IRA killed a total of 184 civilians accused of spying during the War of Independence. The religious denomination of nine of those killed is unknown. Of the remaining 175 whose religious affinities are known, forty-two (24 per cent) were Protestant and 133 (76 per cent) Catholic, so in terms of religion Protestants were a small but significant minority amongst those executed by the IRA as spies. No Protestants were killed in twelve counties where spies were shot, which rules out any possibility that the IRA in Armagh, Carlow, Cavan, Clare, Galway, Kildare, Kilkenny, Limerick, Louth, Meath, Waterford and Wexford used the issue of spies as a pretext for sectarian activity against, or the ethnic cleansing of, Protestants. If the seven counties where no suspected spies were executed are also taken into account, then it can be shown conclusively that no Protestants were executed on suspicion of spying in nineteen.' (Ó Ruairc, *Truce*, 105).

17 Paul McMahon, *British Spies and Irish Rebels: British Intelligence and Ireland, 1916–1945* (Suffolk, 2008), 45.

18 Oliver Coogan, *Politics and War in Meath 1913–1923* (Navan, 1983), 188 and Ultan Courtney, *Mapping the Revolution: Maps, Mayhem and Murder in Meath, 1919–1921* (Meath, 2019), 186. The nature of the death of the military casualty Sergeant Herrod will be dealt with below.

19 In his Bureau of Military History Witness Statement #1060, Séamus Finn, Meath Brigade second-in-command, claims that 'In all there were ten individuals executed in the brigade area.' Detailed research by this writer and a number of others suggests a maximum of eight, including one unidentified victim ('Michael O'Brien'), one British soldier (Herrod) and William Gordon, the murderer of Mark Clinton.

20 Military Archives, Bureau of Military History Witness Statement WS#1622, Michael Hillard, 7/8. Unredacted statement – the online

version has deleted Hilliard's admission that he personally shot 'O'Brien'.

21 This emerges, in particular, from the work of local historian Ultan Courtney in works already cited.
22 Peter O'Connell, Bureau of Military History Witness Statement #1659, 16.
23 Seán Boylan, Bureau of Military History Witness Statement #1715, 29.
24 Oliver Coogan, *Politics and War in Meath 1913–1923* (Navan, 1983), 180.
25 Military Service Pensions Collection, MA/MSPC/RO 489, 1st Eastern Division, 3rd Brigade (Meath) GHQ & 1st–4th Battalions.
26 Matt Govern, Bureau of Military History Witness Statement #1625, 7.
27 Matt Govern, Bureau of Military History Witness Statement #1625, 7–8.
28 Petty Sessions Order Books, CSPS 1/10320. County Meath, 1 November 1920.
29 *Drogheda Independent*, 6 November 1920.
30 *Weekly Freeman's Journal*, 23 December 1922.
31 *Weekly Freeman's Journal*, 23 December 1922.
32 Seán Farrelly, Bureau of Military History Witness Statement #1734, 46.
33 Andy Bielenberg and Pádraig Óg Ó Ruairc, *Shallow Graves; Documenting and Assessing IRA Disappearances during the Irish Revolution 1919–23* (forthcoming 2021). With thanks to Pádraig Óg Ó Ruairc for supplying the statistic (email 27 November 2019).

Chapter 8: The Fourth Killing

1 'Tales of an Old Fenian, memories of Matthew Gilsenan' (born 1856), recorded by P.J. Gaynor in 1946. Supplied by Danny Cusack.
2 Michael Hopkinson, *The Irish War of Independence* (Montreal, 2004), 77.
3 Paul McMahon, *British Spies and Irish Rebels: British Intelligence and Ireland, 1916–1945* (Suffolk, 2008), 46.

4   *Meath Chronicle*, 25 September 1920. My thanks to Professor Linda Connolly for bringing this incident to my attention.

5   1911 Census records, Patrick Keelan, Form B.1 – House and Building Return.

6   Petty Sessions Order Book CSPS 1/10349, 4 September 1913.

7   Petty Sessions Order Book CSPS 1/10346, 6 December 1900, CSPS 1/10347, 2 February 1905.

8   Deaths registered in the district of Nobber, in the union of Kells, 1916, 79.

9   1911 Census records.

10 WO 35, Report on raids carried out in Kilbeg, 23.3.21.

11 WO 35, Raid report 1 S.W.B., 21.4.21.

12 *Drogheda Independent*, 2 April 1921.

13 Seán Farrelly, Bureau of Military History Witness Statement #1734, 46.

14 *Meath Chronicle*, 2 April 1921.

15 *Drogheda Independent*, 28 May 1921.

16 J. Bowyer Bell, *The Secret Army* (London, 1997), 24.

17 Marie Coleman, *The Irish Revolution 1916–1923* (London, 2014), 87.

18 WO35/91/12, 2 July 1921.

19 Clarke and Smyth are identified as IRA company captains in the 3rd Meath Brigade Brigade Activity Report, Military Service Pension Collection, MA/MSPC/RO/489 – the Carnaross company was A Company 2nd Battalion, Kilbeg was E Company 1st Battalion.

20 Information supplied by Danny Cusack, email 31 October 2019.

21 Military Archives, Military Service Pensions Collection, Peter Clinton, MSP34REF36826.

22 Military Archives, Military Service Pensions Collection, Peter Clinton, MSP34REF35849.

23 Inspector J. Bergin, Kells to Chief Superintendent's Office, 23 February 1924, JUS/2019/58/85.

24 William Armstrong to the Secretary, Ministry of Home Affairs, 11 January 1924, JUS/2019/58/85. My thanks to Padraig Óg Ó Ruairc for bringing this file to my attention.

25 Secretary, Ministry of Home Affairs to Garda Commissioner, 16 January 1924, JUS/2019/58/85.

26 Deputy Commissioner, Garda Síochána to the Secretary, Ministry of Home Affairs, 31 January 1924, JUS/2019/58/85.

27 Secretary, Ministry of Home Affairs to William Armstrong, 25 April 1924, JUS/2019/58/85.

28 *Irish Times*, 14 April 1923.

29 Patrick A. Mooney to Secretary, Minister of Justice, 23 March 1931, JUS/2019/58/85.

30 Ireland, Criminal Injuries to Private Persons (Meath), CO 905/15.

31 The information in this section comes from Joe McKenna, son of John, from my sister Teri (Mary Theresa) Dungan, and from a number of anonymous sources.

Chapter 9: Argentina

1 David Fitzpatrick, *Politics and Irish Life, 1913–1921*, 225.

2 John Buchan, *The Three Hostages* (Edinburgh, 2010), 19. Cited in Maurice Walsh, *Bitter Freedom: Ireland in a Revolutionary World* (New York/London, 2015), 163–4.

3 Marie Coleman, *The Irish Revolution 1916–1923* (London, 2014), 78.

4 Tom Barry, *Guerrilla Days in Ireland* (Tralee, 1955), 189–90.

5 Michael Hopkinson, *The Irish War of Independence* (Montreal, 2004), 201.

6 David Fitzpatrick, *Politics and Irish Life, 1913–1921*, 230.

7 4th Brigade, 1st Eastern Division, Intelligence Report, October 1921, 30 October 1921, Military Archives, Collins Papers, IE/MA/CP/5/2/29 (xciv).

8 1st Eastern Division, Monthly Intelligence Report, 9 December 1921. Military Archives, Collins Papers, IE/MA/CP/5/2/29 (cxvii).

9 David Fitzpatrick, *Politics and Irish Life, 1913–1921*, 31.

10 *Meath Chronicle*, 7 February 1914.

11 3rd Brigade, 1st Eastern Division, Intelligence Report, October 1921, 1 November 1921, Military Archives, Collins Papers, IE/MA/CP/5/2/29 (xciii).

12 The words of the compiler of the Brigade Activity Report for the 3rd Meath Brigade, Military Archives, Brigade Activity Reports, BAR, Meath 3rd, MA, MSPC, RO/489.

13 Military Archives, Military Service Pensions Collection, MSP34REF35849.

14 *Meath Chronicle*, 16 July 1921.

15 Military Archives, Bureau of Military History Witness Statement #1060, Séamus Finn, 26.

16 Military Archives, Military Service Pensions Collection, W1RB4154.

17 Military Archives, Military Service Pensions Collection, WDP9489.

18 Military Archives, Military Service Pensions Collection, W34E1843.

19 Military Archives, Bureau of Military History Witness Statement #434.

20 Charles Dalton, *With the Dublin Brigade* (Dublin, 1929), reprinted by Mercier Press with an introduction by Liz Gillis.

21 Dáil Éireann public session, Tuesday 10 January 1922.

22 *Meath Chronicle*, 1 April 1950.

23 Séamus Coogan, *Politics and War in Meath 1913–23* (Meath, 1983), 188.

24 *An tÓglach*, 15 January 1920.

25 *The Carnaross and Mullaghea Story*, 78.

26 Ultan Courtney, 'The War of Independence in County Meath, 1916–1921' in Arlene Crampsie and Francis Ludlow (eds), *Meath: History and Society – Interdisciplinary Essays on the History of an Irish County* (Dublin, 2015), 680.

27 Military Archives, Military Service Pensions Collection, 24SP12899.

28 Thomas Gorman, Army Finance Officer, to the Secretary, Department of Finance, 16 November 1926.

29 Stephen McKenna, *A Gallant Soldier of Ireland* (London, 2019), 51–52.

30 Stephen McKenna, *A Gallant Soldier of Ireland* (London, 2019), 61.

31 *Meath Chronicle*, 23 February 1929.

32 T.P. McKenna Jr. to Minister for Defence, 20 May 1928, Military Archives, T.P. McKenna, MSPC 24D38.

33 Stephen McKenna, *A Gallant Soldier of Ireland* (London, 2019), 65–66.

34 T.P. McKenna Sr. to Military Service Pensions Department, Minister of Finance, Dublin, 8 May 1929, Military Archives, MSPC 24D38.

35 Stephen McKenna, *A Gallant Soldier of Ireland* (London, 2019), 67.

36 Mullagh Historical Committee, *Portrait of a Parish: Mullagh, County Cavan* (Mullagh, 1988), 98.

37 With thanks to Joseph McKenna for allowing me access to a copy
    of the handwritten manuscript. The piece has been published in its
    entirety in Stephen McKenna, *A Gallant Soldier of Ireland: The Life
    and Times of T.P. McKenna Jr.*

38 My thanks to Erna McKenna (daughter of Justin) for supplying me
    with the text of 'Mullagh Hill'.

Epilogue

1   Friedrich Engels and Karl Marx, *Ireland and the Irish Question*
    (London, 1869) – quoted in Richard English, *Irish Freedom: The
    History of Nationalism in Ireland* (London, 2006), 235.

2   http://www.theirishstory.com/2012/02/10/eunan-o-halpin-on-the-
    dead-of-the-irish-revolution/#.XZebNyoZO1u.

Image credits

1. © Roseanne Feeback/Mary Frances Clinton.
2. © Mrs Angela McNicholas.
3. © Arizona Historical Society.
4. © Frank Cogan.
5. © Estate of T.P. McKenna.
6. © Estate of T.P. McKenna.
7. Courtesy of Ultan Courtney.
8. © Estate of T.P. McKenna.
9. © Estate of T.P. McKenna.
10. © Estate of T.P. McKenna.
11. © Estate of T.P. McKenna.
12. © Mrs Angela McNicholas.
13. © Mrs Angela McNicholas.
14. © Joseph McKenna.
15. © Myles Dungan.
16. © Myles Dungan.

About the Author

MYLES DUNGAN is a broadcaster and historian. He presents *The History Show* on RTÉ Radio 1 and is an adjunct lecturer and Fulbright scholar in the School of History and Archives, University College, Dublin. He has also compiled and presented a number of award-winning historical documentaries. He is the author of numerous works on Irish and American history and holds a PhD from Trinity College, Dublin.

Index